THE TWO IMPOSTORS

THE ARCH OF TITUS

THE
TWO IMPOSTORS

DANIELE VARÈ

If you can meet with Triumph and Disaster
And treat those two impostors just the same.
RUDYARD KIPLING—*IF.*

LONDON
JOHN MURRAY, ALBEMARLE STREET, W.

In every boy there is a dreamer that the man survives.
To the dreamer that I was, and others with me, this
book is dedicated.

FIRST EDITION . . . 1949

MADE AND PRINTED IN GREAT BRITAIN BY
BUTLER AND TANNER LTD., FROME AND LONDON

CONTENTS

CONTENTS

PART II. HARVESTING OF A DREAM

PART III. SHADOWS

PART IV. THE DREAM SHATTERED

LIST OF ILLUSTRATIONS

PREFACE

WHILE talking to the faithful Eckermann about the works of contemporary writers, Goethe returned frequently to the distinction between the flesh and the spirit, the outer form and the inner meaning, *das Aussere und das Innere.* The first comprises the narrative, the descriptions, the historical background, the plot of the romance (if it is a romance), the essential unity of the drama. *Das Innere* is the revelation of the author's inner self, the spirit of the man that gives to his work the breath of life ; his character, his culture, his religion, his very soul.

An author can open the door to this Inner Shrine in various ways. But the most difficult is by writing Memoirs. You can reveal much more about yourself by writing fiction, for only in fiction can you be honest.

When telling a story, or presenting a play, it often happens that the writer, himself, acts a part. Sometimes he is only pretending to do so, but—like Hamlet—is very near being what he acts. Pirandello juggled with this theme, playing tricks of mental sleight of hand that left the reader puzzled as to where reality began and where it ended. In imaginative fabrication we can be daring ; in autobiography we must be reticent, if only out of respect for other people. Sometimes we must be content to be judged by our omissions, and follow the running chronicle of our lives, with much left out.

When you write Memoirs (and nowadays, this has become a minor industry !), it is like showing people over your house and garden. You linger, perhaps, before a picture, or to point out some pleasing prospect, and then you go on to the stables, to give carrots to the horses. And whereas you may live modestly, as I do, your Memoirs can be laid out in stately dignity, like the grounds of Versailles.

Some day, perhaps, when I am quite old, with one foot in flannel

[1] Here I sit and shape men after my image, a race that shall be like me.

and the other in the grave, I will attempt a portrait in the grand manner, and present myself to posterity, as Edmund Gosse once put it, in a tight frock-coat, with a glass of water in my hand and one elbow on a desk, preparing to say : ' Ladies and Gentlemen ! '

For a few years more, let me write as I have always written, dwelling on the little things as on the big, even if I seem to show an imperfect sense of proportion.

In that little masterpiece, *The Life of Cardinal Wolsey*, by George Cavendish, written (but not published) in 1557, the biographer occasionally hunts very small game, as when he says : " The Bishop of Carlisle, being with him on his barge, said unto him, wiping the sweat from his face—' Sir, it is a very hot day ! ' "

Such endearing pen-strokes bring Wolsey and his times nearer to me than the mighty struggle between Henry VIII and Rome. It is as if, against the Tudor background, these trivialities acquired something of the majesty of the History of England !

★   ★   ★

I was not yet in my teens, when I first began to spoil good sheets of paper with compilations of my own, and sometimes I would go to a neighbouring printing-press and have these fragments set up in type. One of them bore the pretentious title of *La Musica*. A few days after it had come back from the printer, Mother took me to the Quirinal, to see Queen Margherita. There were no lifts in the Palace in those days, and while we were mounting the shallow, red-carpeted steps of the spiral staircase, I wondered how I could justify myself in offering to the Queen a copy of the poem that I fingered in my pocket. Fortunately, she asked me what I had been doing lately, and this gave me the required opening.

In our family and in my generation, there were two of us with literary proclivities. The other was my cousin, Patrick Chalmers of Aldbar. I had the advantage over him of being able to write in several languages. But he revealed more of *das Innere* in his brief poems than I in my lengthy prose. Anyhow, I like to think that sometimes, when not wasting time on politics, both of us could catch an echo of the Pipes of Pan.

D. V.

ROME, 1949

PART I

ITALY WITHOUT TEARS

A Singer in the Night

HOUSES are no longer built with windows like that, so high and set in such thick walls ; windows that might almost be embrasures through which cannon are pointed. The outer frame was of granite —or so I seem to remember—and the woodwork was painted a bluish grey, picked out with gold, as were the inner shutters. I saw them by the light of an oil-lamp that stood on a table, not far from the window.

I can recollect nothing about the house itself, not even in what town it could have been. Somewhere in Italy, of course. A hill-town, I should say, for one looked out over tiled roofs towards the countryside. There was an open space just opposite—a piazza prob-ably—and the view from the window was such as you might have in Siena, from the Chigi palace. But it was not Siena ; of that I am almost sure, though I could not explain why.

My father was standing near the window : a tall man with grey hair. We had arrived in that town, whatever it was, in the evening, and I had been put to bed after a supper of bread and milk. The bed was a large one for so small a child, and placed in a corner of the room, far from the window. It must have been summer-time, for the window was wide open. When the noise woke me, my mother came and took me up and held me in her arms, wrapped in a blanket. What had woken me was the sound of shouting. It came from the street below. They were shouting for Tamagno, the tenor, to show himself at another window, or balcony, on the same floor as we were on. He had been singing at the Opera, and had just come home.

The crowd kept on shouting and clapping, till at last Tamagno stepped out on a balcony. And then he sang again.

I could not see him ; only hear his voice pealing out into the night. Lights appeared at the windows, first near by, then further off. Above the roofs, the stars were shining. They seemed very near, as if they too had lit up at the sound of that Homeric voice.

That is all : the open window, at which my father was standing ;

the darkness outside, and the song. I must have fallen asleep before it ended, my head resting on my mother's shoulder, as she held me in her arms.

First Journey (with a glimpse of Louis Pasteur)

Two opposing laws seem to me now in contest. The one, a law of blood and death, opening out each day new modes of destruction, forces nations to be always ready for the battle. The other, a law of peace, work and health, whose only aim is to deliver man from the calamities which beset him. The one seeks violent conquests, the other the relief of mankind. The one places a single life above all victories, the other sacrifices hundreds of thousands of lives to the ambition of a single individual. The law of which we are the instruments strives even through carnage to cure the wounds due to the law of war. . . . Which of these two laws will prevail, God only knows. But of this we may be sure, that science, in obeying the law of humanity, will always labour to enlarge the frontiers of life.

The above quotation is taken from the inaugural address, pronounced by Pasteur, at the opening of the Institution in Paris to which he gave his name. It is not out of place in these Memoirs of mine, for I am now one of the few persons living who have seen Pasteur himself give an injection as a preventive of rabies. True, I was only five years old at the time, and the episode occurred during my first journey. I have a vivid recollection of it, because it nearly scared me into fits !

This is how it happened.

My father died in 1884, when I was four years old, and Mother and I continued to live in Rome, at the Palazzo Poli. But soon, Mother herself fell ill. After which we went to live in England, to be near her relations.

We were met in Paris by a brother-in-law of Mother's, William Finlay, who was a doctor and practised in Edinburgh. He was a colleague of Doctor Joseph Bell, the original Sherlock Holmes.

My Uncle William seized the opportunity of his journey to Paris, to see something of a certain French doctor, who was supposed to have discovered a way of preventing rabies in people that had been bitten by a mad dog. Why a little boy, like myself, should have been taken along on this occasion, I cannot imagine, unless it was

4

that, my mother being ill, there was no one with whom I could be left. Anyway, my Uncle William and I went together to what may have been a kind of specialized medical aid station : an incredibly dark and dingy place, where everyone went in and out as they liked.[1] This is what I remember.

A big, square, whitewashed room, with the ceiling in deep shadow. There were about fifteen people in it, none of whom was wearing the white linen overalls that we are now accustomed to see on medical men and their attendants. I am standing near the door and holding my uncle's hand, conscious of the fact that he is not thinking of me at all. To our left is a huge window of rectangular plates of glass, set in a metal frame. A little light comes from it still, but evening is drawing in and the room is lighted by a powerful hanging lamp, with a reflector that directs the rays downwards. Under this lamp, a man with a grey beard is sitting on a low chair (I was going to say : on a straw-bottomed chair, but how could I know what it was made of ?). He wears a black coat (a *rédingote*), with coat-tails that fall to the floor. He holds a child by one arm, with no one to assist him in any way. The child is standing between his knees, and he forces it to bend backwards, so as to throw out its chest. It is a little boy, about eight years old, rather fat, and with curly fair hair that is wet with perspiration. The doctor holds a large syringe and is giving an injection in the upper abdomen, while the small patient screams with fright and pain. The other people in the room are looking on, with a puzzled, reluctant interest.

That is all. The scene remained in my mind, because of the child's screams (it was older than I). Unlike my uncle, I was unaware that, with such injections, something new was being born into the world. But perhaps even he had his doubts. Science, and not our moral inadequacy, was still feared by mankind, in those days.

[1] A doctor friend of mine, who in his youth was employed in the anti-rabies institute, founded by the Duke of Oldenburg in St. Petersburg, suggests that the place visited by my uncle and myself must have been a modest experimental laboratory, temporarily lodged in quarters granted to Louis Pasteur by the Municipal Authorities of Paris. He worked there in the years preceding the creation of the ' Institut Pasteur '. There he kept the infected dogs and rabbits, and there again did he make the first daring experiments on human beings, attempting a cure by vaccine, before the special microbe, causing rabies, had yet been isolated.

Agnès

WHEN Mother and I returned from England to Rome, I was eleven years old. She took an apartment at 118 Via Venti Settembre and introduced me to my father's friends, whom she consulted as to my upbringing. No less a personage than the Minister for Public Instruction, Guido Baccelli, put me to school at the Ginnasio Umberto I and he wrote personally to the ' Preside ', Giuseppe Chiarini, pointing out that, having been abroad so long, I might need some coaching in the Italian language.

Meanwhile we acquired a maid and general factotum, one of those domestic treasures, such as appear once in a generation, a combination of Peggoty and *She Who Must Be Obeyed*. Her name was Agnès, and she had been born on the banks of the Neckar, where it enters the plain of the Rhine, between Heidelberg and Mannheim. A willing, honest, single-minded woman, Agnès brought into everything she did the thoroughness (*Gründlichkeit*) that is the result of a German education.

Mother and I had been separated during her long illness ; she had lost the habit of looking after me. I have no doubt that she felt much relieved when Agnès assumed towards me, almost as a matter of course, the duties of a nursery governess. This implied a return to childish things, but it was not unwelcome, as bed to a little boy who has been kept up too long at night. Also it was something pleasantly new to feel I was not a mere supernumerary in somebody else's household (as I had been in England), but a person whose present needs and future development were of primary importance. Such unaccustomed consequence was not without its disadvantages, for Agnès, though full of tender solicitude, was determined not to spoil me. She showed herself conscientiously severe in inflicting punishment. But these painful occasions were few and far between. Agnès found in me an outlet for an unsatisfied motherliness. In my own docile acceptance of her domestic discipline, there was a feeling of relaxation. I had been obliged to face difficulties and to fend for myself at too early an age. I now surrendered my will and my person with a grateful submission, which revealed an unconscious nostalgia for the childhood I had almost missed.

Agnès revelled in any form of labour intended to keep the house

6

THE AUTHOR'S MOTHER

swept and garnished. Hers was the passion for method that Heine laughed at, and the *laboriositas* that Leibniz described as characteristic of the Teutonic race. She would kneel by the hour, polishing floors, and she prowled about, with a cloth in one hand and a *piumino* in the other. A *piumino* is a feather duster, mounted on a pliable wand of osier. Dust and cobwebs were pursued by the feathers ; small rugs and cushions were beaten with the osier wand. If Agnès is now in Heaven, I hope they allow her to scrub the golden floor and dust the cushions of the throne that is reserved for the Deity. Or they might give her an extra long *piumino* to sweep away the nebulæ.

From Agnès I got my first grounding in the German language. I learnt songs by Schumann (*Es war im schönsten Monat Mai*, and *Die beide Grenadiere*). These she would sing, in a husky contralto, while cleaning the boots and shoes, on the kitchen balcony that overlooked a little garden. Sometimes, Anna, the cook (an ancient Roman, out of the Trastevere) would be ousted from her domain by the kitchen stove, so that Agnès might prepare *Fasching's Krapfen*, a delicacy that, by rights, should be eaten only at the end of Carnival.

Agnès explained the solar system to me, with the aid of an orange and a knitting needle, but she lacked a classical education and could not help me with my studies. However, she persuaded Mother to engage a *ripetitore* (or ' coach '), for me, a dear old Tuscan schoolmaster. And she kept a watchful eye on my *pagella* (a bi-monthly school report). She expressed delight when this contained good marks and laudatory comments. But when it testified to lapses from grace, she threatened to use the osier wand of the *piumino* on other things beside rugs and cushions.

She also devised a method of ensuring that I should give the necessary attention to my school tasks. She would take me down to the garden, carrying my copy-books, dictionaries and classical texts, and she would immure me in the tool-shed, where we kept disused boxes and bird-cages, and a store of wood for the winter. While locked up in there, I was expected to remedy the lack of diligence of which I had been guilty when at large. I was allowed to take with me a slice or two of cake, to consume while I was shut up. Mother compared my place of confinement to the Castle of Chillon, and myself to François Bonivard, making friends with spiders in a dungeon.

Though there were times when I found that such humour was misplaced, Agnès's scheme, on the whole, was successful. I did actually
study better for being confined in that place of detention.

I was imprisoned in the Castle of Chillon more often, after an
English girl, Constance Cazenove, came to stay with us in Rome.
Her presence attracted to Mother's drawing-room a bevy of young
men, mostly of the hunting set, and others that were attached to the
Court. Before long, a love-affair began to develop between Consy
and one of the Court officials, the Marchese Ferdinando Guiccioli.
During Consy's stay with us, Mother engaged a housemaid to come
in by day. This annoyed Agnès, who considered that she could do
any amount of extra house-work, unaided. Also she did not get on
with ' the help ', and for some time was very short in the temper,
so that I was frequently in trouble.

One afternoon, while immured in the tool-shed, I heard voices
that sounded familiar. Putting down Xenophon's *Anabasis*, I looked
out through the small window with its cracked pane of glass, and
saw a man and a girl on the path through the tiny orange-grove,
near the fountain with the goldfish. It was unusual for any of us to
invite visitors into the garden, which we shared with other inmates
of the *palazzo*. So I was astonished to see Consy there, together with
Guiccioli. He was impeccably dressed, and wore a glossy top-hat,
and a tie *en plastron*, with a pin in the shape of an M, studded with
tiny diamonds.

I thought for a moment that Agnès might have given them the
key, to let me out, and I felt much ashamed of being found in circumstances so suggestive of chastisement. But it was clear that those two
had no thought but for each other. They were behaving, it is true,
with perfect dignity and decorum, as befitted their times and social
position ; indeed Ferdinand's declaration took almost the form of a
ritual, and he appeared indifferent to the fact that it had begun to
rain.

As a rule, only cats met in amorous rendezvous in that patch of
garden. But before Agnès came down to liberate me, a proposal of
marriage had been made and accepted. The happy couple, all unconscious of having been watched from only a few yards distance,
proceeded upstairs. Consy announced her engagement to Mother,

8

while Ferdinand hurried off to the Quirinal, to inform Queen Margherita. Apart from my own unseen presence, the episode had been ceremonious and graceful as a minuet.

*　　*　　*

I was seventeen when Agnès left us, to go back to her home, near Heidelberg. Her brother, having lost his wife, wanted someone to help look after his farm and his two children. Three years later, after staying a few weeks at Homburg-vor-der-Höhe, Mother and I went to see Agnès on her native heath. She had grown fat and looked prosperous and happy. Her brother's children, a boy and a girl, were pleasant young people, in a Hansel and Gretel sort of way, but shy. I got on better with them, after we had climbed a centuries-old linden-tree together. It stood in a courtyard, and the children told me it had been planted in the time of Luther.

We were given a wonderful repast, with both Rhine-wine and Pilsen. After which, the *Landbauer* showed me over his property, stretching down to willows by the river's bank. There were cows, pigs and ducks, and the still air vibrated to the distant cackle of the successful hen. I almost wished I could stay on there, to be looked after once more by Agnès.

She died in 1912, at the age of seventy, before the era of world wars, conflicting ideologies and will-o'-the wisp promises of a life without fear or want. The part of Germany that was Agnès's home is described in *A Tramp Abroad*. Mark Twain and Mr. Harris sail down the Neckar in a raft, and visit feudal castles, carrying alpenstocks and wearing muslin tails to their hats, in the tourist-fashion of their day. That was the Germany I first knew : a country of great forests, where lurked—why not ?—the elves of the Nibelungen, and of little square fields where cabbages grew red. Music and beer and romantic legends ; firelight glowing on a blue-tiled stove ; flowered cloth round a feather-bed ; corn and wine and pleasant cities ; Rhine-gold in the women's hair. . . . And, at Christmas Eve, children's voices, flute-like, pure, singing carols under the stars : ' *Stille Nacht !　Heilege Nacht !* '

9

' The Gentle Art of Making Enemies '

And the young man's dog went with him.

APOCRYPHA, Tobit v. 16.

A CONTEMPORARY of Agnès in our household at Rome was my dog, Chirillo. Indeed there was a perpetual feud between them. Not a bitter feud, but an agreement to differ.

Chirillo was a Roman *lupetto* and characteristically a *romano de' Roma* in his outlook and general behaviour.

One of the masques that used to figure in Italian comedy was called ' Rugantino '. This was the companion to Harlequin and to Pulcinella. He was supposed to be a representative Roman type, and as such he figured in Punch and Judy shows. The name is derived from the verb *rugà* (in the dialect of Trastevere). It means ' to growl '. And Chirillo was very much in character. He growled on the slightest provocation, and on none at all. And he could vary the expression from a threatening snarl, to a good-humoured protest at delay in taking him out for a walk.

I acquired Chirillo when he was already a full-grown dog, but we had known each other for some time. He belonged to Ettore, the head groom at Pieretti's riding-school and livery stable, where I kept a pony. Chirillo used to come out with me in a dog-cart ; it amused him to seize the reins in his teeth and pull them, snarling in well-simulated rage. His master, Ettore, had the offer of a place with Manolo Prinetti, who was leaving for Constantinople and taking his horses with him. In the end, neither Manolo nor his horses ever went to Constantinople, but meanwhile Chirillo had taken up his abode with me, and he stayed on.

But he continued to frequent his old haunts, and often had to be retrieved from the stables, where I would find him disporting himself with his old chum ' Renz ', a portly fox-terrier with a permanent stiff neck, which he had acquired by having been put into a fountain of icy-cold water, by some fool stable-boy, who saw him panting after a long run with the horses.

Chirillo only realized that I was indeed his new master when I took him with me for a few days' excursion to Porto d'Anzio on the sea. I went to stay there with Augusto Sindici, whose daughter, Magda, had married William Heinemann, the publisher.

Magda was with her mother, in Rome, but Heinemann came down to Anzio, to stay with us, and brought a friend, a thin, angular gentleman with long hair, whose name, at first, I did not catch (he and Heinemann called each other 'Willy' and 'Jimmy'). The stranger had a rather eccentric taste in clothes, and a flippant, sarcastic way of speaking. He and Chirillo disliked each other from the moment they first met. It was a case of hatred at first sight.

'Jimmy' was an artist, and he did a sketch of himself poking Chirillo with his walking-stick, which the latter seized in his teeth, drawing back his lips in a paroxysm of growling. This was one of many similar sketches. It appeared to be a habit of this painter (at least in the few days we were together) of making a drawing of himself every day, and then tearing it up. He signed his sketches— those that he did not tear up—with a W that resembled the outline of a butterfly. Sometimes the resemblance was more pronounced, as if there really were a butterfly in the picture.

The name I saw on his luggage—James McNeill Whistler—meant nothing to me, but he talked to me about George du Maurier, with whom he had lived in Paris. I had just been reading *Peter Ibbetson*, and in this eccentric artist's conversation—witty and satirical as it was—I heard echoes of du Maurier's rose-coloured reminiscence of an older Paris than that which bears the imprint of the Second Empire.

Whistler and I might have got on nicely, if it had not been for Chirillo. He alluded to me, in conversation, as 'the boy with the awful dog'. There was a touch of affectation both in Whistler and in Chirillo. In their hearts, they enjoyed abusing and growling at one another. But one morning, when we should have gone off together for an excursion in a sailing boat, Whistler refused to start, if Chirillo came too. On my part, I refused to abandon Chirillo, so I remained at the Villa, and the others started off across the shallow bay, in the direction of Torre la Stura, on the southern side of Nettuno.

The excursionists returned home about three in the afternoon, extremely sorry for themselves, but thankful to be alive at all.

They had landed on a sandy point, with the intention of taking a walk in the pine-woods near the shore, and of consuming the picnic lunch they had brought with them in a hamper. They were sitting, contentedly enough, on the slope of a sandy dune, eating *pagnottelle imbottite* (a kind of glorified sandwich) and drinking the light wine of the Alban hills, when Heinemann noticed a strange erection at the edge of the sea, consisting of some stout beams, supporting a triangle of timber, painted a dirty grey.

'What's that thing?' he asked.

In his youth, Whistler had been at West Point and in the Coast Survey. Such objects were familiar to him. He answered: 'It looks to me like a target for artillery practice.'

Sindici was an old soldier, who had fought in the battle of Solferino, and he nodded, with his mouth full. 'That's just what it is,' he began. 'A regiment of artillery is quartered down here, and they use this spit of land for . . .'

A strange, whining sound broke the silence of that desolate sea-shore. Then came a thud and an explosion, which sent barrelfuls of sand over the landscape and the luncheon-party. Artillery practice had begun!

The dauntless three rose to their feet. They did not stop to collect the eatables, or the drinks, but ran heavily over the sand in the direction of the pine-woods. They had hardly covered twenty yards, when again there came that ominous whine and a sickening thud. Again they were half buried under mountains of sand. This time, the shell exploded twenty yards before them in the direction in which they were proceeding.

Heinemann was for doubling back, but Sindici knew more about it, and he urged them forward. 'It's all right!' he gasped. 'They are finding the range. The next one will explode behind us.'

So it did. The party reached the shelter of the pine forest and lay down exhausted. After each shot—and they went on for some time—there came a rattling sound against the trunks of the trees. A new type of shrapnel was being tried out, and that was the tap of half-spent bullets.

After two hours, the firing ceased. The excursionists rose up and made their way back to their boat, which was slightly damaged by a bullet-hole or two. A sentinel saw them in the distance and shouted to them that they must not enter the danger zone. When he discovered that they had been in it all the time, he decided not to say anything about it, or he might have got into trouble himself.

Butterflies under the Arch of Titus

> Non curioso a te delle piccole cose io vengo
> chi le farfalle cerca sotto l'Arco di Tito ?
>
> CARDUCCI, *Roma*.

WHEN I went to school at the Ginnasio-Liceo Umberto I, in Rome, the ' Preside' (or Head), Giuseppe Chiarini, was a scholar and litterateur of some renown, author of the *Studi Shakespeariani*. He did much to make known to his nationals the foreign literary masterpieces, both German and English. Before his day, Italians did not read many foreign books ; they were content with the latest French novel.

Chiarini took a kindly interest in me, and did not cease to do so when he left the ' Umberto I ' to direct a department in the Ministry of Public Instruction. He encouraged me to attempt translations from English into Italian, and even suggested I should put Gray's *Elegy* into Italian verse. I did so, not very successfully, and with his help. It was he who pointed out to me the resemblance between ' The Curfew tolls the knell of parting day ', and the verses in the Eighth Canto of Dante's *Purgatorio* :

> . . . *squilla di lontano*
> *Che paja'l giorno pianger, che si muore.*

One Saturday afternoon (I must have been about fifteen at the time), I went to a thought-reading séance, by a magician or illusionist, at the Salone Margherita, in the Via Due Macelli. And I found myself in a row of seats just behind Chiarini, who was in the company of a robust-looking man with a ruddy countenance and an abundant crop of iron-grey hair, matched by a bushy beard. We got into conversation, and I was introduced to this gentleman, who was no other than the poet, Giosuè Carducci, a Nobel prize-winner for literature. During the thought-reading performance (of which I remember nothing), Carducci was invited to go on the stage, where he sat looking rather sheepish. Meanwhile Chiarini mentioned to me that the poet and he were going next morning (it being a holiday) for a walk in the Forum. Would I care to join them there, about eleven o'clock ?

Next day was fine and sunny. I was on the spot long before my time, waiting, as we had arranged, opposite the Temple of Antoninus and Faustina. I sat down on a fallen column, at the side of the Via Sacra, where wild clover and yellow arnica grew between the time-worn flags. For foreign tourists, the Forum is ' one of the sights '. For us, who live in Rome, it is part of our lives. Young couples meet there, children play, and old men doze in the sun on the steps of the Basilica Julia, where once the charioteers and litter-bearers waited for their masters. You can trace, on those marble steps, certain chiselled lines representing a draught-board, or the preliminary marking for ' Noughts and Crosses ', where idle men killed time with a game or two. No doubt that, in their day, as in ours, fat lizards made the most of the last warm days in October, to bask on sun-warmed bricks. And possibly, at the foot of the *rostra*, a cat may have brought out her family of kittens to enjoy the air, as a tortoiseshell pussy was doing on that morning in 1895.

The cat family, so I discovered, had their quarters in a small vaulted room, behind a doorway curtained with ivy, close to the Temple of Romulus, son of Maxentius. Close by, a pile of fragments was topped by an age-scarred piece of white marble, on which was sculptured, in bas-relief, the figure of a girl. Only the lower half of the figure remained, for the marble was broken at the height of the thighs. A pair of slim, bare legs were visible, under a swirl of draperies that lifted as she danced. The modelling of those feet was delightful ; they looked so light-hearted and happy ! No doubt that they were dancing (and must have been doing so, throughout the history of Rome).

I pointed out those little feet to Carducci and Chiarini, when they turned up. Something of my own interest must have infected them, for they stood there, speculating as to where the fragment might have come from. Possibly it was once part of a frieze in the Golden House of Nero, high up near the cornice of a banqueting hall.

Then we strolled up the slope, towards the Arch of Titus.

In Carducci's ode, *Roma*, inspired by the grandeur that was Rome, there is a famous verse, in which the poet disdains any curiosity as to the little, transient things of life. He asks : " Who would look for butterflies under the Arch of Titus ? "

Chiarini recalled this verse, as we approached the arch, where it stands proudly, on the rising ground between the Colosseum and the Forum. And sure enough there *were* some butterflies fluttering among the ruins on the slope up to the Palatine and through the arch, where are the bas-reliefs of Roman soldiers carrying the seven-branched candlestick that came from the Temple at Jerusalem.

I am more inclined now than I was then to philosophize over Carducci's simile of the butterflies and I am inclined to disagree with him ! Small personal incidents often interest us more than big events. Who would remember the harvest gathered in by the reapers of Boaz, were it not for the gleanings of Ruth that followed after ? In his *Apology for Idlers*, R. L. Stevenson quotes Saint Beuve who, as he grew older, came to regard all experience as a single book in which to study for a few years, ere we go hence ; and it seemed to him all one whether you should read in Chapter XX, which is the differential calculus, or in Chapter XXXIX, which is hearing the band play in the gardens.

I had not, when fifteen years old, the knowledge and the book-learning fully to appreciate our national poet. But I knew his fame. And I gazed with awe at the man who had put into verse so much of contemporary Italian thought and feeling, and so much of the greatness of our past. Carducci was part of Italy's resurrection, no less than Mazzini, Cavour and Garibaldi. Of his ode on Clitumnus (*Alle Fonti del Clitunno*), Sir Arthur Quiller-Couch said ' few nobler poems have adorned our time '. And he describes that poem in his own book *On the Art of Writing* :

He (Carducci) visited the beautiful, everlasting source, and of what did he sing. . . . He sang of the weeping willow, the ilex, ivy, cypress and the presence of the god still immanent among them. He sang of Umbria, of the ensigns of Rome, of Hannibal swooping down over the Alps ; he sang of the nuptials of Janus and Comesena, progenitors of the Italian people ; of nymphs, naiads, and the moonlight dance of Oreads ; of flocks descending to the river at dusk ; of the homestead, the barefooted mother, the clinging child, the father, clad in goat-skins, guiding the ox-wagon ; and he ends on the very note of Virgil's famous apostrophe

Sed neque Medorum silvae, ditissima terra . . .

with an invocation to Italy—Italy, mother of bullocks for agriculture, of wild colts for battle, of corn and of the vine, Roman mother of enduring laws and mediaeval mother of illustrious arts. The mountains, woods and waters of green Umbria applaud the song, and across their applause is heard the whistle of the railway-train bearing promise of new industries and a new national life.

E tu, pia madre di giovenchi invitti
a franger glebe e rintegrar maggesi
e d'annitrenti in guerra aspri polledri
Italia madre,

madre di biade e viti e leggi eterne
ed incliti arti a raddolcir la vita,
salve ! a te i canti de l'antica lode
io rinnovello.

Plaudono i monti al carme e i boschi e l'acque
de l'Umbria verde : in faccia a noi fumando
ed anelando nuove industrie in corsa
fischia il vapore.[1]

Reapers in the Moonlight

THERE is an episode of my childhood that would not be worth recording, were it not that it had a sequel after I had grown up and begun a diplomatic career. It is as if a melody that I had known when I was a little boy had been interrupted, and concluded only when I was a lively Attaché of twenty-seven.

Sometimes, in the summer months, I used to be asked to stay with Romeo Gallenga, at Mandoleto, near Perugia, on the road to Lake Trasimene. Romeo and I were of the same age, and we must have been eleven, or twelve, when we started to pass a month of June together, with no one to look after us but Nazareno, the coachman, and his wife, Lucia.

[1] And thou, pious mother of bullocks, unequalled for breaking the glebe and restoring the fallow, and of rough colts, neighing in battle—Italy mother.

Mother of corn and vine and laws eternal, and noble arts our life to sweeten. *Salve !* To thee I renew the songs of ancient homage.

The song is hailed by the applauding mountains, the woods and waters of green Umbria : there, before us, smoking and panting for new industries, whistles the train.

This unaccustomed, but to us entirely satisfactory, situation had arisen in consequence of the fact that the Signora Gallenga herself stayed on in Perugia, in her beautiful Palazzo, whereas Romeo and I were sent out to the country-house, as being more healthy for two rapidly growing little boys. It would have been absurd to have kept open a huge villa, for the benefit of a couple of ragamuffins like us ; so we were given a nice, cool bedroom in the building that contained the stables, and where Nazareno and Lucia also dwelt. They looked after us, or tried to. The Signora Gallenga sacrificed her comfort by this arrangement, for she deprived herself of her coachman, and therefore of the carriage and pair. She had to be content with a *biroccino*, a rustic conveyance, driven by a groom. Sometimes she drove out to see us, and at last was so horrified at our appearance and conduct that she decided to hasten her own arrival at the Villa by a few weeks. Even so, Romeo and I went native for a month or more.

I remember those days with feelings of amazement, nostalgia and pride. Never again was I destined to live so close to Nature and to the land. Romeo, who in later days became a real dandy, insisted on going about barefoot like the peasant children. To be able to do this, the soles of your feet must be hardened by constant contact with mother earth. I was less advanced than he in this respect, but I made up for it by an even greater neglect of my personal appearance. Romeo and I might have passed for Tom Sawyer and Huckleberry Finn. We never wore more than an old pair of pants, held up by one brace, and an old cotton shirt. The more rents and patches there were in these garments, the more we liked them. After some futile attempts to keep us clean and tidy, Lucia gave it up as a bad job. We were indistinguishable from the peasant children on the hillside.

In one of the neighbouring farms, or *fattorie*, a couple of foreigners were rusticating in the hot Umbrian summer. We heard them spoken of as *i due forestieri*, and we did not take the trouble to enquire who they were, or whence they came. We thought they might be Germans, but later we discovered that they were Austrians. Romeo and I were much impressed by their good looks, for they were typical examples of a nordic beauty. He might have posed as Lohengrin, and she as Elsa. The fact that they were not man and wife meant little to Romeo and me. We passed an occasional afternoon in their company, and they learnt some Italian from us. I remember his asking me how we said 'reapers'. I answered '*mietitori*' and he repeated to himself: '*Mietitori al chiar di luna.*' 'Reapers in the moonlight !'

This was because, down in the plain, the reaping was done at night, by the light of the full moon, which pleased the lovers enormously. They insisted on going down to help fill the granaries. Their clumsy efforts to bind the corn into sheaves were not much help to anybody, but they looked so happy that the hard-working peasants could not but grin appreciatively.

Sometimes, while they reaped, the peasants would sing. Their voices mingled with the song of the crickets in the willow-trees, along the irrigation-ditches. Fireflies rose from the stubble, and in the distance, blue hills, only a shade darker than the sky, were starred with white villages, ghostly in the moonlight.

'*Dans ton cœur dort un clair de lune !*'

I remember his whispering these words to her, as they passed close to me, with their arms full of corn-sheaves. A quotation, evidently, but I did not know where from.

★   ★   ★

Now let us pick up the scent again, further on . . .

It concerns what you might call my first diplomatic mission. And there is something almost symbolical in it, for the interests in my life have centred round three things : Italian emigrants abroad, animals, and beautiful women. There is a little in this story of all three.

The emigrants that I was instructed to help were Italians, but not human beings. They were cows. A question had arisen concerning the rights of pasturage in the Alpine valleys of the Dolomites. During many centuries, such matters had been regulated to the satisfaction of all concerned, by the so-called *Regole Cadorine*, local regulations dictated by a long experience. The number of cows that might be put out to graze in each valley was carefully considered, so that the pastures should not be overstocked during the summer months, when the herds came up from Venetia, to grow fat on the rich clover and lush grass, on the borders of mountain torrents.

But since the year 1866, there was a political frontier half-way up the mountain valleys, and almost every summer this caused trouble to the Italian cows. I imagined them mooing pathetically, to be allowed to pass the black and yellow barriers under the Marmolada and the Tre Cime di Lavaredo.

On one occasion, the First Secretary of the Embassy told me to go round to the Ministry of Agriculture, and see what I could do about it.

The Ministry of Agriculture, in Vienna, was situated not far from where I lived, in the Dominikaner Bastei. In due course I was ushered into a waiting-room, decorated with portraits of the Habsburg Emperors. A young official came to enquire the nature of my errand. The *Sekstionschef* competent to deal with my case (or that of the cows) was absent. The underlings who worked with him were not considered worthy to discuss the matter with the representative (however junior) of a foreign embassy. So it was decided that I should be received by the Under Secretary of State. Would I have the kindness to wait a few minutes, till he should be free?

So I sat on a sofa upholstered in green plush, and waited.

The name of the Under Secretary was familiar to me, though I had never met him. He was to have dined at our embassy a week or so before, and at the last moment had failed to turn up. His wife had come without him. This had caused me much mental agitation, as I was responsible for placing the guests at dinner. The last-minute alterations had not been satisfactory and my Ambassador had expressed disapproval. The Under Secretary's *Frau Gemahlin*, however, had enjoyed herself. She was a fat, comfortable-looking woman, with grey hair and rosy cheeks, and might have been handsome, except for a too-prominent nose. She was a jovial soul, with a fund of stories that had the genuine Viennese flavour.

I had placed her between a young arch-duke and the British Military Attaché, who was then the Duke of Teck. She kept the arch-duke in fits of laughter, but with the Duke of Teck, who was getting deaf, she had less success. I was just near enough to be able to catch a phrase or two, without being able to follow all that was said. During a lull in the general conversation, I gathered that she was describing a festival at the Capucine monastery in Linz, which her husband had attended in his official capacity. Some pretty girls had danced the peasant-dances of Ober Oesterreich, and His Excellency had admired them so much that he had paid scant attention to the local authorities who were there to receive him.

The arch-duke remarked : ' You should keep your husband in better order, *Gnädige Frau* ! '

' My husband has a roving eye for a pretty woman. What can you expect, when his wife has a nose like mine ? '

The arch-duke laughed and said something I did not catch for talk had broken out again along the dining-table. I asked the Councillor of the French Embassy, who was sitting near me, if he could tell me anything about the Under Secretary for Agriculture. His answer was contemptuous : ' A typical character out of Viennese operette. A *Zigeunerbaron*, whose love affairs keep perfect waltz-time. His wife offers comic relief.'

While I waited in His Excellency's anteroom, I wondered if I would find out what all this meant.

A few minutes later, I found myself in the presence of a good-looking man of about fifty, with fair hair that was turning grey and weary grey eyes. I could see nothing in him to remind me of Viennese operette, and certainly nothing gipsy-like (to justify the term *Zigeunerbaron*). Indeed, he was the typical Austrian official of the best class, stiff in manner, precise in speech, and hiding a touch of arrogance under a formal courtesy.

What struck me immediately was that I had met this man before. But I could not remember where, and there was no sign of recognition in his greeting. The effort to recall where and when I had met him in the past almost made me forget the matter in hand, and it was with some hesitation that I presented my case. I kept on thinking that not only his face was familiar. His voice, his gestures, a little trick of smoothing down his hair while talking : all these things I remembered.

His Excellency was very polite, very suave, full of apologies for the delay, but apparently there was a hitch. This was not due to any alarm of foot-and-mouth disease, but to some disagreement between the local authorities. But he hoped that, in a week or two, before the harvest . . .

20

The harvest ! That gave me the clue I had been hunting for, and without thinking, I said out loud : ' *Mietitori al chiar di luna !* '

His Excellency was puzzled. Evidently, he spoke some Italian, for he answered : ' Reapers . . . ? No. They are herdsmen, coming to the higher pasturage.'

I murmured softly : ' *Dans ton cœur dort un clair de lune.*'

He started, as if something had stung him.

' Who are you ? '

The question rang like a pistol-shot. The man's face had grown tense and pale. Even his eyes changed colour, and from grey they became almost white, as if from some hidden fire.

I pointed carelessly to the visiting-card that was lying on his desk, and answered : ' That is my name.'

' Yes . . . But . . . how do you know ? '

' I was one of the little boys you used to talk to at the *fattoria.*'

' Little boys ! What boys ? There were only some barefooted peasant children.'

' We went barefoot, certainly. But one of us was heir to the land, not to mention a Renaissance palace in Perugia.'

I meant Romeo, but His Excellency may have thought I was speaking of myself. He said nothing more, only got up from his chair and went and stared out of the window, while his fingers drummed gently on the panes. I could guess that it was not a Viennese street that he saw at that moment, nor the distant spire of the Stephansdom. More likely, the plain between Perugia and Assisi, a group of farm-houses on the hillside, and against the Raphaelite background of distant hills, a woman's face, fair, sweet, and gentle . . .

He seemed to be talking more to himself than to me (indeed he had his back to me), when he said : ' If you have been a lover in Italy, when you were young, it is as if you felt the pulse of the world throb through the fragrant earth in measure with the beating of your heart . . . '

He turned back to his desk, and stared down at me with a look that was slightly quizzical. ' I seem to remember,' he said, ' that there was a dog there, a *lupetto*, that used to growl at me when I patted him. . . . '

It was my turn to be surprised, and I exclaimed : ' So there was !

And to think that I should have forgotten him ! That was my dog, Chirillo.' And I added : ' What has happened to . . . ?' I had meant to ask what had happened to the lady. But perhaps it was tactless to enquire. However, he understood and answered the unfinished question :

' There is a reaper, and his name is Death. He cuts down the corn and the flowers that grow between.'

It ended that the cows got over the frontier to their pasturage. The French Councillor had been right : lovers and moonlight and a peasant chorus. Lehar might have set it all to music.

Calling up the Carriages

I BEGAN going out in society much too early in life. My *début dans le grand monde*, or coming-out party, was a ball at the Austrian Embassy to the Quirinal, to which I went with Mother in 1896. The Ambassador was Baron Pasetti. He occupied the first floor of the Palazzo Chigi.

I danced there many times in my youth (when the Austrian Ambassador was Count Lutzow), and I regret that the fine old palace should have been turned into a beehive of offices, even though, in the years 1923–24–25, I occupied one of those offices, myself.

On the occasion of Pasetti's ball, the walls of the long gallery had been decorated, for the occasion, in the Austrian colours. These should have been black and yellow, but to make them less sombre, the black of the *Schwarzgelb* had been substituted by its opposite. White walls were starred with bunches of daffodils. As the King and Queen moved about among the guests, they were preceded by the Embassy Secretaries (Flotow, Dumba, Fürstenberg), who gently persuaded people to make room : ' *De grâce, messieurs et dames, un peu de place pour Leurs Majestés !* '

In the Hall of the Galleys, the dancers were almost swamped in the crowd. I remember a radiant apparition suddenly emerging through a doorway, vivid, arch and eager—the Countess Annina Morosini. And later, a desultory conversation, overheard in the embrasure of a big window. Manolo Prinetti, who was getting very deaf, but would not admit it, asked the Contessa di Santa Fiore :

THE HON. MURIEL BECKETT, 1912

'Did you go to the opera last night, Countess?'

'No. I was tired. I went to bed.'

'Were there many people?'

*   *   *

In those days, there used to be a little lame man in Rome, whose profession it was to call up the carriages of the revellers coming out of dances and receptions, or the Costanzi opera-house. He has disappeared, together with the hostesses of his day. But he left a son, who reigns in his stead. There are fewer dances and receptions now, and people have acquired the habit of parking their own cars. The business is not what it used to be.

But sometimes, when I walk home at night and pass a familiar doorway, I hear in memory the lame man's voice, pealing out along the street, '*La carrozza di Sua Altezza la Principessa Hohenlohe!*' followed, as often as not, by muttered objurgations in the gruff voice of a surly coachman, thankful that his mistress (mentioned in disrespectful terms) has at last condescended to come home : '*Ah! Glie l'ha fatta, quella . . .*'

Only when Mother, on pleasure bent, went out at night, did I hear my own name called out and repeated, as in an echo, down a line of carriages, while men waited in opera hats, and ladies with jewels sparkling in their hair. This inevitable end to our revels seems to have acquired an almost symbolical significance, like a roll-call of the Past.

There is a story that, one evening, when the last guest came out from the Palazzo del Drago, where Mrs. Lee had been giving a dance for her grand-daughters, the lame man was heard to call out ironically : '*Le galosce del Conte de Witten!*'

Pippo de Witten, whose modest equipage consisted in nothing more imposing than a pair of galoshes, was an old bachelor, who never missed a party of any kind ; one of those people whose meals seemed to consist principally of 'refreshments', partaken of at crowded buffets, and interrupted by the obligation to bring a glass of lemonade and a sandwich to some weary dowager, chaperoning her daughters. Old de Witten—so a nephew told me—died in harness, that is to say, in his swallow-tailed coat and white tie, having been taken with a stroke, while preparing to go to some reception. Possibly, he was putting on his galoshes, when his name was called by a voice that was not that of the little lame man of the carriages. Could it have been Charon, waiting to give him a lift home, across the Styx?

Mrs. Lee's carriage has also been called, and so has that of her sister, Mrs. Hulbert. They lived in Rome for more years than I can count, but not together. It must have been that they both enjoyed society so much, and the pleasure of receiving in one's own house, that they would not divide these joys by sharing them. So Mrs. Hulbert had her own apartment in the Palazzo Sciarra, on the Corso.

Mrs. Lee's daughter, whom I never knew, had married Ernest Beckett (Lord Grimthorpe) and had three children : Lucile, Muriel and Ralph. She died young. Mrs. Lee's principal mission in life was to be a grandmother, and the children were brought up partly by her, when they stayed in her house in Rome, in an American, cosmopolitan atmosphere.

When her grandchildren were there, Mrs. Lee's apartment in the Palazzo del Drago was open to all her friends, and we would go in and out, on one excuse or another, every day and all day.

My own excuses were numerous and varied, but they centred round the youngest granddaughter, Muriel, or ' Moony '.

She was my first love. And I doubt if either of us were ever so happy again, as when we used to meet, in the springtime of the year and of our lives, in the del Drago garden, when noon was on the roses. We shared, as young people do

> The love of higher things and better days
> The unbounded hope and heavenly ignorance
> Of what is called the world and the world's ways.

Does Moony's ghost look over my shoulder, I wonder, as I write these lines? If so, she will smile at the echo of a youthful ardour, in this old man with white hair.

' Never fear, Moony darling ! I am not going to claim that you loved me better than you loved Mrs. Lee's adorable puppy, that was always getting into trouble, and howled when it was left at home. When I suggested marriage, you did not agree. And though it is first love that gives the freedom of the city, I might say to you, as Cyrano to Roxane, in the last act :

> ' Non, non, mon cher amour, je ne vous aimais pas ! '

Marriage has been described as a state of antagonistic collaboration :
much too serious a proposition for the likes of us. But it was sweet
—April sweet—to be together and enjoy what our world had to offer.
We meet again, after all the years, on this page !

In our halcyon days, England and Italy, Paris and Dresden, Lombard
lakes and Scottish moors, were one happy playground. And the
centre of it all was Rome. What was Rome, to you and me ?

The breath of tall pines round the Piazza di Siena, and daisies
underfoot ; roses and lilac in the spring air ; violets nestling in the
shade of cork woods ; fumes of incense from the open door of a little
chapel. The stately gait of women, carrying burdens on their heads ;
splash of water falling into fountains in squares with medieval names ;
bells in the steeples, with pigeons flying round them ; little lights at
the corners of old palaces, underneath an image of the Madonna ;
rust-coloured walls bathed in the afternoon sun ; children selling
flowers on the steps of basilicas ; lovers in the straight paths, among
the box-hedges of the Villa Medici ; the sheen and coolth, when
streets were watered on hot, dusty afternoons ; cats sunning themselves on broken columns in the Forum of Trajan, and being fed by
charitable old ladies ; women chaffering at the rag-market in the
Campo dei Fiori ; old men watering their plants on roof terraces,
while swallows swoop and shrill in the sunset glow.

And rides in the campagna, where the wild thyme was crushed by
the hooves of our horses ; excursions to the Alban hills, on donkeys
from Albano, to the sacred grove of Ariccia ; home-comings, laden
with cyclamen and wild anemones ; other home-comings in the
small hours, when the dawn came stealing over the roofs, and the
sleeping city had scents and sounds that are unknown during the day.

Rome seemed so small to us then, almost as if it were one house :
the squares our own rooms, and the villas our own garden. And yet
so big ! Bigger than London, or Paris, or New York . . . for it
contained our dreams.

Sad that Italy having brought us together, the next link between
Moony and myself should have been a doctor, and his Klinik in Berlin !

Ernst von Leyden was one of a group of German scientists
(Senator, Fresiche, von Strumpell, Moebius), who—like their contemporary English surgeons and bacteriologists—created a new epoch

in medicine and gave their names to various illnesses, for which they discovered a cure. These men were real pioneers, and they made possible the conquests of our present-day virtuosi in the realm of surgery.

I first knew Leyden in December 1899, when I was a student of music in Berlin, and Mother came to see me there. He attended her in a brief illness. At that time, there used to be a bullfinch that fluttered and hopped about his study, sometimes alighting on his shoulder even when he was interviewing a patient. Later on, he was Moony's doctor, and she was devoted to him. He might have saved her, if anyone could. But she went to him, I believe, when other doctors had lost time with ineffective cures.

I went to Berlin to visit her in hospital, but was not allowed to see her, for she had just had an operation. I had to leave again, before she got better. I said something to Leyden about my not having known that he was going to operate. He answered that she herself had insisted on keeping it dark, because her sister was expecting a baby and Moony did not want to cause her anxiety.

In illness, she revealed a strength, indeed a nobility of character that I have seldom seen equalled.

Sparrows in the Chandelier

IN Anthony Hope's novel, *Simon Dale*, a young man from the country, in the days of Charles II, comes up to London and meets an enchantress, called Nell Gwyn. In the contest for her favours, he almost becomes a rival of the King himself. Extreme youth and inexperience sometimes find doors open that are shut to wealth and power and worldly wisdom.

If I were to assure the reader that I never was the lover of Lina Cavalieri, he might think the disclaimer unnecessary. But a man of the world would smile and say that I am lying like a gentleman. With this premise, let me tell a story, on the lines of *Simon Dale*.

I have met amiable cynics in my time, but none who equalled Carlo di Rudinì in his disregard for the ordinary reticences of good society. He was the son of the Marchese di Rudinì, one time Italian Prime Minister, and perhaps the wealthiest land-owner in Sicily.

Carlo's favourite occupation was gambling for incredibly high stakes. A passion for the card-table made all other interests pale by comparison.

Once I met him at the Bar of the Grand Hotel in Rome, and he surprised me by asking casually : ' Would you like to see a photograph of Papà ? '

The Marchese di Rudinì had died many years before, and I did not remember that his son, during the old man's lifetime, had shown much filial affection. But I expressed a suitable interest, whereupon Carlo took out his pocket-book and extracted from it a snapshot representing a small and seedy-looking individual, with a squint and side-whiskers.

I protested : ' This man is about half your father's size. And where are his beard and monocle ? '

' I never said it was the father you knew. This is another one, a cobbler in Budapesth. He has been kind enough to adopt me. So I call him Papà.'

Carlo and his wife (the daughter of Henry Labouchère) had decided to seek a divorce, and had become temporary citizens of a country where divorce was possible. Carlo had acquired Hungarian nationality, by the simple method of paying a cobbler in Budapesth to adopt him as his son.

I became unexpectedly intimate with Carlo Rudinì many years before his adoption by the Hungarian cobbler. This was after I had been asked to stay with friends at Monte Carlo. My host who, for obvious reasons, must be nameless, was a married man, but—so I was given to understand—did not get on very well with his wife. Nevertheless, when I appeared on the scene, she was expected to arrive from Paris a few days later.

Among the domestic staff was a pretty housemaid, who gave me a friendly warning to clear out, before the châtelaine arrived at Monte Carlo. That house, she told me, was no place for anyone so young as I. Evidently she had some reason to dislike her mistress. She said of her :

' *Elle cherche de se faire pincer en flagrant délit.*'

I have not ventured to translate this phrase, lest I should modify the sense in any way. I was not slow to take the hint. Before my hostess arrived, I had left for the Hôtel de Paris.

I gave as an excuse that I had some friends there, who wished me to join them. This was true only in part. Carlo di Rudinì was about the last person in the world to desire my company in ordinary times. We moved in different circles.

Carlo was the classical *viveur* of the last century, and he was careful to live up to his legend. He had brought with him to Monte Carlo a girl who, not very long before, had been selling flowers in the streets of Rome (here you have the analogy with Nell Gwyn, who sold oranges in Old Drury). Lina Cavalieri hailed from Viterbo, and was more familiar with the woodcutters' paths on ' the Ciminian Hill ' than with byways of the Riviera.

She was in her first youth, and resembled the girl in Goldsmith's *Deserted Village*, ' Sweet as the primrose peeps beneath the thorn.' Her beauty (and in a short time, the fame of her beauty) easily eclipsed that of the bejewelled courtesans (Cléo de Merode, la Belle Otéro, etc.) who queened it in the demi-monde of the Gay Nineties. But when I first met her in Monte Carlo, she was as yet unknown and glad to find in me someone with whom to talk in her native dialect. A bond between us arose, incongruously enough, owing to the fact that we were both rather bored with Monte Carlo. Indeed, had not Carlo introduced me to her and allowed a certain intimacy to grow up between us, I would have left again for Rome. To Lina and to myself, those worldly cosmopolitans appeared dull beyond words ! We were not up to their standard and did not want to be. Russian Grand-dukes, North American and South American millionaires, ' mediatized princes ' from Germany and Austria, English peers and brewers, Jewish moneylenders, Frenchmen whose names were synonymous with the best chocolate and the most expensive perfumes, Indian rajahs and Scandinavian Kings—they were all very well as a spectacle, and some of the stories about them were amusing, as their mistresses vied with each other in the richness of their toilettes, and the sparkle of their jewels. But they were no fit company for a boy in his teens. And Lina, as yet, did not dare to cope with them.

You might have thought that Carlo Rudinì would object to any close familiarity between myself and the girl whom he had ' launched ' so successfully. Instead of which, he encouraged it. At the time, I was puzzled. Now that I am old and worldly-wise, I can guess his motive. There were many well-known owners of yachts and villas on the Riviera, who would willingly have carried Lina off from under Carlo's aristocratic nose. To have lost her to some other cut-throat of his own magnitude would have wounded his vanity. But he did not mind if she took a liking for an inexperienced, insignificant Venetian boy, like myself. Indeed, it did not matter to Carlo, even if the *cavalier servente* were to become an *amant du cœur*. These technicalities of gallantry mattered not at all to a cynic of his calibre. What he wanted was that I should keep the girl amused, while he went hunting more profitable game. He was quick to notice that neither Lina nor I were fascinated by the glitter and glamour of our surroundings. And he watched us good-humouredly, as we sat and yawned at a little table at Ciro's (at two in the morning) and agreed between ourselves that the boiled egg which cost 15 francs (three dollars), even though the charge included the privilege of sitting in the same café as the Prince of Wales, tasted not so good as the eggs that in Rome cost a halfpenny each. In that over-heated, cigar-laden atmosphere, we would recall the *porchetta* that one bought off stands in the Piazza Navona, and ate standing in the street, and the artichokes (*carciofi alla giudia*), as they fried them, in oil, in the Ghetto.

I ought to have been going back home, but meanwhile Lina fell ill. It was not much of an illness, and after ten days in bed, she was up and out again, looking lovelier than ever. During those days, the hotel management provided a French nurse to look after her. But Lina did not like the French nurse. She would send me running to the chemist's, to procure medical products, which I need not specify. It ended in my nursing her, myself. Carlo smiled, and raised no objection.

I remember one evening after she got well again. We were all three together, in her bedroom. Lina was seated at the toilet-table, doing something to her hair. Carlo was all ready to go out. I was in an armchair, revelling in the sight of the loveliest bare arms and shoulders, and the beautiful face reflected in the glass.

Lina said she would have a light supper sent up to her room, since Carlo evidently proposed making a night of it, first at the Casino, and later at the Cercle Sportif. He did not want any woman near him, while he was staking huge sums on the turn of a card. Yet he could not refrain from a jibe that included both Lina and me. I can see him now, with the little pointed beard that made him look like the satyr that he was, and the mocking smile that showed his white teeth (faun-like, he should have been vine-crowned, to hide his pointed ears !). He stood with a black overcoat over one arm, the lights from candles on the toilet table reflected on the satin lining, as on the white expanse of his shirt-front. And he stared down at us through his monocle.

' Do you know,' he asked, ' what you two remind me of ? Of those sparrows that, for some extraordinary reason, have made a temporary home in the chandelier at Ciro's. They hop about under the tables. A schoolboy and a peasant-girl are just as out of place in Monte Carlo ! '

I did not answer, nor did Lina. We both felt that the comparison was rather apt. And Carlo concluded :

" Well, good night, both of you. Heaven knows at what time I'll be back. I won't disturb you, Lina. If tomorrow morning we're awake about nine, I'll come in and have breakfast."

With a casual nod, he passed out of the room, humming an air from Le Roi d'Ys. And the door closed behind him, and I sat on, still saying nothing, while Lina went òn attending to her hair, her eyebrows and her lips. Then she glanced round at me and said :

' You will stay and have supper, won't you, my fellow-sparrow ? '

★   ★   ★

Lina married more than once. For a few days, her husband was an American. For a few years, she was the wife of Prince Bariatinsky. When she grew older, she published a book of Mémoirs, called Le Mie Verità. I am not mentioned in that book, nor is Carlo di Rudinì.

Not many years ago, I was passing through Rieti, having been on a pilgrimage to the shrine of Santa Rita da Cascia. I stopped for a cup of coffee at the hotel, and noticed a good-looking elderly lady, who had an air of being somebody important. As she passed out, our eyes met, but there was no recognition in them. I asked the porter who she might be, and he answered : ' That was Lina Cavalieri.'

Besides some property near Rieti, she owned a small villa at Fiesole. She was living there when Florence was bombarded, and there she met her death. Her villa was destroyed, with its inmates.

The Cry of the Children

> And the child's sob in the silence curses deeper
> Than the strong man in his wrath.
>
> ELISABETH B. BROWNING.

AN old-fashioned but pleasant magazine that has disappeared from circulation since the days of my youth was *Temple Bar*, once published by Macmillan. The outer cover was of faded rose-colour, illustrated with an engraving of Christopher Wren's gateway, that used to slow down the traffic where Fleet Street meets the Strand, over against the Law Courts. Both gate and magazine have passed away.

In its number for February 1905, *Temple Bar* published a story of mine called 'The Valley of the Bees'. This title veiled, rather than revealed, a subject in which I took a philanthropic interest, when I was a young man, just out of my teens.

Ideals that inspire a lifetime are sometimes born in unaccustomed surroundings. To find the mainspring of endeavour in my public life, I must go back in memory to wanderings that took me far from my habitual environment : to glass-factories in the Valley of the Loire, to railways under construction in the Swiss Alps, and to the highlands of Ethiopia.

An Italian diplomat, the Marchese Raniero Paulucci de Calboli, first drew my attention to the infamous treatment meted out to Italian boys, employed in the French *verreries* in the Departements of the Rhone, the Seine, Puy-de Dome, and the suburbs of Lyons. Paulucci was interested in the different forms of what has been called 'pathological emigration' : the exploitation abroad, by foreign employers, and parasitical intermediaries, of the poorer class of emigrants. The classical type of this white-slave traffic is that of girls exported for prostitution. Paulucci published articles, subsequently collected in a book, in which he followed the migrations of organ-grinders, *pifferari*, glass-workers, unwilling prostitutes and those little boys from Lucca who modelled and sold statuettes in terracotta.

These last were called *figurinai*, or *stucchinai*. They might be seen in the streets of Paris and other big towns, sometimes after midnight, trying to dispose of statuettes representing Garibaldi, various saints, and the crowned heads, past and present, of Europe. If they had not affected a sale, they would hardly dare to go home. The people who took pity on them more often were the women of the streets, whose hearts were touched by the sight of children, trying to earn a living on the same ' beat ' as themselves.

The dealers in terracotta statuettes were dispersed over the West, but the little Italian and Spanish carriers and gatherers in the glass factories were to be found in the valleys of the Haute Loire and of the Seine. Inspired by Paulucci's teaching and example, I took an active interest in them, though I do not claim to have done more than round off some of the work that others had begun.

In a conversation I had with Paulucci, he pointed out the scant effect produced by official protests made through our Ambassador in Paris, Count Tornielli. Diplomacy has limited powers to combat vested interests. But a report of Lionello Scelsi, Vice Consul at Lyons, was given a publicity rarely accorded to official documents of a non-political character. After which a moral and humanitarian crusade was launched, both in Italy and in France. Paulucci's articles in the *Revues des Revues* were followed by editorials in *Le Matin*. An Association was formed in Turin, and two missions of enquiry visited the *verreries* and denounced the evils they discovered. Both the Italian Parliament and the French authorities were roused. At the same time, a Neapolitan lawyer, Ugo Cafiero, toured the regions of Campania and Terra di Lavoro, where the child-emigrants were recruited. Other leaders in the campaign were Professor Schiaparelli, the Egyptologist ; Marchese Sommi Picenardi, and Tomaso Gallarati Scotti (the same who, in 1947, was appointed Italian Ambassador in London).

* * *

Technological progress has put an end to most of the processes of manipulation, which were once necessary to produce an ordinary glass bottle. Pressing is now carried out by a so-called ' plunger ', and the human breath has been replaced by compressed air. But when I was young, boys much younger than myself were so necessary

to the glass industry that in some of the French *verreries* a skilled
'blower' could not get a job unless he brought one or two boy-
helpers to assist him. These were known as *gamins, porteurs* and
grand-garçon chauffeurs.

The *gamin* had to gather a blob of molten glass from the furnace-
mouth by means of a blow-pipe, then roll it on a slab of stone and
slightly expand it with his breath, before handing the tubular iron
to the professional blower, or *ouvrier*. The *porteur* had to catch the
tube on which the half-finished bottle was impaled and which the
ouvrier threw to him from a distance of about six feet, and he had to
run off with it to the cooling room near by, and return *prestissimo*,
to await another. Woe to him if he let a bottle fall! The *ouvrier*
was paid by the piece. Speed interested him more than the well-
being of his subordinates.

In the vicinity of the tank-furnaces, the heat might read 40 degrees
centigrade in winter, and 60 in summer. The mere strain of running
in and out of rooms with different temperatures was ruinous to the
health of undernourished boys. The coal-dust suspended in the air,
and the gases discharged from the amalgam, helped to develop
tuberculosis. The passing of the blow-pipe from mouth to mouth
also facilitated the contagion of syphilis.

Work continued day and night, in eight-hour shifts, the first
beginning at four a.m. till midday ; the second ending at eight o'clock
in the evening ; the third ran from eight p.m. till four a.m. No
ouvrier ever worked overtime. But the supply of boys being in-
sufficient, it was a normal practice of the *verreries* to oblige them to
work in two shifts running. Such a *doublage* was prohibited by law,
but the legal restrictions were difficult to enforce, and a fine of five
francs hardly acted as a deterrent.

The legal age at which a French boy could be employed was
thirteen. Even at that age, very few French parents would subject
their children to such a strain. *Gamins* and *porteurs* had to be recruited
abroad. They came mostly from the two Italian provinces of
Caserta and Campobasso. The demand for children was so urgent
that the parents of several were sometimes offered a job at the same
time, a sinecure bringing in 60 francs a month, whereas the children
were paid from 60 to 100 francs. They themselves, however, only

received a few centimes on a Sunday, the rest was kept by those who had procured them and who were supposed to feed, house, and look after them. Education was not an item of expenditure, for the boys were left without instruction of any kind.

Medical attendance was almost non-existent, for both employers and *incettatori* feared to reveal the unhealthy conditions in which the boys worked, and the dangerous nature of their tasks. A boy with a hideous burn from molten glass falling on his foot had it washed with petroleum, and that's all. Burns were frequent, for the boys ran about in clumsy wooden clogs that left the instep exposed.

Boys who went to France in the care of a parent were not ill-treated, apart from being overworked. But the father of a couple of *gamins* would be encouraged to palm off other children as his own, and thus he became party to a fraud. The privileged ones would be employed in the vicinity of Paris, on less fatiguing work than bottle-making. But the boys who emigrated in charge of an *incettatore* were literally sold into slavery. Yet often it was the children themselves who begged their parents to let them go abroad. They were dazzled by the prospect of travel, and by specious promises of high pay, easy work, good food and fine clothes, in a rich country.

They left Italy, to enter France, as often as not with identification papers that were fraudulently altered in the essentials of age, parentage and even surname. Passports were based on the information contained in birth certificates, delivered by Italian communes, and the *incettatori* were always provided with the birth-certificates of other, older boys. These would be used to palm off a wretched child of ten years old, as a boy of fifteen, or more.

' *Qu'ils sont petits, ces italiens !* ' was the ironical comment of the French employers, who were perfectly aware of the swindle.

To their honour be it said that the French authorities were not indifferent, but the Labour Inspectors had the greatest difficulty in their efforts to put it down. At Rive-de-Giers, in the Richarmes factory, they once found no boys employed at all. A system of vedettes, always on the look-out, permitted the employer to hide the little slaves in a disused furnace while the inspectors were on the premises. A few weeks later, a surprise visit by Italian enquirers (who at first were not recognized as such) discovered the presence

34

of numerous groups of *gamins* and *porteurs* at work before the furnaces.[1]

The local inspectors could not question Italian children who knew no French, and the children themselves were afraid of telling the truth, well knowing what punishments awaited them, if they complained. After a few days at the furnace-mouth, the boys' eyes would become bloodshot, their mouths and nostrils blackened by gaseous emanations from the blow-tubes, their thin bodies scarred with blows and burns. They were fed mostly on black bread, and put to sleep four in a bed, with straw mattresses, in conditions of indescribable filth and misery.

Let me give the name of a victim, one only : Filippo Varallo, whose sufferings were denounced to the police by horrified neighbours, and the police pointed him out to the Italians who came to investigate. The boy could not have been more than eleven years old, but was listed as being seventeen. He was woken up out of a kind of stupor, but could not answer intelligibly, which was not surprising as he had been at work for sixteen hours at a stretch. He did not know his own name. His huge eyes had in them no sparkle of life. There was a woman with him, who claimed to be his aunt, and she succeeded in preventing his being given up to his would-be rescuers. He cannot have lived much longer, where he was found, at the Bâtiment des Combles.

I mentioned the *Verrerie* of Monsieur Richarmes (this name figures in many official reports and in an article by G. Sommi Picenardi in the *Nuova Antologia* on 1st February 1902). It was situated at Rive-de-Giers, where, in a street aptly called La Rue Noire, ten Italian

---

[1] The following is an extract from the *Journal Officiel*, No. 282, of the 17th October 1901 :

". . . C'est surtout dans les verreries que sont constatées les infractions les plus graves et les plus nombreuses. Des jeunes garçons, des petites filles même, y sont occupés dès l'age de dix ans, et c'est par la déclaration des accidents dont ces malheureux enfants ont été victimes q'un certain nombre de contraventions ont été connues du service. En ce cas, l'age des victimes est majoré, et ce n'est qu'après une enquête minutieuse que l'inspecteur finit par connaitre la verité. On ne saurait réprimer trop énergiquement de tels abus.

" Les maîtres verriers se retranchent derrière la difficulté de recrutement de leur personnel enfantin ; d'autre part, la complicité des parents est parfois revoltante.

" Ce genre d'infraction est d'ailleurs très difficile à surprendre, les usines ayant plusieurs issues favorisant la fuite des enfants. Ainsi faut-il quelque-fois déléguer deux ou trois inspecteurs pour faire œuvre utile."

children lived in a stall, where once there had been a stable, and where a disused staircase served as a latrine, so that the stench, as you approached, almost knocked you down.

It is an old trick among the traffickers in human flesh, to camouflage their activities under a cloak of charity. This kind of swindle figures even in literature. It furnished Henry Seton Merriman with the subject for a novel, *Roden's Corner*, and Sir Arthur Quiller-Couch describes, in *True Tilda*, a clerical *incettatore* : the Rev. Dr. Purdie Glasson, Principal of the Holy Innocents Orphanage, of Bursfield, near Birmingham.

Benedetto Carlesimo, member of a family of *incettatori* that ended by being expelled from France, had the bright idea of printing a little pamphlet, purporting to be the statutes and prospectus of a charitable institution presided over by himself. There followed a list of the benevolent persons who gave the institution their backing. The crowning touch (both in the literal and figurative sense) was the claim that the institution enjoyed the patronage of the Queen of Italy.

With such inducements, what wonder that the people in remote towns and villages, made gullible by their bitter poverty, were persuaded to confide their children to a charitable individual, who even offered to give them a hundred lire a year, per child, for themselves.

The end would come, after a year or less, when the little *porteur* or *gamin* became too ill to work any more. Then his owner would take him to the Italian Consul General in Lyons, or in Paris, to be repatriated. And here again, the *incettatore* would pose as a charitable individual, who had discovered the boy's condition by mere chance, and had befriended him, after finding him wandering about the streets. Nor would the child itself dare to contradict this statement, even if he were in a condition to understand what it was all about.

A social evil, such as the white-slave traffic in its various forms, cannot be eradicated in a few weeks or months. It is apt to reappear wherever poverty, *mala suada fames*, makes trustful people easy to victimize. In 1902, the *incettatori*, balked in Italy, began to seek new sources of profit elsewhere. I learned from Monsieur Lépine, Prefect of Police in Paris, and from Monsieur Paturet, a Magistrate in Lyons, that when we had delivered the small Italian boys from the clutches of their inhuman employers, other batches of sallow, dark-eyed little boys began to arrive, not from beyond the Alps, but from beyond the Pyrenees.

An Italian boy, whose parents had begged for his return, was traced to Choisy-le-Roi, but disappeared before he could be rescued. His particular slave-owner took him to England, with the idea of finding employment for him in a glass-factory near Birmingham.

I had seen how much practical good had been done by Paulucci's writings in French, and I imagined that it might be of some use to draw the attention of the public, in English, to a humanitarian cause. But numerous rejection slips from the editors of important reviews showed that the matter had scant interest for them. So I took up my pen again and wrote 'The Valley of the Bees', as mentioned at the beginning of this chapter. In due course, it appeared in the pages of *Temple Bar* : a typical nineteenth-century magazine-story of the mawkish, sentimental kind. By turning myself into an eccentric but philanthropic Roman Prince, in love with a pretty American, I managed to bring in the facts about the glass-factories, and some of my own modest activities.

Another foreigner, writing in English, has written on the same subject, though I did not realize this till a few years ago, when my daughter, Diana, gave me a book that she had picked up in Biarritz. It is called *Memories and Vagaries*, by Axel Munthe. I had never heard of their being published, but some of those *Memories* were already known to me. Munthe himself had told me of them.

Let me re-tell a small incident described in Doctor Munthe's pages about Sœur Philomène, one of the Sisters of St. Augustine, serving in a big Paris hospital.

One evening, a boy who had been found lying unconscious in the street was brought in from the police-station. He was bleeding from an ugly wound in his head, and was stiff with cold. Only some thin, ragged clothes protected him against the winter's night. When Sister Philomène put him to bed, he remained unconscious for some time, and then began to moan. Soon he opened his large, wondering eyes. And his hands groped about, in search of something. He became quieter, after he had got hold of the tiny fiddle, which had been found with him and which constituted his whole outfit.

He could not be got to speak, and the French Doctor was about to write upon the slate over his bed : *Commotion cérébrale ; perte de parole*. But a characteristic southern gesture gave Axel Munthe a clue to the boy's nationality. And he asked him : ' *Tu sei italiano ?* '
' *Sissignore. Vengo da Napoli.* '

The little emigrant had found a friend, but too late . . . The winter's night had been too cold for him. As the day wore on, he began to cough. During three nights, Sister Philomène watched over him, and on the fourth he died. I give the end of the story in Axel Munthe's own words :

No one had taken any notice of him before ; he belonged to nobody as long as he was alive, but once dead, he belonged, according to hospital rules, to the dissecting room. He had hardly grown cold before they came to carry him down to the Anatomical Hall, where his frail little body was soon to be cut to pieces by the dissecting knives of the students. Sœur Philomène and the doctor were standing by his bed, and their eyes met. He who had been unable to save the life of his little friend, now covered his face with the sheet, and beckoned silently to the porter to delay his errand ; and he went down to see *Monsieur le Directeur*. . . .

In the evening a small coffin was carried out of the hospital gates ; the funeral procession was not a long one, only a Sister of Charity and a student. The homeless little vagabond lay there in peace, with his broken fiddle in his hand. And of all the wealth of flowers which the luxury of the winter metropolis borrows each morning from the summer of the South, a handful of violets had found its way into the coffin of the curly-headed little musician, with a fragrant greeting from the land of his birth, where his mother that same evening, in the little church high up on the mountains, implored the Madonna to watch over her child wandering about alone over the world.

The problem of Italian child-emigrants, though not as it existed in my youth, has now re-emerged among the greater problems, left over by two world wars. And these problems are both national and international. A new and vaster community of *Les Misérables* has arisen among the ruins of a world that has passed away. You might seek among those ruins for the ideals that I pursued when I was young.

If I have done nothing much in my life to be proud of, at least it has happened to me, once or twice, to find, far from home, a little boy in tears, and to have left him smiling.

LINA CAVALIERI

Giovanni Colonna di Cesarò

ONE morning, during carnival in 1898, I received a message, asking if —as I played the violin—I would join a party of young bloods, who were proposing to serenade the Fahrensbach girl. I did not know the lady, but I accepted with enthusiasm. At the age of eighteen, the prospect of playing the violin in the street, on a cold winter's night, was more attractive than it would be now.

We met by appointment at No. 75 Via Nazionale, where Giovanni Colonna lived with his mother, née Sonnino (a sister of Baron Sidney Sonnino, who represented Italy, together with Orlando, at the Peace Conference in Paris, after the first world war).

Giovanni's name, as given in the *Almanach de Gotha*, was :

Giovanni Antonio Francesco Giorgio Landolfo Colonna, 8th Duke of Cesarò, Duke of Reitano, Marquess of Fiumedinisi, Count of Sant' Alesio, Baron of Joppolo, etc. etc.

He was the head of the Sicilian branch of the Colonna family, descended from Federigo Colonna, called ' the Roman ', who established himself in Sicily in the year 1223.

The friendship between Giovanni and myself began when our hearts were full of the lighter melodies, which may explain why we should have serenaded the Fahrensbach girl. As a matter of fact we never did so, for we played and sang on the wrong side of the house. The only person to benefit was the cook. Giovanni was not musical, but he contributed to the concert, playing a rustic instrument known as a *pu-ti-pù* : an earthenware jar with the top covered with sheepskin, drawn tight as a drum. Through the skin was stuck a reed, which you rubbed up and down with your hand, producing a sound like a grunt. It was a low-toned instrument, like a double-bass, suitable for accompaniments.

No lily-white hand appeared between half-opened shutters, to throw down a red rose. After a few tunes that elicited no response, we moved off. Just then, a sudden fluttering and squawking in the air preceded the arrival from above of a large gallinaceous fowl, who with many turkey-cock ejaculations, settled at our feet and allowed himself to be caught. From the direction of his downward flight, we

decided that he must have come from the house opposite the Fahrensbach residence. Possibly he had escaped from a cage, or pen, on the
top of a flat roof. We woke up the house-porter and offered to
return the turkey to its rightful owner. But the porter knew nothing
about it and was indignant at being disturbed in the middle of his
beauty-sleep. The turkey came home with me, and some days later
we ate him, before going to a masked ball (or *veglione*) at the Costanzi
opera-house.

During that entertainment, I came in touch, for the first time in my
life, with Far Eastern diplomacy. This was when, in the lightness of
my heart, I pulled the pigtail of a Chinese Mandarin, feeling sure
that it would come off. But it didn't. The wearer was not, as I
had imagined, a masked reveller, but a foreign diplomat : no other
than the Minister in Rome of the Son of Heaven, Kuang-hsu, Emperor
of China !

Having discovered that we were kindred spirits, Giovanni and I
were always on the look-out for some new means to get rid of our
superfluous energy. Among other things, we organized paper-chases
on bicycles, on summer nights, in the older part of the town, through
narrow lanes that bear the names of medieval and papal Rome (the
Street of the Golden Mask, the Court of the Bloody Tower).

' Hounds met ' in front of Latour's Café, where the Colonna Palace
has an outer tower, at the corner of the Via Nazionale. There were
not many social doings in Rome, during summer months in motor-
less days. *Faute de mieux*, smart ladies and their daughters used to
congregate at midnight, round the little tables outside Latour's, and
partake of ices, while they watched us move off. And it happened
that they would sometimes rub elbows with ' ladies ' who were not
listed in the Social Register of Rome (the so-called *Carnet Mondain*).
On one occasion a Member of the Hunt turned up in an open cab, or
botticella, with two girls (described as *chanteuses*) and their maid, in
white apron and cap. The maid was seated on the box, next to the
cabman. I abstain from giving the name of the young man who was
responsible for this turn-out, for he now considers himself a respectable
member of society. Mutual friends may identify him when I add
that some weeks later he went off with a lady who sold neck-ties in
the Via Condotti, and travelled all over Sicily with her. They passed

themselves off as Delegates to an Agricultural Congress, then meeting
at Palermo.

Our nocturnal paper-chases used to finish up with a fish-supper at
Bucci's in the Pescheria. These were the rowdiest meals that I have
ever attended. Only one of our party behaved with any pretence at
decorum, and this was the Baron Kuhn von Kuhenfeld, Councillor
of the Austrian Embassy : an elderly man with a bald head and a
short, pointed beard. Why he should have elected to join company
with us I do not know. He cannot possibly have enjoyed it, for he
had a rather formal manner and was inclined to stand on his dignity.
This is not easy when someone (to be precise, the Marchese Ugo
Spinola) has overturned a soup-tureen full of whipped cream (meant
to be served with the strawberries) over your head, and someone else
has completed the arrangement by pouring the contents of a coffee-
pot on top of the cream-covered cranium.

I only caught a glimpse of Baron Kuhn after he had been tarred and
feathered (so to speak), for the next moment I retired under the table.
Not that I was drunk. But I thought it only prudent to suffer a
momentary eclipse, for a row had broken out that was really alarming.
The trouble arose when the youngest of the de Martinos put his eye
to the keyhole of a door, leading into an adjacent *cabinet-particulier*,
and his elder brother gave him a terrific push from behind that sent
him hurtling through the door on top of the amorous couple in
the next room. During the ensuing pandemonium, nearly all the
members of the supper-party sought refuge under the long table. This
group of revellers included the scions of the oldest Roman families,
answering to the historic names of Colonna, Orsini, Caetani, Odes-
calchi, Chigi, and so on. . . . None of us, on that occasion, showed
any courage whatever. To quote Euripides : " Cowards do not
count in battle. They are there, but not in it ! "

The only one who maintained a bold front, and faced the irate
gentleman from the *cabinet-particulier*, was Baron Kuhn. And I really
think that his appearance, with his bald head crowned with whipped
cream, and his beard dripping coffee, had the effect of sobering the
claimant for our blood. The latter must have thought, not unnatur-
ally, that he had broken in upon a supper of criminal lunatics, or that
he was ' seeing things '.

One autumn, I went to stay with Giovanni at Joppolo, which was one of the original Colonna estates in Sicily. This was during an election, when danger to life and limb was greater on that island of an ancient civilization than in darkest Africa. I remember riding from Joppolo to Raffadali, on the other side of the valley. We were mounted on mules, and rode through vast corn-fields that lay fallow under the autumn rain. Though quite a large party, we proceeded in single file, with a space of some twenty yards between each rider. In this formation, if he had been held up when crossing the stream at the bottom of the gully, only one of the party could have been stopped. The others could have closed in to help their companion.

Giovanni's character made him singularly adapted to combative, militant politics. Absolutely without self-consciousness and affectation ; pleasant to deal with and interesting to talk to, he was yet the most litigious man I ever knew. He paid his lawyers by the year, and was never happy unless he had at least five lawsuits going at the same time. Once, I believe, he had seventeen of them, and like Montmorency, the fox-terrier in *Three Men in a Boat*, thought he had got to Heaven !

There is a story about him that dates from the days when he first entered parliament. In the heat of an animated discussion, Giovanni threw an ink-pot at the government bench. He aimed at Signor Schanzer, but missed him. Some of the ink went over the *rédingote* of the Prime Minister, Signor Giolitti. When the latter got home that night, his wife asked how it was that he had got covered with ink. The Prime Minister answered mildly : ' It is a sign of ducal displeasure.'

This happened in the year 1909. Since then all inkpots in the Italian Houses of Parliament have been firmly screwed to the desks.

The Sunny Side of the Street

Every street has two sides, the shady side and the sunny. When two men shake hands and part, mark which of the two takes the sunny side ; he will be the younger man of the two.

BULWER-LYTTON.

BESIDES rescuing little Italian boys from the *verreries* in France, the heroin ' The Valley of the Bees ', worked incognito as a mill-hand in

Paterson, New Jersey, and later as an overseer on the railway-line over the Albula Pass, in Switzerland. Paterson, N.J. came into the story because the anarchist, Bresci, who assassinated King Humbert I at Monza, in 1900, came back to Italy from the States, to commit that premeditated crime. I took the opportunity of pointing out, in my story, how dangerous was the policy which left Italian emigrants without sufficient aid and protection. Poverty-stricken aliens, they offered a fertile field for nihilist propaganda.

The Albula Pass opens out, on the Engadine side, in the Beversthal, which in the Romanch dialect means Valley of the Bees. This valley is not far from St. Moritz, where I used to go for winter sports, and only a little more distant from Campfer, where Mother and I often stayed in the summer.

I cannot claim, like the prince in my story, to have shared the emigrants' hardships as one of themselves.[1] I lived the life of my own class, and being neither ill-favoured, nor poor, nor adverse to pleasurable adventure, I brought a natural gaiety into the social whirl of my time. But though preferring the sunny side of the street, I was no hedonist, to make the pursuit of pleasure the principal aim of existence. When in the Engadine, winter or summer, I passed much of my time in the Beversthal among my nationals who were engaged in boring the long tunnel through the mountain. Their task was harder, owing to lack of many hygienic precautions, than that of the workers on the Simplon tunnel. The absence of parallel bores made the high temperatures (due to hot springs) difficult to bear, and there were no shower-baths and *vestiaires* for the men as they came out into the open air, which, in winter, was bitterly cold.

The priest who lived among the workmen, at the mouth of the tunnel, was a friend of mine, as were many of his colleagues of the *Opera Bonomelli* that looked after the spiritual welfare of Italian emigrants. Sometimes, when I was in the Beversthal, a storm would blow up, making it difficult to get home again. Once I passed a night in a hay-loft, and another time as a guest of Doctor Bernard,

[1] If you seek a modern counterpart to St. Peter Claver's mission to the slave-ships, you will find it in the work of a little Italian nun, who has recently been canonized as a saint, Madre Saveria Cabrini. She is known in Italy as *la santa degli emigranti*. Hospitals, Orphanages, Schools and rest-houses bear her name all over North and South America, as in Europe.

at Samaden (he had a small collection of pictures by Segantini, that were a joy for ever).

One winter's night, when staying at the Kulm Hotel at St. Moritz Dorf, I had just changed into a dinner jacket, to descend to the restaurant, when they brought me a message from the priest at the Beversthal, to say that one of the workmen was in danger. He was known to have started to walk over the Bernina Pass, on his way to Italy, and to have been caught in a snowstorm.

It took me little more than an hour to organize a rescue-party. We left the hotel in sleighs, to the sound of revelry by night. In the ballroom, old Doctor Holland was directing some form of cotillion that must have dated from the days of Beau Nash at Bath. For the first hundred yards of our drive, the strains of music mingled with the jingling of sleigh-bells and the crunching of the snow under our runners. Violins were playing *Wiener Blut*, and the frosty air, sprinkled with stars, seemed to act like a sounding-board. I felt like the hero in Longfellow's *Excelsior* :

> The shades of night were falling fast,
> As through an Alpine village passed
> A youth, who bore 'mid snow and ice,
> A banner with a strange device
> Excelsior !

Two weeks later, the hall porter of the hotel handed me a letter from Italy, with a golden crown engraved on the envelope above the legend : *Casa di Sua Maestà la Regina*. The priest in the Beversthal had written to the Bishop Bonomelli, at Cremona, and the latter, who was on friendly terms with Queen Margherita, had passed on to her the information about the episode on the Bernina Pass. The Queen sent some money for the man I had rescued. Ferdinand Guiccioli, who wrote to me by the Queen's orders, added his own congratulations. The story, passing from one person to another, had grown beyond recognition. I appeared as having done something heroic.

As a matter of fact, we found the man and brought him back to the little hospital at St. Moritz, where he died a few days later, from mortification following severe frost-bite in the hands and feet. The fore-finger on my own hand got frost-bitten and still bears the mark, in the deformation of the nail that replaced the one I lost. But I took no pride in my prowess. Indeed, I remained with a painful impression that I was partly responsible for the man's death. Having brought him down to safety, I took him, at the first opportunity, into a warm room. This should have been avoided. I learnt too late that the rapid re-establishment of circulation, through the sudden thawing of the blood-vessels, can be a cause of inflammation and gangrene.

I have forgotten the date of this episode, but it must have been in the winter of 1904–05, for I remember coming home, out of the star-filled winter's night, and stopping in the hotel lounge to read the latest telegrams about the Russo-Japanese war.

*   *   *

I shared with Giovanni Colonna, a youthful, but ambitious, scheme, to take peasants from his property in Sicily, or from my native Venetia, and to establish them in our remaining colony of Erithrea. I say 'remaining', for when I was a boy, that is to say from the year 1889 till 1896, all Ethiopia had been an Italian protectorate. We lost our hold on that region, just as the British lost their hold on the Sudan in Gordon's time, after an unsuccessful colonial war.

Giovanni and I obtained official encouragement from the Commendatore Agnesa, who directed our ' Colonial Office ', which then consisted of a few rooms on the ground floor of the Consulta. He promised to grant us a ' concession ', if we found the conditions in Erithrea suitable to our enterprise. But the project came to nothing. Conditions on or beyond the plateau of Asmara offered little security for the peasants, or profit for us. The Abyssinian tribes were still inclined to be aggressive, and made occasional raids on our territory, as on the British-controlled territories on their Western and Southern borders. We came to the conclusion that Italian emigration had better be directed to the U.S.A., which in those days did not discriminate against our peasants, in favour of the nordic races. ' Quotas ' had not yet been devised to exclude us.

Like Pompey, in the days of ancient Rome, I first made the acquaintance of African soil by falling on it (' Teneo te, Africa ! '). I was ignominiously shot off on the ground, when attempting to mount a camel, a pessimistic animal who bore the name of Socrates, possibly because he wore habitually an expression like that of a philosopher fallen on evil days.

45

When Socrates lay down and allowed me to get on his back, I had no idea which end of him would rise up first. When a horse gets up, he rises on his fore-legs, a cow on her hinds legs. But camels, being contrary by nature, do either one or the other according to what they think will most inconvenience the rider.

The camel suffers from all the diseases that afflict man, and all those that afflict the lower animals, besides a few that he cultivates on his own account. Even at the best of times he is so much in the habit of looking at the dark side of things, that it is not easy to know when he *is* ill. I felt that Socrates's idea of a practical joke would be to stop with me a thousand miles from anywhere, and lie down and die. This he would do with a sarcastic smile, as if to say : ' Here is where *I* get off ! '

When travelling in the interior, Giovanni and I slept in *tukuls*, circular tents with a thatched roof. The roof is much more solid than the hut, and it was a common sight to see the natives taking the roof of an old hut, to put it on a new one. The sides of a *tukul* are often little more than a few branches of poles roughly put together, and the wind hums through them like a Jews' harp. My native servant would empty the washing-basin by throwing the water against the side of the hut. Some of it went though, and this he considered enough for practical purposes. Between the roof and the circular chamber below was a sheet of sail-cloth, much frequented by mice. The snakes in the vicinity would come, at night, and hunt the mice. Every now and then, a mouse would fall with a plop into the water-basin, and when I woke up in the small hours of the morning, I would generally see a couple of snakes' tails, hanging down at the side of the sail-cloth ceiling.

On cold nights—so I was told—the snakes might try to come to bed with you, and curl up on your chest, to keep themselves warm. I don't know whether this was true, but it seemed to me that they would be preferable, as bed-fellows, to the local *hetairae*, with hair redolent of rancid butter.

What Abyssinians call ' good water ' for drinking would not be considered that anywhere else, and a draught from a wayside well under a sycamore tree cost me many a day's illness. To fall ill in a *tukul* twenty-five days' journey from the coast of the Red Sea, is not a pleasant experience. Only time and nature can cure you. I realized in those days how big was the world, and how small I was in proportion. I was not sorry to embark once more at Massawah.

When I got home, I found a pile of letters and bills on my writing desk, and on top of them an invitation : *L'Ambassadeur de France et Madame Barrère ont l'honneur* . . . That same night, there was a dinner and a musical evening at the French Embassy. I telephoned to know if there were still a place for me at the bottom of the table, and was told, 'Yes !' Barrère (with whom I occasionally made music) added a message. He said that Debussy's quartet was going to be played for the first time in Rome.

After the lonely spaces, the thorny scrub, and the pitiless sun burning down on dried-up watercourses—the stately rooms and rich Gobelins of the Palazzo Farnese . . . jewelled fingers and women's eyes, sparkling in the candlelight. After the yapping of jackals in the rubbish heaps on the outskirts of an African village—the sweep of stringed instruments weaving the air with scents and visions. After the roasted kid and fermented honey, in the hut of some half savage *ras*—the white table heaped with roses, and set with silver and crystal. Bare necks bending ; bubbles in the wine . . . After weird stories of tribal wars, and brigandage, and snake-bites—the social gossip, and the verbal fencing, with the buttons on the foils.

Young Men's Visions

> . . . your young men shall see visions.
>
> Book of the Prophet Joel, ii. 28.

I DID not feel divinely called to any particular profession. So many paths opened out before me, at a time

> When all the world was young, lad,
> And all the trees were green,
> And every goose a swan, lad,
> And every lass a Queen !

I first got it into my head that I might become a real musician, and went to Berlin, to study with that end in view. But I was advised— and rightly advised—to seek some other means of expressing my personality.

47

Then I took, twice in succession, the examination for the diplomatic service, and failed both times. That is to say, I failed to come out on top. The test being a competitive one, and I half way down the list, none of the vacant posts were assigned to me. I can't say that I was much disappointed. At that time, a diplomatic career did not represent an ideal in itself, but merely a means to an end. Like most young men, who have, or think they have, the world at their feet, I had dreams that hung before me like a beckoning star. In the vision of the part that I might play, my role was a double one : to further the expansion of Italy overseas ; to promote better relations with Great Britain, and inaugurate a common policy of penetration in Africa.

The reader will smile, no doubt, at such presumption. Also, he may point out (with the wisdom that the history has taught us) that these ideals might be incompatible, one with the other.

Be this as it may, I should begin by explaining how a young man, whose outlook on life was gay and light-hearted, could aim so high.

First of all there was the conscious heredity of a family tradition. I don't mean far-off memories of ancestors in armour, but the inspiring tradition of recent generations. A Varè was one of Napoleon's generals. My father, Giambattista Varè, born in Venice in 1817, shared in the youthful strivings after the ideal of Italian unity, liberty and independence.

In an older generation than mine, the names of certain Italian patriots were household words. But few indeed of our younger contemporaries today know about the romantic nineteenth-century movement that was called the ' Risorgimento '. And I wonder how many New Yorkers, when they pass along the asphalt paths in Central Park West, have any idea who that Giuseppe Mazzini could have been, whose bust looks out across the green sward, in the direction of Fifth Avenue. His was the inspiration that went before the Italians in their exodus from servitude, like a pillar of cloud by day and a pillar of fire by night.

I have inherited many relics of Mazzini's, the letters he wrote to my father, and the pocket-book (his own pocket-book) that he gave him, when they parted in exile, after meeting at Lausanne. This was during the period of disillusion which followed the unsuccessful revolutions of 1848–49. A similarity of circumstances brought the two men together as refugees on Swiss territory. Mazzini, with the help of Garibaldi, had set up a republic in Rome (while the Pope fled to Gaeta). At the same time, Daniele Manin and my father proclaimed a sister republic in Venice. The French sent an army, to restore Pope Pius IX to his dominions. The Austrians, after a prolonged siege, reconquered Venice.

Friendships between Italian revolutionists were often made—as my father's friendship with Mazzini—in disappointment and disaster. But these men were destined to feel the bitter-sweet torment that accompanies the harvesting of a dream. Thanks to them, a new Italy emerged, united and independent. They were ardent nationalists, and their nationalism was the expression of collective liberty.

Of the group that centred round Mazzini, Garibaldi and Cavour, there is an appreciation in the first pages of Benedetto Croce's *A History of Italy 1871–1915* (translated from the Italian by Cecilia M. Ady) :

> They are worthy of being held up as examples for the purity of their love of country, which was nothing else but love of virtue ; for the sobriety and dignity of their lives ; for their entire disinterestedness ; for their powers of heart and mind, and for the religious self-discipline to which they had accustomed themselves in youth . . .
>
> Their deeds, and the words that they committed to writing, are a permanent source of moral and political education, warning us, exhorting us, and at times causing us to blush.

It is a fine idea that, in the true patriot, love of country is nothing but love of virtue. Goethe once said much the same thing to Eckermann, when he compared such a man to an eagle, looking down from dizzy heights over the countryside, to discover what he may seize. It is all the same to the eagle, if what he seeks be in Saxony or in Prussia. He knows nothing of state territories.[1]

This is perhaps why the patriots who founded a united Italy were

[1] See the *Gespräche mit Goethe*, by Johann Peter Eckermann.
Der Dichter wird als Mensch und Bürger sein Vaterland lieben, aber das Vaterland seiner poetischen Kräfter und seines poetischen Wirkens ist das Gute, Edle and Schöne, das an keine besonderen Provinz und an kein besonderes Land gebunden ist, und das er ergreift und bildet wo er es findet. Er ist darin dem Adler gleich, der mit freien Blick über Ländern schwebt, und dem es gleich ist, ob der Hase, auf den er herabscheist, in Preussen oder in Sachsen läuft.

admired and loved in many countries beside their own. Their virtue transcends all frontiers.

That period of history had closed ten years before I was born. New ideals had succeeded those of unity and independence. For these, so I decided, I would work in my turn, trying to emulate my father in his disinterestedness and in his honesty of purpose, if not in the greater qualities that I did not possess.

When I sit at his desk (as I am seated now), in his high-backed chair, the same clock ticks out the minutes for me, as it did for him. His portrait looks down on me from above the mantelpiece. Sometimes I half expect his ghost to come out of the shadows and speak to me.

Why not? The spiritual continuity of the race is an eternal dialogue between the quick and the dead.

★　　　★　　　★

There is always unhappiness in the world, and it takes different forms with the passing generations. In every generation, there are young men who have visions of going to the help of those who suffer. Sometimes there is a poet, who interprets the voice of the sufferers.

In the nineteenth century, the social injustice that was at the bottom of class-wars found expression in Elisabeth Barrett Browning's *The Cry of the Children*, and in Thomas Hood's *The Song of the Shirt*.

I made several unsuccessful attempts to write a poem, in which to voice the cry of the Italian peasant, forced to emigrate to foreign lands. Their unhappiness was that which Dante—speaking of his own exile—expresses in the Seventeenth Canto of the *Paradiso* :

> *E proverai si come sa di sale*
> *Lo pane altrui, e com'è duro calle*
> *Lo scendere, e'l salir per l'altrui scale.*

> (And thou shalt prove how salt a flavour hath
> The bread of others, and how hard the path
> To climb and to descend the stranger's stairs.)

It has been calculated that more than fourteen million Italian emigrants left their country during the last decades of the nineteenth century and the beginning of the twentieth, before the outbreak of the first world-war. This is more than the total population of many European states. Such an exodus should have been looked upon as a world problem (connected with unemployment), fit subject for an International Conference. It represented the kind of problem that, in President Wilson's imaginings, the League of Nations was created to solve. Instead of which it was left to chance and to the interference of selfishly interested parties. If the Italy I lived in, in my youth, might be described as being ' without tears ', this could not be said of the Italians who were forced to seek work abroad.

It was in 1926 that I came, by chance, upon an ' emigrant's prayer ', written in prose by Carlo Delcroix, one of our *grands mutilés de guerre* (he was blinded and maimed of both hands, in the first world-war). It consists of two short paragraphs, meant to interpret the feelings of the humbler Italian expatriate, ' in tears amid the alien corn '.

He invokes his native land :

O mother, bless your distant sons, those that left you poor and alone, to offer you from afar the bitter adventure of their lives. Bless the children who learnt to pray in the harmony of your words ; the young men who toil, dreaming of a love that awaits them beyond the far horizon ; the old folk who, on the threshold of death, long to rest in the bosom of their mother-soil, and implore the lament of their native bells, in a last good-bye !

Italy, bless your offspring, those who love you from a distance, those who dream of you without knowing you, those who call upon your name, but cannot see you. Bless them in sweat and tears, in travail, in love, in pain. Bless your children, who have abandoned you only to love you more, in the double exile from the homeland and the heart's desire !

Dr. Axel Munthe

THE physician who attended my father in his last illness was Doctor Ehrhardt. When I knew him, he had an apartment in the Via San Nicolò de Tolentino. Before that, so I have heard, he lived in the Piazza di Spagna, opposite the house which is now the Keats Memorial, and which was then occupied by Dr. Axel Munthe.

After my father's death, Dr. Ehrhardt, perceiving in his widow some premonitions of melancholia, advised her to consult Munthe. That is how she first got to know him.

In his *Story of San Michele*, Munthe writes that Ehrhardt was :

. . . one of the best doctors and one of the kindest-hearted men I ever met . . . Although over seventy, he was still in possession of his mental and physical vigour, day and night on the go, always ready to help, rich and poor all the same to him. He was the most perfect type of the family doctor of bygone times, now almost extinct—so much the worse for suffering humanity. It was impossible not to love him. . . . He was a German by birth, and had there been many like him in the Fatherland in 1914, there would never have been a war.

Ehrhardt died when I was in my teens, but we continued to see Munthe after he introduced Mother and myself to a friend and patient of his, a Mrs. Stephens, who had a suite in the Grand Hotel, close to where we lived, in the Via Venti Settembre.

Mrs. Stephens was consumptive, and when I first met her, it did not seem that she had much longer to live. But Munthe said that, if she did not die within the next two years, she might attain the age of eighty. And this is what she did.

Her Christian name was Ella, and her husband's was Edward. They were rich people and had no children. I imagined that their money might come from Stephen's Ink, but it was not so. Their fortune had been put together by previous generations—so I was told—when the lighting of ships in the British Navy, as in the Admiralty offices, had all been done by candles. The purveyors of these candles had made their pile long before Edward's day. He was a pleasant little man, who did not seem to have much to do, except pay his wife's bills and look after a family of poodles : feeding them, clipping them and taking them for walks in Kensington Gardens.

At Munthe's suggestion, Ella Stephens and my mother passed a winter at Capri, which island had more of Paradise and less of Cosmopolis than it has now. There, they made friends with the various retainers, who helped Munthe run his Villa and his sailing craft. The doyen of these, old Pacciale, was still alive at the time. Of him, Munthe wrote :

. . . A devoted servant cancels the name of master. He had become my friend ; the honour was mine, he was a far better man than I. Although he belonged to another world than I, a world almost unknown to me, we understood each other quite well. During the long days and nights we were together, alone on the sea, he taught me many things I had not read in my books, or heard from the lips of men. He was a taciturn man, the sea had taught him its silence long ago. His thoughts were few, and so much the better for him. But his sayings were full of poetry, and the archaic simplicity of his similes was pure Greek.

The tradition of affection between master and servant, based on other considerations than mere money, is likely to continue in Italy long after it lingers on elsewhere only in the memory of Colonel Blimp and other diehards. That tradition, with us, goes back to the days when Aeneas buried his old nurse at Gaeta. Doubtless she had some of the characteristics that Munthe observed in Pacciale. Today, in most countries, the individual servant merges into a mass proletariat, paid by the hour ; a class of people without roots, without traditions, without a folk-lore, without songs.

*   *   *

No need for me to dwell on Munthe's surroundings at Capri. His book on the subject has been translated into thirty languages, and has had seventy-four printings in Great Britain alone. I sometimes wonder if some merit for such a success is not due, in a small part, to a revision of the manuscript (at Munthe's request), by Sir Rennell Rodd, former Ambassador in Rome, who deleted many paragraphs on alarming medical technicalities.

Though always ready to poke fun at his friend, Sir Rennell was devoted to Munthe, and went to stay at San Michele with his bride, on their honeymoon. Munthe was then passing through a phase of acute asceticism, when he went about barefoot and in rags. He tried to persuade his guests to follow his example and to lead ' the hard life '. But the English *sposa* could not be induced to do without baths. Nor did Munthe himself keep up that particular fad for long.

It was not in Capri, but in Rome, that I saw most of the author of that international best-seller, *The Story of San Michele*. During the bicycle craze that swept over Europe at the end of the last century, Munthe and I taught two ladies to ride a bike. One was the Crown Princess of Sweden ; the other was Ella Stephens.

We would take them to the Viale Parioli, which was then in open country, and let them coast down the slope between the Salarian and the Flaminian roads, on the left bank of the Tiber. Two carriages followed sedately behind. The ladies wore very large hats, sat very straight, and seemed to think they were doing something rather fast.

In those days, Munthe was in his prime. The magnetic qualities of his rather puzzling personality were more noticeable than in his later years. He was undoubtedly a *poseur*, and some people were inclined to believe that even the very real trouble with his eyes was part of his affectation. That he tried to live up to the legend he had created about himself is certainly true, and his pontifical attitudes were sometimes irritating and absurd. But he belonged to a generation that delighted in aesthetic poses. I am not immune from this vice myself.

I have heard Munthe spoken of as a dangerous man and not to be trusted with confidences. Such suspicions may not have been wholly unjustified. Occasionally he could be indiscreet. His practice gave him knowledge of the skeleton in many a cupboard. He was not always reticent about the people whose confidence he enjoyed. He was not malicious, but he sometimes let himself be carried away by his imagination and his sense of humour. He could not resist telling a good story.

His successes (often unsought) provoked the jealousy of other doctors. They said unkind things about him. To these, I paid no attention. But the Princess Antoine Radziwill once told me a piece of gossip that amused me, because it was evident, at the time, that she herself was not aware *who* she was talking about. She had been staying at Karlsruh, with the Grand Duke and Duchess of Baden, and had found her hosts in a state of mental perturbation, because their daughter, who had married the Crown Prince of Sweden, had gone to Italy on the advice of her doctor. The Court of Sweden had not considered that this *Italienische Reise* was really necessary for the Princess's health, and raised difficulties about defraying the expenses. The Grand Duke of Baden found himself morally obliged to furnish her daughter with the requisite funds. And he was annoyed about it.

To accuse Munthe of being a sort of medical Svengali, or a quack and a charlatan, shows only a lack of understanding of his methods. He was a faith healer, and his knowledge of psychology often brought him to pander to the egotism of his patients, by flattery, bluff, sympathy and other tricks of the trade (if you like to call them that). But, apart from a few pious frauds, he undoubtedly possessed the healing touch, which in him was an inborn, personal quality and had

a l'amico
Lord Bristes
dal' amico
Leo Nichelron
Roma 3 magio
1902

DON GIOVANNI COLONNA,
DUKE OF CESARÒ

nothing to do with orthodox medical qualifications. It was this that sometimes provoked the Philistinism of the medical profession. And it is undoubtedly true that, in dealing with various forms of hysteria, he relied more on the hypnotic attraction that he exercised over his patients than on the medical knowledge he had acquired at the University of Upsala, or at the Salpêtrière.

Francesco Crispi and Friendship with England

SINCE 1932 I have lived in the new quarter of Rome, called Prati di Castello, where there used to be nothing but open fields at the back of the Castel Sant'Angelo. This modern suburb was built after 1911, and the streets round my house are named after the patriots of the Risorgimento. My windows look out on the Avenue called after Giuseppe Mazzini, and the side-streets bear the names of men, some of whom, when I was a boy, used to frequent my mother's drawing-room.

That I should have known, in my first youth, such survivals of the past, gives me memories that appear inconsistent with my present age. I heard so much about events that occurred before I was born, stories told by men on whom beat the spotlight of history, that I almost came to consider such happenings as part of my own experience.

One of the national heroes I knew best was Francesco Crispi. He has a street named after him in the middle of the town—the thorough-fare that used to be called Capo le Case. He lived near there, in the Via Gregoriana, and was still an important figure in national and international politics, long after other patriots of his generation were dead or on the shelf. He was twice Prime Minister at the close of the last century. An ardent anglo-phil, though a firm supporter of the Triple Alliance, he based his policy upon that alliance, supplemented with a naval entente with Great Britain.

A fiery revolutionist, comrade of Garibaldi, with whom he organized the expedition of ' The Thousand ' that delivered his native Sicily from the tyranny of the Naples Bourbons, he was a swarthy southerner, with blazing black eyes and (when I knew him) an enormous, snow-white moustache, the walrus moustache that was characteristic of his epoch. A small, nervous man, and a fighter in every sense of the word, in the field of battle and in the political arena. With all this, cool-headed as Sicilians often are (there is snow on Etna !).

I was nineteen when I used to go and see him. He was then out-of-office, in straightened circumstances, and going blind. This blindness accentuated the Homeric touch in the old national hero. His anger, the *saeva indignatio*, that blazed out whenever he deplored the pusillanimity of his political adversaries, had in it something of the wrath of Achilles. And though aged and infirm and on the shelf, ' Achilles was Achilles still '.

Young as I was, Crispi would talk with me as to the son of a patriot like himself. And because I spoke English and knew England, he told me of the opportunity that had been missed by the Italian Government, to initiate a friendly collaboration with Great Britain in Africa. What started the conversation on this subject was my having mentioned that a Scotch uncle of mine, a brother of my mother's, Colonel Norman Chalmers of the 79th Highlanders, was passing through Rome. He had lost part of his left hand, having been wounded in Egypt, at the battle of Tel-el-kebir. Crispi exclaimed : ' Our bersaglieri should have been at that battle, fighting shoulder to shoulder with the highlanders. If I had been in office at the time, I would have sent them ! '

No doubt he would have. This is how the opportunity came and was lost :

On the 24th July 1882, Sir Augustus Paget, British Ambassador in Rome, was instructed to invite the Italian Government to co-operate with England and France in the steps to be taken for the protection of the Suez Canal. The French Government having backed out (when Freycinet replaced Gambetta as Prime Minister), the first communication to Italy was followed by another. This time, Lord Granville informed the Italian Ambassador in London that ' Her Majesty's Government would also welcome the co-operation of Italy in a movement in the interior, which they were of opinion could no longer be delayed and for which they were making active preparations.'

The man responsible for refusing this offer was Pasquale Stanislao Mancini, Minister for Foreign Affairs in the Depretis Cabinet, which had succeeded that of Cairoli. The latter (which included my father as Minister of Justice) had fallen in consequence of the French occupation of Tunis.

When talking to me and telling me the history of past events, Crispi showed me a copy of the letter he had sent to Mancini. He had written from London, after having an interview with Lord Granville, at 18 Carlton House Terrace, and also with Mr. Gladstone, with whom he spoke Italian :

LONDON, *29th July 1882*

MY DEAR MANCINI,

I am most sorrowful (*sono dolentissimo*) that you should have declined the offer made you by England, to intervene in Egypt. Please God your refusal does not bring further misfortunes on Italy in the Mediterranean.

You should have accepted without hesitation. When Cavour received the offer to join the Western powers in invading the Crimea, he did not lose a moment. The Government of little Piedmont possessed the courage that is lacking today in the Government of Italy.

Yours affectionately,
F. CRISPI.

The lost opportunity of taking common action in Egypt did not put an end to further possibility of Anglo-Italian collaboration in Africa. Italy and Great Britain helped one another in their common fight against the dervishes and the Mahdi. The town and *mudiria* of Kassala, lying on the River Mareb, in the Anglo-Egyptian Sudan, was besieged by the dervishes in November 1883. The British garrison held out till the 30th July 1885, when, owing to lack of food, it was forced to capitulate. Kassala was recaptured from the dervishes, by an Italian force under Colonel Baratieri, on the 17th July 1894, and by the Italians handed over to the British (representing the Egyptians) on Christmas Day 1897.

Italians need, every now and then, a statesman of the type of Crispi, to give them a political tonic. Benedetto Croce says of Crispi that he brought to the government of his country

the great benefits and national advancement to be derived from a dominant personality, conceiving the ideas which the Italian people were unable to conceive, opening up paths of which they were unaware, and finding within himself the powers that they did not possess, or could only develop under his rule and leadership.

Ernesto Nathan and a Journey to Albania

VIA TORINO is a street that leads from the Via Venti Settembre, where Mother and I lived, to the Piazza Santa Maria Maggiore, where I went to a day-school.

On my way there, every morning at a quarter to eight, I would meet the porter of No. 122 escorting a fussy and self-important fox-terrier on a constitutional round the lamp-posts. I would stop and ask if the ' Signorino Maurice ' had started out yet. The porter's name was Zeffiro, meaning a soft and gentle breeze. The fox-terrier was more aptly called ' Bulky '. He was stout by nature and inclined to become more so, by over-indulgence among the flesh-pots.

The house that bore the number 122 belonged to Ernesto Nathan, whose son, Maurice, went to school with me. We sat side by side on the same bench and became united in a life-long intimacy, such as school-days leave behind them.

At that time, Ernesto Nathan was Syndic (Lord Mayor) of Rome. And it struck people as incongruous that the capital of Italy, world-centre of Catholicism, should be administered by an English-born Jew. To explain this anomaly, there arose a legend that was generally believed : the legend that Ernesto Nathan was the son of Mazzini. But though it was true that Mazzini, while an exile in London, had frequented the house of old Mayor Nathan and of Sarah, his wife, this was when the future Syndic of Rome was already two years old. So the rumour, as far as he was concerned, was unfounded.

In politics, Ernesto was inevitably a liberal, and liberalism inspired what was called his *irredentismo*, the ideal that claimed for Italy all territories and towns, along the coasts of the Adriatic, that were inhabited by Italian-speaking people and carried on the ancient traditions of Venice.

In the early summer of 1905, while staying with Mother at Campfèr, in the Engadine, I received a letter from Ernesto Nathan, asking if I could meet him in Milan. He had a project for extending Italian influence over Albania, and thought I might be willing to collaborate. So I took the diligence down the Maloja Pass, and, on arrival, found Ernesto in the house of some relations in the Via Bigli.

His idea was that we should begin by buying, or leasing, the island of Saseno, in the Gulf of Valona, with the excuse of making some experiments in the breeding of cattle in a more or less wild state.

Albania was then much as it was when Gibbon described it as being " within sight of Italy and less known than the interior of America ". Since Gibbon's day, we have extended our knowledge of America, but are only a little better informed than Childe Harold about :

> The wild Albanian kirtled to his knee
> With shawl-girt head and ornamented gun.

Behind the plate-glass windows of booksellers in Oxford Street and Piccadilly was put out for sale (at the time I was touring Albania) a book by Miss Edith Durham, *The Burden of the Balkans*. She describes the few people who were interested in Turkey in Europe as believing it to be a spot inhabited by Turks (all Moslems and bad) and ' Macedonians ' (all Christians and virtuous).

Four centuries before Miss Durham and I visited Albania, the all-conquering Ottoman had swept over the land, blotting it out from the world's history. And though in 1905 it was still a part of the Ottoman Empire, the Turkish officials could not give you a safe-conduct that would really be a protection. They were strongly opposed to all progress, and tore up the old Roman roads, to hinder communications. Yet they could not obliterate the ruins of Venetian castles and of the Appian Way, that led from Rome to Constantinople : traces of two stupendous civilizations, overrun by the conquering armies of an Eastern race.

When passing through Rome, on my way to Valona, I talked with the Marchese di San Giuliano, our Minister for Foreign Affairs. He compared Albania to Brunhilde, sleeping politically, surrounded by flames less visible but more real than those with which Wotan enclosed his daughter.

Among my youthful visions, was that of awakening Brunhilde !

Albania's history goes further back than the Nibelungen saga. It claims such old-world heroes as Alexander the Great, whose mother, Olympias, was an Albanian, and Pyrrhus, and Scanderberg, and Mehemet Ali. The Roman Emperors, Diocletian and Constantine, were of Illyrian blood, and the fierce peoples of the Balkan peninsula, once conquered, furnished the flower of the Roman armies. Descendants of Albanian colonists were scattered over the southern provinces of Italy, and over Sicily. The family of Francesco Crispi was of Albanian origin. Their emigration from their native country probably took place when a ' Kingdom of Albania ' was ruled over by Sicilian Kings of the House of Anjou.

When I knew them, at the beginning of the present century, the Albanians possessed a mentality and lived in conditions that were more backward than those of Europe during the Middle Ages. They could hardly be said to have outgrown the tribal state. They were ruled by ' the law of the mountain ', supposed to be the oldest law in Europe. It contained no provision for the trial and punishment of murder.

During my journey, I acquired some first-hand knowledge of the incredible hatreds, from which the Balkan peoples still reap such a bitter harvest. The folklore of what we now call the ' Southern Slavs ' shows that the amiable practice of gouging out a rival's eyes, with a spoon, is both ancient and endemic. During the second world-war and its aftermath, this was done by the Croats to the Serbs, and to Italians, accused of being Fascists. The eyes were then collected and taken to the Slavonic chiefs.

Similar stories figure in a cycle of popular poetry, dating from the fourteenth century, concerning the ' heroic deeds ' of Mark Kraglievich. He even took out the eyes of his own sister, to revenge himself for having been betrayed by her husband. And he carried the eyes home and showed them to his mother, who was much distressed. All this sounds almost unbelievable, but it is confirmed by the legend of an aged Saint, who appeared to a Croat warrior and made him the following offer :

' I will do anything you ask. You have only to command me. But whatever I do for you, I will do again, twice over, for a Serb.'

The Croat thought the matter over and then answered : ' Take out one of my eyes ! '

I discovered that among the sources of hatred and of strife, in Illyria, religious intolerance was not lacking. And apparently it was not limited to human beings ! Even the storks had something to say on the matter. Never by any chance did they build a nest on the roof of a house belonging to a Christian. Only Moslem buildings were honoured by their patronage. Such a preference is not so extraordinary as it might be supposed. To the Moslem, the stork is sacred. To the Christian he may be a legitimate object of the chase ! I was told that, in some provinces of Greece, much as Morea the storks disappeared after the country ceased to be a province of the Ottoman Empire.

I can't say that I made friends with the storks, but I made the acquaintance of a couple, and they treated me with a certain dignified condescension. I got so interested in their doings that I would get up as soon as dawn showed through the window of my bedroom, and watch them sending their children off to school. I don't know of any other animal that does this, but more than once I saw a group of a dozen young storks, performing evolutions in the air under the supervision of two, or three, elder birds, evidently instructors in aviation. Those few teachers could not have been parents of the entire class. The stork is voiceless, though it can emit a sort of melancholy whistle. It keeps up the conversation by a sort of tapping sound, produced by the mandibles of its long beak. This sound can be modulated from a *pianissimo* to a loud rattle, like that produced by a machine-gun, or the back-fire of a motor-cycle.

I was at Valona, Durazzo and Tirana at the season when the storks were training their children for their annual departure for Africa, on the 28th August. This is a fixed date (or at least it was in those years) and never varied, which makes one suppose that those birds keep some sort of calendar in their heads.

The annual flight south, with the recently born young, was evidently a serious business. The sicklier specimens among the juniors were killed off, as it could be foreseen that they might not survive the journey overseas. I was told—though I cannot confirm this—that the parent-birds that hatch out more than two eggs, would sometimes push the heaviest of their offspring out of the nest. It would fall to the ground and be left to die : the reason being that the parents let their fledgelings rest on their backs, during the long flight south, and they can do this for two fledgelings, but not for more. Such ruthlessness contrasts forcibly with the legend of the mother-bird remaining on her nest, with wings outstretched, to protect her young, when the house below them is destroyed by fire.

At Durazzo, I met a crony of Miss Edith Durham's. This was a huge pet ram, called Napoleon, with curly horns and a massive Roman nose, which the serving-men stooped to kiss, as they passed. When Napoleon wanted a drink, he baa'd loudly, and someone would escort him to a horse-trough, in the yard of the ' han '.

I might continue this chapter with the account of how, during my stay in Albania, I prepared the ground for some events that followed after. But of the seed that I sowed in that field, as in many others, nothing now remains. Memories are left to me of the storks at dawn, of long rides on mule-back, sometimes through rich lands, sometimes through a fragrant scrub, sometimes in the shade of giant olive-trees that had never been pruned. I vaguely remember my escort of Turkish mounted-police (*suvarris*), each man armed with a Peabody-Martini rifle, a sheath-knife and a revolver. These men (so I gathered) were unpaid, and had to cater for themselves as we travelled, except for what I gave them. Their uniforms were ragged, and often in strong contrast with the smart fustanella of the wealthier civilians. But they had good horses, of which they seemed to be fond.

Around me, as we moved from place to place, I saw evidences of a primitive life, such as is described in Isaiah :

". . . and they shall fight every one against his brother, and every one against his neighbour, city against city, and kingdom against kingdom . . . and a fierce king shall rule over them."

Lest I should give a wrong impression, I must add that the country-folk were hospitable, as only a primitive people can be. And the Christian women-school-teachers in the larger centres, seemed active, intelligent and enlightened.

Sometimes the school-marm can do more for a country than the diplomats and politicians.

Pure Economics and Practical Politics

> In the Carboniferous Epoch, we were promised
> abundance for all
> By robbing selected Peter to pay for
> collective Paul ;
>
> But though we had plenty of money
> there was nothing our money could buy
> And the Gods of the Copy-book-headings said :
> ' If you don't work you die ! '
> RUDYARD KIPLING, *The Gods of the Copy-book-headings.*

MAFFEO PANTALEONI—DAVID LUBIN—OLIVIA AGRESTI ROSSETTI

IT was said of Gladstone that not only did he make of Finance an art, but that he could speak of it, as if he were the Tenth of the Muses. I owe my first grounding in economics to Maffeo Pantaleoni, who could make even Finance amusing.

He taught ' pure economics ', political economy in the abstract. This science starts from the hedonistic premise that men are moved to act exclusively by the desire to obtain the greatest possible satisfaction of their needs, by means of the smallest possible individual sacrifice. Such a science, considering man as an object of thought, supposes him to be, in every deal, a complete egoist. But in the abstract science, man is represented as an intelligent egoist, who knows what is good for him and is willing to further his own interest by every possible means. In practical economics, this is not so. One must take psychology into account, such things as the pride of doctrinaires in their orthodoxy ; ignorance and the greed that overreaches itself.

If it had been possible—or were still possible—to overcome the selfish policies of the trade unions and their political bosses, and to apply the science of pure economics to such problems as immigration and emigration, it is probable that ' labour ' (in the meaning of labourers and producers in the aggregate, not as the label of a political party) would by now have certain inalienable rights internationally recognized, to the greater advantage of Peace. Without quoting the almost utopistic declarations of the Burlinghame Treaty between the U.S.A. and China (in 1868), the outstanding example is that of

63

Australia. In his book, *The Steep Places*,[1] Sir Norman Angell refers twice to this subject. He writes :

More than a generation since it became evident that if the British Commonwealth, including as it does great empty territories in Canada, Australia, New Zealand and elsewhere, was to duplicate the history of the United States, and become a series of powerful and rich nations, it would be by adopting what was, in the years of American expansion, the American policy of fairly free immigration. All Dominion governments have until yesterday refused even to consider putting down the barriers . . .

In the concluding chapter of the same work, the author demands, for the British Commonwealth, policies permitting a much greater and more rapid development of its resources than do the present restrictive policies. " In the way of the best use of the existing opportunities stand the ingrained habits of thought and feeling, still so strong in Britain and the British Dominions (especially in relation to immigration)."

There is something in Sir Norman Angell's views on economics which makes me think of him as a Maffeo Pantaleoni, brought up to date, and without Maffeo's Voltairian irony. I remember that the latter compared those dog-in-the-manger colonists, who reserve for themselves territories that are too vast for them, to the savages who have need of a large country to hunt in, hunting being their only means of livelihood. Pantaleoni was especially bitter against the supercilious type of philanthropist, who preaches birth-control to the peoples that are poor in territory. He quoted Dickens's *Christmas Carol*, where Scrooge champions a similar selfish philosophy to cut down the surplus population, and is reproved by the Spirit, who tells him not to speak till he knows what the surplus is and where it is.

There is an article about my old teacher in the Supplement to the *Encyclopædia Britannica* (thirteenth edition, 1926). He is described as the founder of a new scientific tendency in economics. Pantaleoni was well known in eight Universities, including that of Geneva. His *Principii di Economia Pura* (translated into English by T. B. Bruce, London, 1898) set forth the mathematical foundation on which

[1] Published by Hamish Hamilton, London, 1947.

political economy is based. He always managed to weld theoretical principles with the elaboration of concrete facts. As Financial Adviser of the League of Nations, he worked on various Commissions for restoring the world's finances after the first world war, and generally found himself on the opposite side of the barricade to the pundits that Kipling calls The Gods of the Copy-book-headings.

The following are some typical extracts from a Memorandum of his, prepared for the International Financial Commission in Brussels. It should appeal to present-day permit-ridden victims of that controlled economy that appears to be inspired more by proletarian envy than by any aspiration to give back to Europe and to the world their former prosperity.

Governments have everywhere, but in different measure, taken into their management and away from private management, a very large series of services for which they are utterly unfit, as ancient and recent experience has proved, viz :

(*a*) They cannot manage railways ;
(*b*) They cannot manage shipping ;
(*c*) They cannot manage harbours ;
(*d*) They cannot manage international commerce ;
(*e*) They cannot manage the commerce in bills ;
(*f*) They cannot regulate the prices of commodities, and
(*g*) They cannot conserve and distribute commodities after requisition.

They have done and are doing all this and more, neglecting their proper functions.

Governments have taken to what is called State Socialism and Paternalism, or general tutorship of citizens, creating innumerable State monopolies, privileges ; laming private efficiency, destroying speculative commerce and industry, turning into crimes absolutely necessary ways of doing business, such as contracts *à terme avec prime*, combines, trusts, competition, hoarding or deferring consumption, refusing to sell under one's own price. . . .

Everywhere, more or less, Governments pay a corrupted Press, forming public opinion, and strong Governments pay foreign Press, bamboozling public opinion in those countries.

Public opinion should be awakened to the economic value of Governmental honesty. Private dishonesty is repressed by courts of law. Unfortunately there are no prisons for statesmen and political bodies.

Every fool can put on taxes. Ability consists in : (*a*) Reducing expenses by giving efficient service for tax-money ; (*b*) Putting on taxes which do not hamper production and trade, or do so less than any other.

If present methods continue, defaulting will be the consequence. The rope will break. In their own interests, strong Governments ought to learn salmon-fishing, and weak Governments not to be their instrument.

Pantaleoni believed that *pour gouverner bien il faut gouverner peu*. This does not mean that he was an uncompromising supporter of the *laissez faire* capitalist system, as I have heard it upheld, with becoming gravity by serious-minded people such as old Mr. Fisher-Unwin, President of the Cobden Club (he had married a daughter of Richard Cobden). But Pantaleoni could not resist a slightly mocking attitude, and enjoyed blowing the froth off the flagon of any inflated eulogy, such as is only too common in public assemblies.

My own friendship with him dated from the day when I went up for the *viva voce* examination in political economy, on the occasion of my taking a degree at the old University of La Sapienza. There were three examiners, of which Pantaleoni was one, but it was not he that conducted the examination. He merely presided, as a sort of arbiter. Without quite knowing how we started such an argument, I found myself upholding the following contention : that in practical politics, no economic theory should be accepted as entirely true, or turned down as entirely false. A principle, sound in itself, may be pressed too far. All theories are good up to a certain point, and could be expressed graphically in the form of a parabola, the curve giving varying degrees of usefulness in time and space. Also, the accepted faith of one generation is the heresy of another.

I had been reading a pamphlet by Mr. Balfour, on the subject of Tariff reform, in his usual style of philosophic doubt. He showed his habitual dexterity in evading any expression of his final opinion. While maintaining the view that true wisdom lies in not going too far, I may have used arguments furnished by A. J. B. Anyhow, I found myself getting the better of the two examiners, who were questioning me. Pantaleoni, after listening with an amused smile on his face, decided suddenly to intervene in my favour, and together we carried all before us. I was given a maximum of marks !

This was the beginning of an acquaintance that ripened into friendship. I used to go and see Pantaleoni in his apartment in the Via Giulia, and would find him, in winter-time, wrapped in a huge rug, for the room was unheated, and there were other rugs lying about on various chairs, for visitors to use, if they wanted them.

There were also various domestic pets : dogs, cats, birds, and a tortoise, for whose benefit the house (apparently) was run. This was a bond of sympathy, for in Mother's house and mine, it was much the same.

It was in Pantaleoni's house that I met David Lubin, the American who, with the support of the King of Italy, founded the International Institute of Agriculture. This Californian from Sacramento was the first real internationalist I ever met, and unlike a good many whom I met later, he was a practical idealist. His was no cloudy ideology. Economic justice was his lodestar, in home politics and in international politics. He viewed it as the outcome of a slow process of constructive organization, which would bring about an ever increasing degree of equity in human relationships, and first of all, equity in exchange. He considered this equity as an essential condition, to ensure the life of Democracy.

From the first page of his biography, written by the Signora Agresti Rossetti, I quote the following extract, taken from a letter, in which he tried to interest Mr. Gifford Pinchot (a member of the Theodore Roosevelt Administration) in the International Institute of Agriculture.[1]

. . . I think you follow me. But, human-like, you want to know my motive before you can trust me. Well, my motive is not a salary, not a medal, nor social scintillations, nor is it to be Count of Sacramento. I wish to serve the dear old Uncle, Uncle Samuel, and you laugh ! But how many better men have given their lives for the Uncle. But there is a higher service still, and that is for the United States of the World. And I am happy to be an humble soldier, a private, in this Army. Do you understand ? And when one is such in dead earnest, the Almighty does not mind that he is an ordinary scrub and no educated diplomat. That same Almighty makes him a *persona gratissima* just everywhere ; because this is His great fun in His Divine Comedy. And that is the reason that He took common scrubs for His prophets and His great workers, and ' who shall say Him nay ? '

I mentioned David Lubin's biographer, the Signora Olivia Agresti Rossetti. She also belonged to the group that sometimes met in Pantaleoni's house. And she, with myself, is one of the last of its survivors.

[1] See *David Lubin*, by Olivia Rossetti Agresti (Little, Brown & Co., New York).

The Signora Agresti is English-born, though her family is of Italian origin. She is a niece of Dante Gabriele Rossetti, poet and painter, who with Holman Hunt, Madox Brown and Millais, founded the Pre-Raphaelite Brotherhood. Though spiritually Italian, the Signora Agresti carries with her an atmosphere of Chelsea, London's Montmartre, where, in her uncle's day, you could wander down, so to speak, most of English art and letters. She is just what you would expect a Pre-Raphaelite to look like : not colourless, but faintly coloured, like an illustration by Max Beerbohm. Indeed, she might have figured in Max's delightful little book, *Rossetti and his Circle*.

Max Beerbohm includes John Stuart Mill in this circle, so perhaps it is not to be wondered at that it should have given birth to a girl who, in her day, has become an authority on practical economics. The Signora Agresti is at home in several languages. She has acted as interpreter in many International Conferences, before the first world war and after the second. Modest and unassuming as she is, her long experience, combined with a clear and simple style in writing and speaking, has conferred on her a genuine authority in international economics. Her opinion carries weight even within so closed a community as that of the experts in world-finance. She is known as a formidable opponent of international usury. Her ideal is still that which David Lubin brought over from California half a century ago : economic justice in international affairs. This aspiration cannot be classified under any sectarian label.

She acquired her first notions of economics in the years when the misery and exasperation, that were responsible for the conflict between labour and capital, nearly led to bloody revolution. Absorbed, as they are, in the rivalry between present-day ideologies, people have forgotten—or so it would seem—the struggle that, in the last century, almost took on the aspect of organized warfare : the Trafalgar Square riots, and the Chicago bomb outrages, with hired thugs firing on the mobs in free America.

The struggle generally ended in defeat for the workers, who in sullen anger were forced back to their long hours, starvation wages, and dangerous conditions of work, described by Cronin in *The Stars Look Down*. But in time, as their organization became more powerful, the workers were able to force from their employers some grudging concessions, thus securing for themselves a higher standard of living and some degree of social security.

These concessions staved off revolution. Had similar concessions been made in the realm of international economics, two world wars might never have broken out.

Final Choice of a Profession

IN the spring of 1906, Alberto Sabbatini, brother of an old school friend of mine, came back to Italy from British Central Africa, with a proposition that attracted me, for it offered practical means of settling some Italians on African soil, and offering them work.

Sabbatini had been acting as an overseer, on a plantation belonging to a Scotsman, at Blantyre. He ran the plantation, while the Scotsman drank the *vin ordinaire* of his native heath. He drank so much whisky that he died, and the property passed to his heirs, who were living in Scotland. Sabbatini came to Europe, to get in touch with them and possibly to buy the plantation. Not having enough money, he appealed to me. I furnished the requisite funds, and introduced Sabbatini to my cousins, the Dick Clelands, in London, also to my mother's solicitors, Lindsay & Howe, in Edinburgh. With the latter's help, the property was bought and I arranged to go out with Sabbatini. We were to take with us a group of young Italians who wished to try their luck in new surroundings.

I had my passage reserved, with the others, from Naples to Mombasa, and arranged to meet Sabbatini in Milan, three weeks before the date of sailing. We foregathered at the Hotel Cavour.

Among the guests, staying at the hotel, was the Contessa delle Somaglia, a pleasant, kind old lady, sister to Prince Doria, and to the Princess Colonna. She had often taken a mildly benevolent interest in my doings, nevertheless she surprised me by asking me to her sitting-room and enquiring as to my future plans. Had I given up all idea of entering the diplomatic service? I answered that, for the moment, I proposed to go to British Central Africa, to become a colonial.

In the course of the conversation, I gathered that it was not me the old Contessa was interested in, but her own nephew, Ascanio

Colonna. Like myself, he had taken the examination for the diplomatic service, but had finished up among the 'also ran'. However, a new *concorso* was coming on. It would serve as an encouragement to Ascanio—so his aunt told me—if I were to try again. However, at that moment, I could not offer the desired incentive.

Then Sabbatini, much to my astonishment, asked me if I still meant to go out to Mombasa with the others. I answered in the affirmative, and noticed that he looked disappointed. It transpired that the ship was crowded and no further accommodation available. Still, I could not see that this mattered.

'We all have our cabins,' I said, 'or at least a berth. What do you want an extra place for?'

'The truth is, I was thinking of getting married.'

'Do you mean that you want my cabin for your future wife?'

'That was the idea.'

'And who is *die Betreffende*, as they say in German?'

'Well, so far, she doesn't exist.'

'You are thinking of getting married, before the ship sails, and you do not know who to?'

'Yes.'

'And what steps do you propose to take, in order to secure a wife?'

He explained. And the explanation sounded more reasonable. It appeared that there were some cousins of his, living at Asti. He had not heard of them for some time, but he remembered that, when he had seen them last, there had been a little girl.

'She must be seventeen or eighteen by now. They are nice people. I'm sure I could not do better.'

'Do you mean to tell me that you contemplate asking this girl, who probably does not know of your existence, to marry you off-hand and to start with you for Central Africa by the first boat?'

'Yes.'

'Well, you have nerve! If I had told you that I did not need my cabin any more, what would you have done?'

'Started off, this evening, for Asti, to arrange matters.'

'Far be it from me to shatter love's young dream! If the lady

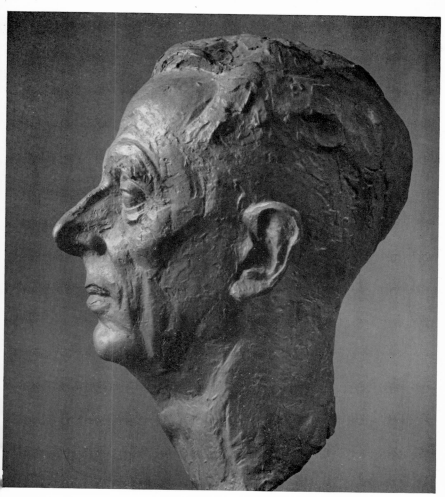

THE AUTHOR
Bust by Alexander Peikow, 1942

will have you, my cabin is yours. I will come on later. You are probably right that one requires a wife out there. But nobody would marry *me* on such short notice. I wish you good luck ! '

This conversation took place on a Wednesday. On the following Saturday, Sabbatini reappeared in Milan, and said that everything was settled.

I asked : ' You are really going to be married ? '

' Yes.'

' Congratulations ! What happened, exactly ? '

' Well, it was a little difficult at first. You see, I arrived just in time for the father's funeral.'

' Not a propitious moment, certainly. And then, what ? '

' They all thought, naturally, I had come for that. And they were much touched at my kind sympathy. While we were on the way to the cemetery, I kept looking round to see which of the mourners might be my possible fiancée.'

' And you spotted her ? '

' Yes.'

' And, later on, you proposed ? '

' Yes.'

' And were accepted ? '

' Yes.'

' Well, if you do not make a successful colonist, no one will. You are welcome to my cabin.'

Sabbatini was duly married and started off, with his bride, to Mombasa and Blantyre. The marriage turned out very well.

But I never went out, after all. Ascanio Colonna and I both took the examination for the diplomatic service. And this time our two names appeared at the top of the list.

And that is how I became a diplomat.

But I was sorry to renounce the hope of leading our emigrants to a Promised Land. Like the men and women of other races, who have created new worlds for themselves beyond the sea, those hard-working Italian peasants had nations in their eyes.

Official Interlude in a Changing World

EXTRACTS FROM "THE HANDBOOK OF THE PERFECT DIPLOMAT"

Hic videbis, fili mî, quam parva sapientia regatur mundus.

The CHANCELLOR VON OXENSTIERNA to his son, when
sending him on a diplomatic mission abroad, A.D. 1632.

IN May 1907, I went to my tailor, Filippo Mattina, to try on an
Attaché's uniform. When it was ready, I took up my duties at the
Italian Embassy in Vienna, and began to learn such lessons as a
diplomat's life could teach me.

I also began to jot down thoughts and impressions, as I went along :
a rudimentary *Esquisse psychologique* of the people with whom I had
to deal. Part of this ' Handbook of the Perfect Diplomat ' [1] has been
published, in the form of extracts, interleaved with the Memoirs of
my official career, as set forth in *Laughing Diplomat*. I do not claim
that the thoughts and commentaries thus collected were either original
or very new. But they may serve—as Samuel Butler once said of
his own books—to give me something to read in my old age.

In the following pages are some further extracts. They will serve
as an interlude to beguile the way and as a dividing line between my
recollections of the years before I entered government service, and
the years that followed my return to private life.

[1] If some explanation is needed for the peculiar construction of this book
(other than the fact that the story of the years 1907-32 is told elsewhere), I offer
the following :

A diplomat's autobiography is the story of a person who might be nameless,
even as the designation of the host in an invitation-card, ' *L'Ambassadeur d'Italie
et la Marquise Imperiali ont l'honneur*. . . .' (only the wife's name is mentioned).
In our public career, we are puppets. Only when we pass in through our own
front door, do we become ourselves.

The story of a man's private life, though he may be working for the same
ideals that he pursued in an official capacity, is a personal chronicle. His responsi-
bilities are his own. He is not acting under instructions. Thus, when serving
in the Section of the Ministero degli Affari Esteri that dealt with our occupation
of Lybia, I was a cog in a machine. When taking an active part in Italy's
expansion overseas, as in the defence, by speech and writing, of such expansion,
I did so as Daniele Varè, on my own initiative.

The autobiography enclosed between the covers of this volume may not
appear to be a consecutive story. Nevertheless, it is an unbroken chronicle of
the author's own hopes and endeavours, his successes and his failures.

THE ITALIANS (A FRAGMENT)

I REGRET to say that in my country there are fewer patriots than partisans. It may have something to do with the soil and the climate. Ours is a wonderful country, infinitely varied. And the people are more varied than the landscape, so much so that I sometimes ask myself if there are any Italians at all. We are such a mixed lot !

When the Roman Empire declined and fell, there were very few of the old burgesses left : the so-called Quirites. And since then the peninsula has been invaded by Visigoths, Ostrogoths, Byzantines, Lombards, Franks, Frederick Barbarossa, the Normans, the Suevi, the Angevins, the Aragonese, the Spaniards (united under Charles V), the French, the Austrians, Napoleon, the Austrians again, the Germans and the Anglo-Americans. I have not counted the Saracens, who made raids on our coastal provinces and left the hill-towns battered and scarred.

All these have left traces, but a remnant of the original stock remains, underlying the racial strata of foreign importation. Italy might be described as the rest-house of an eternal cavalcade. Our ' yesterdays ' are like the ' days ' in the first chapter of Genesis (" and the evening and the morning were the second day ").

*　　　*　　　*

Rome organized the Christian religion and carried it over the world. But this was not an unmixed blessing to the Italians. With the Papacy, there arose in their midst an international institute, which looked beyond the national life of the people, and was a source of weakness, in as much as it opposed the realization of those national ideals : Unity and Independence.

Yet in the papacy itself we may perceive a characteristic of the Italian people : their tendency to centralize. One infallible Pope stands between humanity and the Creator, in contrast with the nordic creeds that allow each human soul to stand alone, facing the Divinity.

The same centralizing tendency can be observed in Italian art. In Dante's masterpiece, we find the whole material world, and the worlds to come, held within the Cantos of a single poem, the *Divine*

Comedy. In the greatest masterpiece of nordic literature, Shakespeare's plays, the characters portrayed are as varied as humanity itself. And whereas the personality of Dante dominates his work, the personality of Shakespeare is hidden behind those of his creations.

*   *   *

On every nation, at its birth, some good fairies confer blessings, and one bad fairy lays a curse. The curse that was laid on Italy in her cradle would seem to be this : that when she grew up and had children, she would see the labour and the intelligence of her sons exploited by others, so that she and they would remain always in a position of inferiority. As late as 1918, when ' peace ' was being negotiated at Versailles, Clémenceau resented our claiming parity with the other powers, and said so, with his usual bluntness, to Guglielmo Marconi.

But the bad fairy's curse goes back further than that. In his book on *The Italian Renaissance*, John Addington Symonds describes the supreme part played by Italians in what—to use Michelet's phrase—was " the discovery of the world and the discovery of man ". The Sybil of the Renaissance had been offering her books in vain to feudal Europe. They were accepted in Italy. But " an alien monarchy, greedy for gold, a panic-stricken hierarchy in terror for its life, warped the tendencies and throttled the energies of the most artistically sensitive, the most heroically innovating of the existing races ".

There is no poetic exaggeration in these statements. No other people have given to the world such a galaxy of heroic figures in the domain of science, of politics and of art ; such navigators, saints, pioneers, poets, mathematicians, discoverers. But as a nation, this has availed us little. Italy's great men have not always contributed to *her* greatness. It was typical of this fact that Columbus should have discovered America, when serving a foreign queen, and the Cabotos given Newfoundland to an English King.

And how often has the inventive genius of an Italian been exploited by foreigners, as with Antonio Meucci, the real inventor of the telephone (this was admitted in the Supreme Court of the United States, in October 1888).

Marconi once told me that he would have been a far richer and successful man if he had submitted to the pressure brought to bear on him, to change his nationality. Having refused to do so, he had to defend *unguibus et rostro*, his right to the priority in the invention of wireless telegraphy. The matter was settled once and for all, in a court of law. The judgment of Judge Townsend, in the U.S.A. Circuit Court (May 1905), is also a very fine piece of English prose :

> Other inventors, venturing forth on the sea of electrical movement, met the rising tide of the Hertzian waves and allowed them to roll by without appreciating that this new current was destined to carry onward the freight and traffic of the world's commerce. They noted their manifestations, suspected their possibilities, disclosed their characteristics, and hesitated, fearing the breakers ahead, imagining barriers of impracticable channels and shifting sandbars. Marconi, daring to hoist his sail and explore the unknown current, first disclosed the new highway.

★   ★   ★

If I can be described as ' a patriot ', it is in the sense that was given to the word in the eighteenth century, when it meant a discontented man, as opposed to the courtier, who professed himself satisfied with present conditions. For me, that mystical, mysterious thrill of veneration for one's fatherland, that we call love of country, does not necessarily imply the same feeling for my countrymen. I have been exasperated by the Italians more often than by any other people with whom I have had to deal. And I sympathize with Dante, who peopled Hell with his fellow-citizens.

> *Godi, Firenze, poi che se' sì grande,*
> *Che per mare, e per terra batti l'ali,*
> *E per lo 'nferno il tuo nome si spande.*[1]

Even when they don't annoy me beyond endurance, I can see—as no foreigner could—the absurdities in the Italian character, and I must laugh at them. But *on se moque de ce qu'on aime.*

THE AMERICANS (A FRAGMENT)

WHILE writing a contemporary History of England (in Italian), I came to the conclusion that the British often brought heroic remedies to

---

[1] Rejoice, oh Florence, for you are so great,
   That your wings beat over land and sea,
   And your name is famous throughout Hell !
                                      Inferno, canto 26, *v.* 1.

counteract colossal mistakes. In this—so it now seems to me—the Americans tend to follow their example ; indeed, to outdo them.

One of the boasts one hears more often among the less cultured Americans is that something of theirs, such as Niagara Falls, the Morgan collections of Chinese porcelain, or a bridge over some estuary, is ' the greatest in the world '. They might say the same of some of the mistakes in foreign policy, made by their leading politicians, and of the relief-measures that the American nation has to pay for, in order to remedy the consequences of such mistakes. Luckily, they are wealthy. With nations, as with individuals, the rich can afford to make mistakes. A millionaire can sometimes take in his stride the troubles caused by his own imprudence and lack of foresight. The poor man goes under for a very similar fault.

So it is with nations. And because political morality is selective and judges by results, what in a great power is condoned as an error, in a small one is condemned as a crime.

I am always a bit afraid of the Americans, not because of anything *they* do, or don't do, but because so many other countries offer them the sincerest form of flattery. You will find an imitation U.S.A. almost everywhere : East and West and North and South.

Also it seems to me that they lead us in the field of advancing technology, at some risk to our personal, spiritual, inner progress. An advance in the standard of living is sometimes obtained at the expense of other, more valuable, things. So it has been in those apocalyptic processes of agriculture, in which the Americans are the world's pioneers. They sometimes make progress at ruinous cost, squandering Nature's irreplaceable resources. Are we to follow their lead in this too ?

I remember (at the end of the second world war) the contempt expressed by American soldiers of the Army of Occupation, when they observed the mellow folkways and certain century-old methods of cultivation, still in use in hill-farms on the Apennines (where the peasants sometimes dwelt in rock-houses). I doubt, myself, whether Italian *contadini* were ever much worse off than American tenant-farmers in the South, and in these difficult times they are certainly more prosperous than the white-collar workers in our cities. But no doubt their methods of cultivation contrasted forcibly with those of the Middle West. Yet Italian agriculture is far from being backward ; it represents the fruit of a long experience, and an expert knowledge of modern conditions. Large-scale methods, used on our soil, would soon reduce it to a collection of ' dust-bowls '. And even if it be true that in some parts of Italy the peasant's life is archaic, does this mean that he is to be pitied or despised ? It was of very similar agriculturists that Virgil wrote : " O fortunatos nimium . . ."

I can only express in the form of a platitude the obvious truth that, even if they hitch their wagon to the Stars and Stripes, Europeans should try to preserve their national characteristics (otherwise the tourist trade will suffer !). Bernard Shaw makes this truism the subject of an amusing dialogue in the second act of The Apple Cart. King Magnus does not share the American ambassador's enthusiasm at the prospect of the British Commonwealth ending up as a new group of stars in the American flag.

CLÉMENCEAU AT VERSAILLES, AND SOME FRENCH CHARACTERISTICS

AFTER a long world war, the moral cleaning up is more difficult than the material recovery. Any fool—said Bernard Shaw—can make war, but it takes a real statesman to make peace. At the moment when law and order are to replace violence, all the masks should come off, and the cards be laid face upwards on the table. The process is not a pleasant one. When the hypocrisies are dropped, we must expect some disappointments and the revelation of national egoisms and characteristics.

The peace terms that concluded the first world war disappointed many Italians like myself, who had expected to see assigned to Italy one at least of the colonial mandates. Instead of which the German–African empire was divided up between powers that were already surfeited with colonial possessions. Article 13 of the Treaty of London (26th April 1915), defining the terms for Italy's entry into the war on the side of the Allies, was ignored. So were the promises made us at the Interallied Conference at Saint Jean de Maurienne, in April 1917.

The atmosphere in Paris, during the peace negotiations, could hardly have been more unfavourable to a fair consideration of Italy's aspirations. Mr. Herbert Hoover described that atmosphere in an article, 'The First American Crusade', published in the *Saturday Evening Post* of the 1st November 1941 :

One day, after the President arrived, he asked me what I thought of the situation in Paris. I remarked that the whole air had suddenly become impregnated with currents of indescribable malignity. . . . I was convinced that America was accepted in Europe as the golden-egged goose—as such, our life would be safe, but not the eggs. He was shocked and expressed disagreement that such expressions should be used in respect of men who led those glorious triumphs of democracy. About two months later, he recalled that conversation and remarked : ' I have often agreed with you.'

Here we have an example of that demoralizing sickness of the spirit that brings even victorious peoples closer to defeat than the foe ever could have done. As an instance of that ' indescribable malignity ', mentioned by Mr. Hoover, let me outline the policy that Clémenceau recommended that the French should adopt towards Italy. He expounded this policy, during a meeting of the leaders of the French Chamber, on the 21st of January 1919, that is to say, at a time when we and the French were still Allies, and the war not officially over. I cannot guarantee a verbal accuracy, but the spirit of ' the Tiger ' is evident in every page :

The mistake that Napoleon III made, in allowing Italy to accomplish her unification, was no less than the other mistake in allowing the unification of Germany. Italy grows in proportion to the demographic diminution of France. In ten years' time, the Italians will be approaching 50 millions, and the French will be 35. Add to this that in Italy there is a re-awakening of all national energies, and the present crisis will only temper them for the future. From this double dynamic plenitude, it follows that Italy, poor as she is in territory and in raw materials, feels an irresistible need and at the same time a formidable force of expansion. . . . The field of this fatal expansion is the same that is held by France, and which France not only cannot exploit, but even has difficulty to keep a hold on, owing to her poverty in men. The substitution of Italy for France is therefore inevitable, unless France succeeds in preventing, or at least in paralysing, the development of Italy. How can it be paralysed ?

By keeping Italy as much as possible in economic subjection, in denying her any Mediterranean colonial possession that might be sufficient to give her the raw materials of which she is in need, and obliging her to disperse and to lose her growing demographic strength in transoceanic emigration, such as can more easily be denationalized, and finally leaving her with a thorn in her flesh, both from the sentimental as from the strategic point of view, so that she shall be hampered in any broad-minded Mediterranean policy. . . . In other words, create for her enmities in the Adriatic and in the East ; crush all possible future allies of Italy in the Adriatic and in the Balkans, among the Bulgarians and the Hungarians ; draw the Rumanians away from her ; deny to Italy any growth in Africa ; measure out in the most miserly way any part she may be assigned in Asia Minor ; again, in other words : oppose globally the entire Italian programme of peace. This policy, among its other advantages, may oblige the Italian demographic plethora to flow, at least in part, into France and into French colonies, so as to act as a blood-transfusion of men, made necessary by French sterility.

A policy of delending of Carthage, to be followed towards an ally, as soon as the common danger was over, was selfish, spiteful and mean. It was also short-sighted, for more could have been gained by keeping Italian friendship, while we grew strong, than by fostering our enmity in the attempt to keep us weak. But outspokenly inimical as it is, I can appreciate such frankness better than the plausible pretence at goodwill, in less honest, more self-righteous opponents : such foreign politicians who blandly assure us that, in denying to the Italians what *they* have (and stick to), they have only *our* interests at heart. Colonies would not be good for *us*, even in territories which Italians have made prosperous by their labour. They are too expensive to maintain, and much less profitable in the long run than we were led to suppose.

On the whole, if I am to have an adversary, I prefer a Frenchman to some others I could mention. There is nothing smug about him ; he is avowedly out for the main chance, and the devil take the hindmost. If French diplomats have a weakness, I think it lies in ignoring the truth of their own proverb : *On n'attrape pas les mouches avec du vinaigre !*

Their particular school of diplomacy, which alternates *le beau geste* with a certain ruthlessness, can be explained by the history of France. We find in it, again and again, the old policy that was formulated by the Cardinal de Richelieu : ' My neighbours are my enemies, the neighbours of my enemies are my friends.' To reverse such a policy, we would have to guarantee to France the security that in the past she has never attained.

Speaking about his own nickname, Clémenceau once said that every Frenchman was half tiger and half monkey. But their characteristic touch of *sauvagerie* helps to keep them immune to one of the greatest of contemporary evils : the mechanization of thought through propaganda.

The Parisian mind is the only part of French public opinion (and it is not only French) with which I can claim acquaintance, having been in touch with it since the days of the two Cambons, and Diaghilev, and Boni de Castellane. In those days, the Parisian was always *à la page*, and his mind was merry and subtle and fine, with a wit that snapped and crackled.

And the rapid intellectual grace of their causeries ! Even simple, homely men were often in touch with the great world of thought, and one might converse with them, with pleasure, on a penny steam-boat on the Seine.

CHANGES IN THE BRITISH CHARACTER

DURING the last hundred years, the mentality of most people in this world has changed more rapidly than in any preceding period of history. I wonder if I am right in saying that the British have changed more than any other people, since Latin quotations left English public life ? One still perceives in them traces of the old strains, that of the Puritan and the Cavalier, but mellowed by the passing of time, and by the industrial revolution.

In the Preface to his book of drawings, illustrating *Rosetti and his Circle*, Max Beerbohm says that Byron, Disraeli and Rossetti seem to him the three most interesting men England had in the nineteenth century. Of these three, only Rosetti could possibly figure as a contemporary of our own. Byron and Disraeli, were we to meet them today, would appear hopelessly outdated. But though Rossetti —as Max Beerbohm says—would not have seemed out of place in the Quattrocento by the Arno, he *was* born out of his time in London, " in the great days of a deep, smug, thick, rich, drab, industrial com-placency ". He and his fellow Pre-Raphaelites revolted against that complacency, and they heralded a revolution that extended far beyond the field of art.

I once heard from Rudyard Kipling an authoritative comment on the changes in the British character. This was when he made a speech at the Royal Society of St. George, on the 6th of May 1935. He mentioned Great Britain's quota of dead in the first world war, and spoke of those who had burned out half a life's vitality in three or four years : men who had been incapacitated from effort by the effects of shock, gassing, tubercle, and the like :

' All these men were of average physique, and, but that they died without issue, would have continued the race. The selective elimination of so many men of one type, and their replacement by so many persons of another type and their children, led to an extensive revision of all standards of English thought and action. . . .

' A little later our electorate was enlarged by the enfranchisement of all English women over twenty-one. This gave renewed impulse to the national ideal of an ever-rising standard of living, and the removal of want, discomfort and the accidents of life from the lives of our people. To this end they built up, and were now building, gigantic organizations to control and handle every detail of those lives.'

An important factor in the change that recent decades have brought about in the British character, was foreshadowed by Harold Nicholson, in a ' Rede Lecture ', at the University of Cambridge, on the 23rd of April 1937. His subject was ' The meaning of Prestige', and he concluded with a query concerning what might happen to the British character if Great Britain did not achieve again the unchallengeable power in international politics, which even in 1937 she had admittedly lost. He asks : ' Is there danger lest that character may also decline ? ' And he adds :

I have not that complacency which would lead me to believe that our people are possessed of nobler virtues than are other peoples. We could afford the luxury of gentleness, because we were unafraid. Now that we have lost our sense of security, shall we always maintain our good-humour and our objectivity ? Will even our honesty, our candour and our truthfulness remain undimmed ? . . . If we are alert and determined, these great blessings will each one be preserved. Yet if we forfeit them, then (however great may be our physical power, however thunderous our guns) British prestige will perish from the earth ; and mankind will thereby lose one of the last citadels of tolerance, of gentleness and of reason.

There is, however, one symptom of strength—as far as I can judge—still noticeable in the British people. I once heard it defined by Monsieur Laval. He said : ' *L'Angleterre ne désire ni comprendre, ni être comprise !* ' This trait corresponds, in foreign politics, to a similar one in private life. What the typical Briton likes best is to be regarded as a private gentleman, or in other words : to be left alone.

The English are sometimes unconscious of the extent to which they remain isolated from the currents of continental opinion, or if they do realize this, they take pride in it. Yet such isolation is sometimes responsible for what John Morley calls ' epidemics of unreason '.

On the other hand, it would seem to be a contemporary British characteristic to keep abstractions (in which they sometimes include both politics and religion) away from their daily lives. This may explain in part their not un-merited reputation for tolerance. The Covenanters, in Cromwell's day, adopted a creed of religious uniformity and would have compelled it at the point of the sword. But in the nineteenth century we find Lord Melbourne saying : ' Things have come to a pretty pass, when religion is allowed to invade private life ! '

*　　　*　　　*

The daily Press has changed the character of the nations, but not so much, in essentials, as one might suppose. Henry VIII discovered, before *The Times*, that it pays to have a good motive to put forward in justification of British material interests.

Though he is careful not ' to theorize ' over the drama of history, James Anthony Froude draws a philosophical conclusion from the fate of the great expedition, sent by Philip II to restore the Papal authority over England :

> The English nature on that occasion was seen at its very best. The days had not yet come of inflated self-praise ; and the spirit which produces actions of real merit is usually simple in the description of such actions. Good wine needs no bush ; the finest jewels need the least gaudy setting ; and as the newspaper correspondent was not yet born, and the men who did the fighting wrote also the reports, the same fine and modest temper is equally seen in both.

HABIT-WORDS AND THE MECHANIZATION OF THOUGHT

SEVERAL new factors have entered world-politics during the first half of the twentieth century, though it may be that they are nothing more than new names for old ideas. Bolshevism, Fascism, Democracy, Internationalism are labels slapped on many parcels, with different contents. Future historians may get grievous headaches, trying to find correct definitions corresponding to the habit-words of successive generations.

We are told in Genesis how once the whole world was of one language and of one speech, but while building the Tower of Babel men came to have different languages and were confounded and dispersed over the earth. Having different words for the same thing, they could not understand each other.

Later on, a similar curse was again laid upon humanity. It is not that men use different words for the same thing. They use the same words for different things. But the result is the same. ' Communism ', ' Fascism ', ' Democracy ', mean different things to different people. We use these words as sticks, to beat each other's dogs with.

Words are not like crystals, transparent and unchanging. They vary in colour and content according to the circumstances and the time when they are used.

Look what the English and the Americans, between them, have done to that poor little Italian word, ' propaganda ', after adopting it into their own language ! With us, it used to mean ' propagation of the Christian faith '. Now it has acquired an almost diabolical significance !

While names change, like lights and shadows on a high mountain range, the elemental factors in history are eternal as the eternal snow. They are the same as those that Machiavelli pointed out in the days of Alexander VI and Caesar Borgia. Men persist in seeing things, not as they are, but as they wish them to be. We put our signatures to paper reforms, but still the conqueror behaves towards the vanquished as Achilles did, when he dragged the dead body of Hector at the wheels of his chariot, and sacrificed twelve young boys on the funeral pyre of Patrocles. While Christianity makes the highest attempt of which the human intelligence is capable, to interpret the universe on a principle of justice, mankind continues, always and everywhere, to bow its neck to force.

But force tires, and as it does so, existing situations are revised. This is what is called History.

*   *   *

An ominous change has come over the civilized world, by the mechanization of ideas. Humanity, like Faust, is on a fair way to sell its soul for that mental ease, which is vouchsafed to those who do not think for themselves. Nations tend to live on infused opinions and to have knowledge pumped into them mechanically, as in Huxley's *Brave New World* (which may be nearer than we think).

Most of our convictions today are nothing more than the reflected image of certain collective movements of ideas. Kinglake pointed out in *Eothen* how difficult it is for anyone living in the East not to be influenced by the general belief in magic, so that one ends by sharing that belief.

The contagion of mass-psychology is exploited by official and non-official propaganda. Through its publicity-bureaus, a government sells its policies to the tax-payer in his own money. Avenues of information are controlled till ' public opinion ' becomes almost a meaningless expression. Sometimes, these exaggerations defeat their own ends, and statesmen are hampered or driven to excesses by their own Press and radio campaigns that have got out of hand.

James Truslow Adams writes in his *Epic of America* :

> It has been said, not without a show of reason, by those familiar with the most recent advertising methods, that only cost limits the delivery of public opinion in any direction desired, on any subject. The more money available, the larger the slice of opinion that can be delivered.

These lines describe the situation in U.S.A. under President Taft. It would seem that they are no less true today. But here and there a reaction is visible. The very excesses of propaganda cause a boomerang-return of his weapon on the head of the propagandist. A situation changes overnight, and then we may observe a transfer of intolerance from one side to the other.

Navigation is not easy, as tides alternate over shifting shoals, in shallow waters. But the more light-hearted politicians soon acquire the art of trimming their sails to changing winds.

One of them should write a *Philosophy of the Vicar of Bray*.

PART II
HARVESTING OF A DREAM

> Try as he will, no man breaks wholly loose
> From his first love, no matter who she be.
> Oh, was there ever sailor free to choose,
> That didn't settle somewhere near the sea ?
>
> Parsons in pulpits, tax-payers in pews,
> Kings on your thrones, you know as well as me,
> We've only one virginity to lose,
> And where we lost it there our hearts will be !
>
> RUDYARD KIPLING, speaking of his first mistress,
> the *Indian Civil and Military Gazette*.

IN the Italian Legation at Copenhagen, one of the pleasantest rooms
is the pantry. It is a corner room on the first floor, with two big
windows, looking out on the royal palaces of Amalienborg. There
are four of these palaces, built round a square ; the King lives in one
of them and receives in another.

You might describe that pantry as a sunny room, if there were any
sun to speak of in Denmark, even in summer, when the nights last
less than two hours. Anyway, it gets all the light there is and is much
brighter than the poky, low-ceilinged rooms on the ground floor,
where I worked (when I was Italian Minister to Denmark) and
received visitors.

I rarely set foot in the pantry, but Bettina, my wife's, household
duties often took her there, and on the morning of the 1st of August
1932 I went to seek her among the silver and the china, to show her
a telegram they had just deciphered in the Chancery. The Foreign
Office in Rome informed me that I had been placed on the retired
list, and instructed me to approach the Danish Government, to obtain
their *agrément* to the appointment of my successor.

Thus began, for me, what you might call a second incarnation ;
the first having been my career as a diplomat on active service.

The telegram, signed ' Suvich ' (the newly appointed Under Secretary of State, acting for Mussolini) came as a bolt from the blue.
Nothing in the previous correspondence had led me to expect anything of the kind. I was only fifty-two and might have looked
forward to many more years of work.

The discharge did not concern me only. Nineteen of my colleagues were put on the retired list at the same time. This wholesale *dégommage* became known as 'The Massacre of the Innocents'. At the head of the list was our Ambassador in Paris, Baron Romano Avezzana. He told me later that the Quai d'Orsay had manifested a natural astonishment at the sudden dismissal of so large a portion of the Italian diplomatic service, and asked if anything had happened to justify such a liquidation. Baron Romano answered No. It was merely the preliminary to a transfusion of new blood. The French official answered : '*Je comprends ! C'est de la ventilation qu'on fait chez vous.*'

A 'United Press' telegram, dated Rome, 5th August, mentioned the matter under the heading : "Mussolini names young Fascists as Ambassadors." It pointed out that only two of the men appointed to replace those who had been dismissed were professional diplomats (one of the two was Augusto Rosso, Ambassador to Washington). The others were newspaper men, who had already been sent by the Duce on diplomatic missions and who had decided to take up diplomacy as a career. My own successor in Denmark was a former journalist. I have no criticism to offer. . . . But I cannot refrain from quoting a phrase of Scialoja's concerning the most flashy of our new representatives abroad : "When he should be a diplomat, he is a journalist, and when he should be a journalist, he is a diplomat."

There is a certain *esprit de corps* among career diplomats, which is not limited to their own nationality. Though I had never cut much ice in diplomacy, my own dismissal caused a certain stir. Sir Miles Lampson (later, Lord Killearn) wrote to me : "I'm rather glad this country's destinies (and mine) do not lie in the hands of these supermen. But frankly, is it not rather monstrous as far as you are concerned?"

Hardly 'monstrous', though perhaps a little unfair. But it is a custom in many countries to consider diplomatic posts abroad as plums with which to reward services to a political party, and as a means to feather the nests of personal adherents to those in power. This tendency is accentuated in times of political change. A new régime takes more interest in distributing lucrative posts among its supporters than in choosing the most suitable men to occupy those posts.

An editorial in the London *Times*, with the title ' The Tallest Poppies ', commenting on the Fascist system of making changes in government personnel, contained criticisms that would have been equally pertinent in other times and in other countries, besides Italy.

I must admit to have felt some pain at the sudden uprooting, though I was careful to utter no complaint. Among others, Ciano (Mussolini's son-in-law), who had been my secretary when I was in China, was prompt to express sympathy. At that time he held the Ministry of Press and Propaganda, and he encouraged me to make use of an unwelcome leisure by writing for the papers. This was a poor substitute for my own chosen profession. I had hoped, some day, to end up as Ambassador in Washington or London. In the ordinary course of events, that is to say, if Mussolini had never come to power, or if he had not felt the need of making transfusions of Fascist blood into Italian diplomacy, it is more than probable that one or the other of our principal embassies would have been mine for the asking. But new brooms sweep clean, and new régimes make room for their own supporters. I might add that just as peasants are suspicious of city-polish, so are the parvenus in politics suspicious of the more stream-lined diplomatists, even when they are as unpretentious as I am.

All men, who are happy and successful in their work, gain by experience and by training a special kind of strength, suited to their particular environment. I do not think I am boasting when I say that I was well suited to that much abused, much laughed at, profession, the diplomatic service. I sometimes feel a little homesick for it, even now.

When I got back to Rome, I went to see Mussolini. He received me, standing behind his writing-table in the corner of that huge hall, the Sala del Mappamondo, in the Palazzo Venezia. He asked, rather brusquely :

' Well, Varè. What do you want from me ? '

I answered : ' Nothing.'

Then, for the first time since I met him in Lausanne in 1922, I saw a look of real astonishment come into his face. That anyone, in my circumstances, should come to see him, merely out of courtesy and not to ask for anything, must have appeared to him almost miraculous. Yet, why should I have wanted anything from him ? Nothing he could offer was worth to me what he had taken away.

After a brief moment, he smiled, and we talked amicably for a little while, still standing, one on either side of the table. He asked me if my daughter, Margherita, continued to ride in international horse-shows, since her marriage to Ranieri di Campello. But he did not wait for my answer, and the conversation—as so often with him—ended abruptly, with a wave of his hand to dismiss me.

Retirement

Retirement, like matrimony, is an honourable estate ; and nowadays is becoming an important one. This is due to two reasons. On the one hand, this is, as we all know, the Age of Youth. In every business and profession, the leading figures tend more and more to be (in theatrical parlance) juvenile leads. . . . Early retirement is the order of the day. But if a man nowadays is frequently too old at forty, the advance of medical science provides that he should usually be too young at sixty. Thus the elder generation is quietly getting a bit of its own back.

C. R. BAINES, *Retirement*, ' G. K.'s Weekly ', 28th May 1936.

IF I may compare little things to great, I would say that my mentality, in the first years after my dismissal from the diplomatic service, was similar to that of Machiavelli, when in March 1513 he retired to his farm near San Casciano. After he came home in the evening, he used to take off the clothes in which he had tramped round all day, and which were often covered with mud, or dust. And he would put on his best velvet robe, and light the candles, to commune with the great spirits of the Past.

I might, of course, have given myself the airs of a martyr and posed as a victim of Fascism. Who knows if that would not have procured my nomination to a professorship of diplomacy in some foreign university ? So many seats of learning had their tame victim (or pretended victim) of totalitarian ideologies ! To figure abroad as an anti-Fascist, persecuted for his opinions, became for many non-entities, a lucrative profession. It was the same, just after the Bolshevist Revolution in Russia. Every smart hotel on the Riviera, and not a few in Switzerland, had then their refugee Russian Princess. *On leur donnait la chambre et deux repas.* (I have been assured that this was true by no less an authority than Monsieur Albous—the director of the Ritz Carlton, in Madison Avenue, when I was last in U.S.A.)

My situation was paradoxical. I had been removed to make place for the special protégés of Mussolini's, but I remained on good terms with him, and even more so with Ciano. I did not figure as a Fascist in Italy, but put my name down on the 'Fascio' of London ; an arrangement which made me practically independent of any Fascist authority.

Among the members of my family, the news of my retirement was received with mixed feelings. They expressed the opinion that I had been badly treated. But they were pleased, every one of them, to return to live in Italy. Bettina liked seeing new places and learning new languages (as well as having new landscapes to paint). But it bored her to be continually giving balls and dinners for people she hardly knew, and having to go out in society, when she would have much preferred to stay at home.

The person who took it most to heart was my youngest daughter's governess. She belonged to that class of people to whom 'diplomatic privilege' (which she shared indirectly) represented a foretaste of heaven. And she made quite a nuisance of herself by shedding tears over our fall in the social scale. Fortunately she left us to look after the children of an Ambassador in Poland, where I presume she found happiness in Paradise regained.

Also Curry, the rough-haired fox-terrier, resented the change in his habits. Copenhagen suited him, and he approved of the local custom of eating between meals. When we went for walks along the Lange Linie, Curry would find little groups sitting on benches or on the grass, consuming smörbrod, the national sandwich, containing unlimited butter. He would go up to the picnickers and beg : rarely in vain.

When Curry got home and was taken for walks in the Villa Borghese, he would run up to similar groups of people. But these were Italians. They would pat him and say he was a good dog. But rarely, if ever, did they offer him food. And Italy suffered by comparison.

On the whole, I owe a debt of gratitude to Mussolini for having turned me out of the diplomatic service. I would have been miserable if I had had to represent Italy abroad, during the second world war or after it. Instead of which, by that time, I had succeeded in finding a little corner for myself in literature.

The Spring of 1935—Stresa and the Jubilee

LOOKING back on it, the year 1935 appears to have been full of travel, incident and activity. But it began quietly enough.

I stayed a few weeks at Baveno, on Lake Maggiore, to put the finishing touches on two books in English : *The Last of the Empresses*, and *The Maker of Heavenly Trousers*. Afterwards, I meant to go on to London, to look for a publisher who might be willing to accept them.

The Lago Maggiore represents for me the ideal of a peaceful country life, without the heartbreaking anxieties and catastrophes of agriculture and farming. The view out towards the St. Gothard, with Pallanza and the Borromean Islands, and south towards Stresa, is one of the most restful in the world, even in the full glory of spring, when it all seems almost too beautiful to be true. I have happy childish memories of Baveno, and others, more poignant, when I was there in my first youth. But that, as Kipling would say, ' is another story '. Some day I may tell it you, if you would like to hear.

In April 1935, the English, French and Italian statesmen were meeting at Stresa. I saw something of them both before and after their labours. No one, then, at any apprehension of a dangerous crisis impending between England and Italy. It was hoped, not unreasonably, that England, France and Italy might form a United front against an aggressive Germany. The murder of Dollfuss had occurred eight months before. Germany had withdrawn from the League of Nations and was re-arming.

Mussolini's *riposte*, when he massed troops on the Italo-Austrian frontier, after the assassination of Millimetternich (as the little Bundskansler was called), received, at the time, no effective support either from France or Great Britain, and this slightly modified the Duce's outlook. He complained that the English and French governments had egged him on to an anti-German policy and then left him in the lurch. But eight months later it was hoped that a meeting, on the shores of Lake Maggiore, would strengthen the bonds between us.

At Stresa, Great Britain was represented by Ramsay MacDonald and Sir John Simon. France by Flandin and Monsieur Laval. When we consider the result of their discussions round the green baize table, it is difficult not to come to the conclusion that most of what was said and done was beside the point. Much time was spent in discussing the situation in the Balkans and in preparing for a meeting of Balkan statesmen, who should have foregathered in Rome (but never did). A lot was said about the attitude of the Powers towards Hungary, whose revisionist aspirations were considered dangerous by Jugoslavia and Czechoslovakia. The other powers looked upon these aspirations with a platonic and ineffectual sympathy.

With regard to Nazi pressure on Austria, the French spoke of applying sanctions to Germany, but MacDonald said that such sanctions were likely to do more harm to those who applied them than to the power against whom they were directed. There followed a game of battledore and shuttlecock, in which each delegation tried to make out that the fate of Austria was of supreme interest to some other power but not to themselves. Monsieur Laval maintained that the independence of Austria was principally an Italian interest. Mussolini (after the others had had their say) answered that he had no reason to be nervous about Austria. Even if it were to be invaded by Germany, this would not necessarily imply a danger to Italy. There was an excellent frontier. He felt quite capable of defending it. If to anybody, the Austrian question was primarily of interest to England. Its occupation by Germany would be a first step towards the Bosphorus and the East. Ramsay MacDonald seemed to find this argument rather far-fetched. And he added that, in his opinion, Austria was a ripe fruit, ready at any moment to fall into the lap of Germany. This could not be prevented. (I spoke about the matter, later on, with Ciano, who agreed with MacDonald. He believed that, if Italian troops had entered Austria after the murder of Dollfuss, they would have found more than half the population ready to oppose them, and siding with the German Nazis.)

No mention was made of Ethiopia.

Yet, at the time of the Stresa Conference, the Gavinana and Peloritana divisions had been mobilized in Italy, and our military stores were daily passing through the Suez Canal. The British Government was well aware of Mussolini's intention to move into Abyssinia. They expected our action to be in the nature of a protracted and increasing military pressure ; not a sudden concerted attack, with the intention of going through with it, once and for all. This may, indeed, have been Mussolini's first idea on the matter, and it might have been possible to carry out, if the Negus had not been given every reason to believe that he would receive effective military support against the Italians. But, at Stresa, the future was still nebulous. The Italian experts could not enlighten anybody on Mussolini's intentions, for they did not know what these were. Probably he did not know himself. His projects changed according to circumstances and his own varying moods.

The British Delegation at Stresa numbered among its members the Foreign Office expert on Ethiopian affairs, Mr. Thompson. He sat about on the hotel sofas and discussed things in general with his opposite number in the Italian Ministero degli Affari Esteri, Signor G. B. Guarnaschelli. The opportunity was there for the British to have made known their opposition to any move of ours in Abyssinia before Mussolini had irretrievably committed himself. And it may be added that, if the Foreign Office was anxious about the matter, at that time, it was for no reason that could be described as hostile towards the Italians. Our collaboration in Europe was then considered indispensable, if concerted opposition was to be offered to German action in Austria and elsewhere. It was feared that a colonial campaign might weaken us, just when it was essential that our military efficiency be in no way impaired. Of all the moral crusade that later on was engineered in England, to ensure a majority in the coming elections, there was, at the time of the Stresa Conference, no foreboding and no trace. All was peace and amity.

The minor lights of the British and Italian delegations partook of a convivial ' fish lunch ' at the Isola dei Pescatori. The African experts, who had come to the Conference in case they should be wanted, gave each other some assurances about the undefined Somali frontier and the flow of the waters of the Lake Tsana down to the Nile. This was a matter that the British Government had once tried to settle directly with the Ethiopian Government, and had failed to come to an agreement. The mere fact that the question was discussed with the Italians, even *sub rosa*, was proof positive that a move of ours into Abyssinia was considered with no great disfavour.

94

I learnt afterwards that members of the British Delegation had discussed among themselves whether, or no, to raise the question of Ethiopia. I do not know why they did not do so. Perhaps they felt hurried, in view of the imminent meeting of the League of Nations Council at Geneva. At most international conferences, the principal anxiety of the delegations is that some formula be found by next Saturday, so that they may conclude their labours before the week-end !

Sir John Simon was once accused, by Lloyd George, of " sitting on the fence till the iron entered into his soul ". He appears to have done so at Stresa. Whether it is fair to blame him for this, I cannot say. But Christopher Hollis, in his very impartial book, *Italy in Africa*, writes : " It is perfectly certain that, through their egregious silence at Stresa, the British Government must take a certain share of the responsibility for the subsequent catastrophe."

Mussolini himself might quite safely have taken the initiative and played his hand boldly, but with diplomatic subtlety. He might have expressed frankly what were his thoughts at the time :

' We are here to measure the forces that we can oppose to the Germans if they continue to advance and to threaten. Each of us should specify his own quota, his possible contribution to the common action that may become necessary. For my part, I am willing to do so. Indeed, I have already proved my goodwill after the assassination of my friend Dollfuss, who was murdered while his wife and children were my guests in Italy. You may count on me to be at your side. But this must not exclude any action that I may consider necessary to safeguard Italian interests and realize Italian aspirations in Africa.'

Even if it is true that Mussolini, like Sir John Simon, never used the diplomatic instruments that were there, at Stresa, to do his behests, he did not fail to make his meaning clear, or his intentions. The Conference concluded with a final resolution, that afterwards figured in a communiqué. The text was circulated at the last meeting, so that the delegates might signify their approval, or their dissent. It spoke of " opposing by all practical means any unilateral repudiation of treaties, which may endanger peace . . . " Mussolini took out his pen and added in his own handwriting the significant words " in Europe ". And he looked round to see if his colleagues had any

95

objections. Laval merely smiled. Ramsay MacDonald said ' Yes.
I know your views . . . '

I must add (as I was not present) that I have heard another and
slightly different account of this episode. One of our own delegates
told me that, as far as he remembered, the words " in Europe " were
already there, in the final resolution, as prepared by the drafting
Committee, and Mussolini merely drew attention to them at the last
meeting of the Conference.

Anyway, the expressive gesture of Mussolini's was afterwards confirmed by Monsieur Flandin and recalled by the Duce himself, in an
interview with Mr. Ian Munro, for the *Morning Post* (17th September
1935). Later on, when in conversation with Alberto Pirelli, Mussolini listened without animosity to a criticism of his handling of the
Ethiopian question, and he said that he had thought himself authorized
to proceed as he did, both by the talks he had had with Monsieur
Laval, in January 1935, and by the silence of the British Ministers at
Stresa.

★   ★   ★

From Baveno, I proceeded, in April, to London.

I do not think that anybody loved the British Isles more than I
did, since my first youth and well on into middle-age. I even thought
it incumbent on me to get my countrymen to know the English
better and to appreciate them more. With this object in view, I
wrote, in Italian, a contemporary *History of England* and published
it, at my own expense (old Commendatore Bemporad would risk
no money himself on such a venture). The book was intended
originally to cover the period between 1837 and 1919. But because
I described the relations between Italy and England as being those
between two democratic states, and this, under Fascism, was no longer
the case, the third and fourth volumes, although ready to print, were
never published. My superiors at the Ministero appeared much
impressed by the laudatory reviews of the first two volumes, in the
Westminster Gazette and *The Times Literary Supplement*. Mussolini
remarked that it was a fine edition, adding however that he had no
time to read it.

Like Fritz in *La Grande Duchesse de Gerolstein*, who wanted to be a
schoolmaster in order to learn how to read and write, I wrote my

History of England in order to learn something about it myself. It was a labour of love.

Since I was a boy, England and Scotland offered a happy hunting-ground for my holidays. Whenever I arrived in London, I felt a thrill as the boat-train approached Charing Cross, with a view over the roofs and the smoky, wind-blown chimneys (but sometimes there was a fog, and then it seemed as if London were no longer there !).

The English smells would greet me : smells of bacon, of tea, of soot and Harris tweed, of stout and whisky and newly-mown lawns. In my youth, the station platforms were dimly lit by gas, and there were, of course, no taxis (when they made their first appearance on London streets, they were hailed as ' sparrow-starvers '). The drive to my grandmother's house in Collingham Road, South Kensington, would be taken in a four-wheeler, with straw at the bottom of the cab. Often, some poor wretch would run behind, to earn a few shillings by carrying heavy trunks into the house and up numerous flights of stairs.

I have pleasanter recollections of the hansoms, taking the dip in Piccadilly with a jingle of the harness bell accompanying the clip-clop of hoofs, when I went out to dinner at dusk on a summer eve, with my shirt-front catching the light as I leant forward (unless the weather was bad and the cabby had to lower the glass window against the splash of rain). As late as 1939, it sometimes happened that I heard a double whistle on a London street, and I would look round, half expecting to see two hansom cabs race for a fare from opposite directions, and draw up with a slithering of hoofs and mutual abuse by rival Jehus.

Besides echoes and ghosts of Victorian England, other things lingered on unchanged in recent years : week-ends in country houses ; running horses and silken jackets at Ascot ; muslins rippled by the breeze, and long cool days by the river, with lunch under a club-tent at Henley.

The ' season ' of 1935 represented a very creditable effort on the part of the Old Order, to make us believe it could still hold its own in a world where the great, small courtesies had been voted obsolete, and pounds were no longer made of gold. I got caught in a social whirl that brought to my mantelpiece a pile of invitations to luncheons and dinners, balls and week-end parties. The excess of demand over supply enhanced the value of a former diplomat, old-fashioned enough to leave cards where he had dined and sometimes even to send flowers to a head-hunting hostess. My diary of those hectic months reads like extracts from the Society News in a penny newspaper. Even *The Times* found space to announce that I was present at a dinner-party, together with the Duchess of Norfolk and the Marquess and Marchioness of Salisbury. If I remember that dinner, it was for another reason. I found myself seated between Marta Abba, the actress who is supposed best to interpret Pirandello, and the Hon. Mrs. Walter Runciman. The latter said a thing that left me gasping with astonishment : the sort of remark that Dickens might have put in the mouths of the Brothers Cheeryble. Our conversation had got round to the subject of Happiness and its rarity. Mrs. Runciman did not share the common opinion as to its being uncommon, or fleeting. ' I,' she said, ' have always been perfectly happy. I *am* perfectly happy, and I never expect to be anything but perfectly happy ! '

I asked : ' Have you any children ? '

She said she had, and they had never given her any anxiety. I went on to enquire if the fact that her husband was in the government did not occasionally represent a source of mental worry. She answered : ' Certainly not ! '

Mrs. Runciman's appearance carried out her claim to bask in un-broken rays of felicity : a good-looking and rather plump lady, with rosy cheeks and grey hair. I never met her again, but I have often envied her tranquillity of mind in a world so full of *malades imaginaires*. But I confess that I found Marta Abba more human. She told me she was having a humpy time learning enough English to act the part of the Russian Princess, turned lady's maid, in *Tovarich*.

Meanwhile, people's thoughts were directed to the coming celebration of the Jubilee.

I believe I am not far wrong in saying that it was a happy event in the chimpanzee family at the Zoo, which inspired the subsequent festivities to commemorate King George V's accession to the throne, twenty-five years before. Many of the pundits of the Zoological Gardens used to congregate for lunch at the round table in the corner, at the Brook Street end of the Savile Club dining-room. It was their idea to give the name of Jubilee to the baby chimpanzee. Their decision was announced in an article that appeared next Sunday in the *Observer*, and this was the first time that the sabbatical year was brought to the notice of the public, as with a flourish of trumpets.

As the preparations for the Jubilee grew in intensity, my second daughter, Diana, came over to share the fun. She had a room at Claridges, and I a guest-room at the Savile, so we lived next door to one another, and I spent in a week what she did in a day. Diana did not much enjoy London society : she complained that it was too large a community for one foreign girl to make herself at home in. You never seem to meet the same people twice.

She and I motored down to Knole, where she found a kindred spirit in the American-born Lady Sackville. The latter did not take kindly to the English habit of the hostess pouring out tea for everybody, so I enjoyed the unusual sight of a daughter of mine performing that ceremony in the stateliest of the stately homes of England.

I had made myself a mental picture of Knole, when reading *The Edwardians*. After seeing it, I have remained with a confused memory of russet roofs and squat grey towers, of Water Courts, and Pheasant Courts and Brown Galleries, of tapestry in a Venetian room and Jacobean wainscoting in a ballroom. Also of two long wine-glasses for stirrup-cups, one called My Lord's Conscience, and the other My Lady's Conscience. One is taller and more capacious than the other. I can't remember which.

British castles and Italian palaces required more of their owners than money, supposing that to be forthcoming. They ask each successive generation to sacrifice itself to a tradition of magnificence that no longer impresses young people, or attracts them. When Diana and I left Knole for London, her first remark as we drove through Sevenoaks was : ' How I understand that the younger members of the family don't live there ! '

At Knole one breathes the air of Elizabethan England. It would hardly be surprising to meet Robert Dudley, Earl of Leicester, riding up to the outer doors, wearing a hunting-suit of Lincoln-green. I stayed a few days at another country-house where the atmosphere was Victorian. But the ghosts of the Past were no less characteristic of a golden age.

My wife's cousin, Lady Normanby (known in the family as ' Bee ') asked me down to Mulgrave for Whitsuntide. As Yorkshire is Bettina's home-county, I wrote to her from there, endeavouring to describe surroundings that had been those of her youth. Bettina kept my letter. In reading it over, today, I seem to find in it something more than the account of a week-end in a pleasant country-house, in sight of the grey North Sea. Like some of the chapters in *Tom Sawyer* and *Huckleberry Finn*, it recalls a vanished civilization : the gilt-edged, candle-lit days of Merry England !

MULGRAVE CASTLE
Saturday, 8th June 1935 (written between
11 p.m. and midnight, before going to bed)

I travelled down here by the Great Northern as far as York, and thence in a local train that crawls through the East Riding and up the coast, with prolonged sojourns at every station and not a few sidings. We ambled along in so leisurely a fashion, we might almost have dallied with the butterflies, afloat over the meadow-sweet and the forget-me-nots.

Gazing drowsily out of the carriage window, I saw the names of places that must be familiar to you : Kirkham Abbey on the banks of a little river (you may know what it is called) ; Howard Castle among thick woods ; Melton, where a charabanc of excursionists waited at the level crossing, and some boys on an orchard fence waved their caps at the passing train. Rooks called to one another in the high elms ; children picked flowers in the meadows ; girls in cottage-gardens hung out the washing to dry, and cotton garments swelled out in the sea-breeze. Just outside Rollington, an adverse signal kept us waiting long enough for the engine-driver to exchange gossip with some navvies at work on the line, while a pair of huge Shire horses, their fetlocks well feathered, grazed amicably a few yards off. There is an Arcadian sleepiness about English landscapes in summer-time, nor is a freckled Amaryllis lacking, with a wreath of cowslips, to dump on Strephon's brow !

Although we are in June, the big trees are just beginning to come into leaf, and the hedge-rows are gay with flowers that in Italy are long since over. The honey-bee is on the broom, grey sheep are fattening in the valley-pastures . . . The little amber-coloured streams all seem to run *away* from the coast. Are they loth, I wonder, to plunge into the cold North Sea ?

Bee has put me in a downstair suite. The furniture, I think, is Georgian (if not older), but the bedroom must have been done up afresh in the days of the Bedchamber Question. You remember the story ? When about to take office, in 1839, Sir Robert Peel objected to Lady Normanby, wife of one of the principal Whigs, remaining on at Court, as the closest household companion of the young Queen Victoria. But the latter would not consent to a dismissal that she conceived to be contrary to usage and was repugnant to her feelings. Peel refused to modify his request, so Lord Melbourne returned to power, or rather crept again into office behind the petticoats of the ladies-in-waiting.

I also have a ' bedchamber question', which puzzled me very much, but now I have solved it ! There are two peculiar pieces of furniture on either side of my bed, the nature of which I could not understand. They are funnel-shaped (the smaller end rests on the floor) and topped with pink marble and a decorative edging in gilded metal. The wood may be rose-wood. It looks very precious. But there is no door, or opening, as in a *table de nuit*. Yet some vertical and horizontal fissures show that the contraption *could* be opened, if one knew how.

While I ought to have been dressing for dinner, I kept fidgeting with the dam' thing, pushing and pulling. Only when I essayed to lift the marble top, was the mystery solved. Then the apparatus sprang to life, like a Jack-in-the-box, revealing what the French call *une chaise percée*. Such were the ' conveniences' of aristocratic bedrooms, before the days of modern plumbing. A future generation may turn them into cocktail-bars !

In my bedroom, there are pictures of the Royal children (Edward VII and the Empress Frederick, when still in the nursery). Also a portrait of the Prince Consort, wearing a complete suit of armour. His fat, bourgeois face with its Victorian side-whiskers, looks out incongruously above the shining cuirass and steel gorget.

A more interesting picture hangs over the grand piano in the drawing-room. It dates from the year 1605 and represents a good-looking young woman, in deep mourning, but with a tantalising, ironical smile that seems to mock the onlooker, whose eyes meet those in the canvas. This is the daughter of James I (and therefore a granddaughter of Mary Queen of Scots). Her first husband was the Earl of Anglesea ; when he died, she married a Normanby. The background to the portrait is a view of the royal palace of St. James, and up near the top is an inscription in French rhyme :

> *Puisque le Comte d'Anglesea mourut sans remords,*
> *J'avons que mon deuil n'est qu'un dehors !*

The lady in the picture does not look as if her character was hard or bitter. It must have been nothing more than a whimsical sincerity that admitted to feeling no regret for husband No. 1.

My fellow-guests are Lord and Lady Rockley. Before being raised to the peerage, he was the Hon. Evelyn Cecil. It surprises me that anyone who bears the historic name of Cecil should condescend to accept the title of Baron, but I suppose there are advantages. Lady Rockley is an authority on gardens, and recently she has been writing articles in the papers about them. She gets five pounds apiece for these articles. She said : ' Evelyn is rather ashamed of me ! '

There are also a mother and daughter, and the latter has the most beautiful hair I have seen for a long time ; the real Titian bronze, which is erroneously supposed to be common in Venice. Her name is Ann Hope.

Bee is much shocked because I told her that Diana has had an offer, in Paris, to do a film with Josephine Baker.

' *My* cousin ! My beautiful cousin ! To go on the stage with a negress ! ' Anyhow, I don't suppose that anything will come of it.

I like this place, even if I don't fit into the landscape as well as I should. It is pleasant to retire every now and then into this older England, with *chaises percées* on either side of your bed, and family portraits of royalties that were taken more seriously then than they are now.

But I regret not being able to find any portrait of the Marquess of Normanby who was once British Minister at the Granducal Court of Tuscany. In my mind, I can see him strolling up the Lung 'Arno, in a brown frock coat and a top hat of light-coloured beaver. He is still remembered in the City of the Red Lily, as having kicked up the hell of a row, because he had not been given his right place at table, when dining with the Grand Duke.

It seems to me more fitting that a Marquess of Normanby should be a diplomat than a clergyman, as Bee's late husband was. You must have known him better than I did. I was a young sprout of eighteen, when we first met in Scotland, and we motored together from Montrose to Glamis. In those days, motors were a novelty, and we caused quite a sensation, as we puffed wheezily up the Vale of Strathmore. Lord Normanby was a friend of the old Earl, whose golden wedding was about to be celebrated in a few days' time. After our call, when we started back, the younger members of the Bowes-Lyon family stood outside the hall door, to watch us depart. They expected, no doubt, that we would dash off at a terrific speed. Instead of which we crawled up the avenue even slower than the train that brought me here today.

The almost pastoral tranquillity of Mulgrave (where there was not even a telephone) was a pleasant rest after the hectic life I led in London, looking after Diana, especially when Ciano and Edda Mussolini came over for a few days and stayed at our Embassy.

Ciano loved London and said that the climate suited him. Edda, I saw little of, but I got mixed up in a visit she paid to *The Times* premises. Geoffrey Dawson, the Editor, was an old friend of Bettina's, and I went to a tea-party in the little garden of his house. Hearing of Edda's intended visit to Printing House Square, Dawson asked me to come along too. But I mistook the hour, and Geoffrey Dawson never learnt that Edda was on the premises till she was

DIANA

actually getting into her motor, to leave. He missed her by a split second. On the whole I think he was relieved to have avoided a *corvée*.

Ciano showed me an article in the French *Journal des Débats*, which alluded to the possibility of the Germans endeavouring to put the Powers in the presence of a *fait accompli*, such as the military occupation of the Rhineland. The article concluded by saying that, in this case, France could count on the support of Italy. I asked Ciano if this were true. He said that he could not predict the future, but it was certain that our relations with France had never been better than at that moment. This was regarded with suspicion by the champions of the *status quo* (he mentioned Titulescu), who feared any Franco-Italian collaboration, because of its realistic tendency to treaty-revision in the matter of agreements concerning the Danube.

Meanwhile Diana complicated our existence by acquiring a parrot. I suggested that, like the chimpanzee at the Zoo, it should be called ' Jubilee'. Instead of which, it was named Loreto.

I do not know to this day who gave the parrot to Diana, for she had forgotten the donor's name. She described him in her rather peculiar English : ' Oh, Loreto was given me by a man . . . a lovely man . . . He is as pale as a sheet. He lives in an apartment all panelled in black velvet, with bowls of yellow orchids. He has a lapis-lazuli bath. And he sits all day in the house and sews . . . '

Austen Chamberlain asked us to lunch. Diana told him about the parrot, adding the description as quoted above. A frosty light shone for a moment in Chamberlain's eye-glass, as he remarked : ' *Not* very good company, I think ! '

Diana left for the continent rather suddenly. There was no cage to put Loreto in ; only a perch, and they travelled by air. I found the whole business so nerve-racking that I refused to see Diana off.

Half an hour after her departure, there was a telephone message from the French Embassy : ' *Prière de dire à Mademoiselle Varè que les perroquets ne peuvent pas entrer en France.*'

I wondered what would happen to poor Loreto when he reached the aerodrome of Le Bourget and was refused admittance. Anyway, I could do nothing about it. Next day I received a telegram from Paris : ' All well. Love. Diana.' No mention of Loreto.

It was only when I arrived back in Rome, that I heard a garbled version of what had occurred. Diana was off again, this time to Vienna, where she was staying somewhere in the Wienerwald, taking part in the shooting of a film, *Marie Berchirtcheff* (or some such name) with Hans Jeray in the principal part. But Loreto was at home, and he had eaten most of the wooden frame of a tall, leather arm-chair that stood opposite my writing-desk.

It appears that, on the day of their arrival in Paris, the Customs officials had begun by saying that parrots could not enter the country. To which Diana replied that he *had* entered the country. There he was ! And that, if they would send someone with her (and Loreto) to the Quai d'Orsay, she could arrange matters to the satisfaction of all concerned.

This was done. I don't quite know *where* they actually went, but in the end, Diana and Loreto (after some parleying) were ushered into the presence of some former colleague of mine. I think it must have been the Comte de Martel. He asked what the devil she wanted.

' *Damien ! Faites moi entrer en France avec cet animal !* '

De Martel stared indignantly at the parrot, who met his gaze with indifference, and croaked ' Loreto ! ', as if introducing himself.

De Martel answered : ' Diana ! You may come into France with a tiger for all I care, but go away and leave me in peace ! '

On the strength of this authorization, Loreto was allowed to stay a few days in Paris, on his way to Italy.

*   *   *

If there is one form of brag that sets my teeth on edge more than any other, it is the kind that boasts of literary success. Despite this premise, I must admit that my stay in London, during the spring of the Jubilee year, was eminently successful. Not only were my books accepted for publication, but the *Heavenly Trousers* was promptly taken up by the representative in London of a leading American firm, for publication in U.S.A. An unknown author, as I was, writing in a language not his own, I felt that I had conquered the Land of Canaan. And I decided to go to New York, to keep in touch with my publishers there.

I was encouraged in this project by Ciano, who found me one day, after my return to Rome, sitting on the sands by the sea at Castel Fusano, correcting the proofs of the *Heavenly Trousers*. He sat down beside me and picked up a sheet of the galley-proofs, to see what it was all about. He happened to light on a page where I quoted the Chinese proverb : *He who rides the tiger cannot dismount.*

' That,' said Ciano, ' is very true ! '

When I told him that I was thinking of joining Margherita, who was over in the States, staying with the Crane family at Cape Cod, Ciano said : ' When you go, get in touch with our embassy in Washington and see if you can't give Rosso a helping hand. He is having a difficult time, for public opinion is dead against us in the Abyssinian question.'

I said I would do my best, but that I did not want to tour the United States as a propagandist.

I think it was only then that I began to realize how the Ethiopian question had grown in importance and even changed its character, since the placid days of Stresa.

' Hail Columbia ! '

AFTER going with Bettina to Siena, to see the ' Palio ', in August 1935, I embarked at Naples on the *Rex*, for New York.

I had a fellow traveller in a young Italian diplomat, Bergamaschi, who was on his way to our embassy in Washington. He was an excellent pianist, and soon found a kindred spirit on board, in the shape of Mr. Murray Jacoby, a gentleman connected in some way with Wall Street (he telephoned there every day, to find out what stocks and shares were doing). But he looked upon himself also as a retired diplomat, like myself, for he had been Ambassador Extraordinary of the United States at the Court of Ethiopia, on the occasion of the coronation of the Negus.

When not playing duets with Bergamaschi (on two pianos, in the ship's concert room), Mr. Jacoby would give me his views on the political situation. He seemed to be under the impression that if he and I were to agree to some solution on the Abyssinian question, we could obtain the approval of our two governments (and of other governments as well), and they would get our proposals carried through.

His mission to Addis Ababa had left Mr. Jacoby with a marked sympathy for the Ethiopians. On the other hand, he showed a singularly open mind in the matter of Italy's needs and aspirations. And he suggested to me, quite seriously, that we Italians should leave Abyssinia alone, on condition that France should cede us Tunisia. I cannot imagine any Italian statesman that would not have jumped at the offer.

Without any prompting from me, Mr. Murray Jacoby saw for himself the injustice of a country like France, with a rapidly decreasing population, holding a colonial empire of four million square miles, while a country like Italy, whose workmen had to emigrate in order to earn their living, was accused of selfish imperialism, for claiming that her birthright be not so utterly disproportioned to her birthrate. In 1935, France's population was steadily approaching what it had been in Napoleon's day (when she sold Louisiana to the United States). Her colossal dominions overseas had to be governed by a skeleton crew of French officials, policed by black troops and defended by the British Navy !

Our crossing of the Atlantic was not uneventful, as is shown by the following entry in my Diary, dated 27th August :

Gulf Stream. Very hot and damp ; the air steamy, with lowering clouds. Stopped engines and stood by to pick up the owner and crew of a small skiff (three tons), carrying Mr. Welch and four sailors. They had left Bermuda on the 18th. Their craft was disabled and they had been four days at the pumps. I hear that ' Welch's Grape Juice ' used to be almost a national beverage during Prohibition. Mr. Welch was on his way to join his wife on the Riviera. She had advised him to take a liner, like everybody else, and not risk his life on a cockleshell. He has now sent her a wireless message : ' You were quite right ! '

We docked in New York on the 29th. My eldest daughter, Margherita, was at Chelsea Piers to meet me.

*   *   *

My letters to Bettina from New York, Washington and the houses of friends in the country, have this in common with similar epistles, written in those years from England, France, or Italy. They do not illustrate any prearranged activity, as they might have if I had been still in the Diplomatic Service. My time was my own, and I used it to look on at the pageant of life in a foreign country, without having to send reports home, or await instructions concerning this question, or that.

In New York, as during the preceding months, I corrected proofs and debated questions concerning wrappers, illustrations and publicity. Meanwhile, my former colleagues at the Italian Embassy in Washington came to regard me as a sort of ' elder statesman ', and were pleased to have me round.

Though I refused to make a tour of lectures, I was willing to speak informally whenever, by doing so, I could give some encouragement to my nationals, during a period of political tension.

Though I had left for the States with a bundle of introductions, I began by making a friend on my own. Her name was Rose : a ' non ruminating artiodactyle ungulate mammal ', otherwise the hippopotamus in the small zoological garden at the Prosperity Fountain end of Central Park. Rose's ancestors are disrespectfully mentioned in the Book of Job. The family name, in those days, was Behemoth (" The shady trees compassed them with their shadow ; the willows of the brook did compass them about").

I presume Rose's name was given to her in view of the lovely shade of pink round the eyes and jowl. She had a nasty, hard, concrete floor to lie on, instead of the nice soft mud along the banks of the White Nile.

I generally found Rose half asleep, with her chin resting against the vertical bars of her cage. When she saw me, she would open her mouth wide, as a hint that I should throw something into it, despite a notice to the effect that you might not ' feed, or annoy, the animals '. These two injunctions contradicted one another. If you didn't feed the animals, it annoyed them extremely. I compromised (and avoided the 25 dollars fine) by feeding Rose with buns when nobody was looking.

The seals seemed fairly happy, playing ' king of the castle ' in their swimming-pool. But Chang, the elephant (habitat, India), walked round and round his narrow cage, doing figures of eight, the picture of tragic boredom. And the otter scratched despairingly at the hard concrete floor, in the vain hope of making a hole.

Sometimes I took a bag of peanuts and sat on a bench, along one of the asphalted paths in the Park, and the squirrels came and helped themselves, darting about silently as beams of light, eating out of their little hands, their heads shaded by their tails. Doubtless their ancestors held the whole land thereabouts, and the fruits thereof, in feudal tenure from the Creator, before Giovanni Verazzani sailed up the river that now bears Hudson's name.

The Italian Consulate was then in 69th Street. I sometimes strolled up there, coming out of Central Park, to go and pick up Guido Colonna. There were always four negresses walking round and round with expressionless faces, like Chang the elephant in his cage. They carried placards on which was written : ' Hands off Ethiopia ! ' I wondered if they knew that the Abyssinians were more nearly related to the Jews than to them, and that darkies were bought and sold as slaves in Ethiopia !

One woman, not a negress, asked to see some official in the Consulate and was received by Guido Colonna. She then gave expression to her political opinions by throwing a bottle of ink over his tweed suit.

It is odd that America—perhaps the most truly hospitable country in the world—should be so full of people who are in a hurry to hate. In the nineteenth century, the foreign immigrant was told that, if he wanted to be a true American, it was England that he must hate. ' To twist the Lion's tail ' became a national sport, and Theodore Roosevelt made good use of the ill-feeling, to build up a real navy.

When I arrived in New York, we Italians were the principal objects of animosity. A first deliberate injury was done us by discriminating against the Italian immigration quota (this was done by selecting the most unfavourable years, on which to base the estimate of that quota). Thus our country was deprived of that export of services, which had been a major asset in balancing our budget of international payments. Then came the prohibitive duties of the Smoot-Hawley tariff, in which a deadly blow was dealt to our exports even on such un-competitive items as olive-oil and pecorino cheese. Yet, at that time, Italy purchased from the U.S.A. four times as much as she sold. It is this sort of economic pressure that forces a country to seek terri-torial expansion, as a means to procure raw materials and markets.

Then, in June 1935, with no attempt at justification, American banks cut off all commercial credits, at the instigation of British bankers, in an attempt to exercise further pressure on the Italian government, in its colonial policies. This economic warfare was in no way dissimilar to that which the French government waged against the Austrian government, in 1931, forcing it to abandon the tariff-union with Germany, that seemed to be the only way that might allow Austria to continue to exist economically (the episode greatly strengthened the hands of the Nazi extremists in Austria).

There is nothing new in the use of money-power, in time of peace, to produce a catastrophe in a rival nation. But Dante tells us it *was* new in his time :

> Già si solea con le spade far guerra :
> Ma or si fa togliendo or qui, or quivi
> Lo pan ch'el Pio Padre a nessun serra.[1]

Letters from my Skyscraper

This must be the first time I write to you from a skyscraper. I call it that, but it does not really puncture the clouds. It is merely a very tall house, and I live on the eighth floor, which, of course, is nothing. When I look out of my window in 46th Street, I see the towers of Manhattan foreshortened. In the evening, when there is a mist, they have something spectral about them. Fifth Avenue reminds me of the Yangtze Gorges : the same precipitous sides to the canyon, and peaks disappearing in the clouds above. Instead of seething waters, the stream of traffic.

They seem to consider me here as a sort of ' ambassador at large ', and the management of the hotel have put me into a suite of rooms, worthy of a delegation. There is an electric clock in every room, each marking a slightly different hour, but all animated by a jerky movement, like a hiccup.

On the whole, I find so much luxury depressing. My sitting-room is un-compromisingly tidy. If I could persuade Margherita to come down from Cape Cod, things might be livelier. These rooms would have flowers in them, and boxes of chocolate, novels, fashion-papers, and so on. When I come home, and enter the little entrance-hall, I would be met by whiffs of

---

[1] In other days, one made war with the sword ; now it is waged by taking away, sometimes here, sometimes there, the bread that Our Father in Heaven would deny to no one.

scent and cigarette-smoke. A gramophone would be pouring out the latest tunes. There might even be a dog, causing trouble.

But, of course, my expenses would be trebled ! I can imagine Diana, emerging through that door, leading now to an unoccupied bedroom :

' Papa ! There's a lovely evening frock at the corner shop in Forty-seventh Street ; black veil over painted chiffon. Do you think I might . . .'

I wonder if it wouldn't have been cheaper, in the long run, if we had sons, and not daughters. The latter are always wanting frocks, and stockings, and undies . . . But I suppose, if they had been sons, I would have to keep them, and also pay for frocks, and stockings, and undies, for ladies that were no relations of mine !

BLUEMONT

VIRGINIA, *September 1935*

I came up here, via Washington, to stay with the Ambassador, Augusto Rosso. Margherita is here too.

Rosso and I had never met before. He is very popular—so I am told. A quiet, prudent, pleasant man, too modern to be spoken of as belonging to ' the old school '. But with all the experience of a career diplomat. He is a bachelor, and his family, at present, consists only of two dogs, spaniels, called Tobia and Tobiola, with whom, needless to say, I immediately made friends.

Margherita rides Rosso's horse, *Water Baby*, and disappears down in the Shenandoah Valley, where there are grasslands. Up at Bluemont, it is all woods and steep hills. There is nobody here except our host, ourselves, part of the embassy staff, and Bergamaschi, who came over with me on the *Rex*. In the evening, Bergamaschi plays the piano, Margherita curls up on the sofa and knits, and I and Rosso talk shop.

When I read books on contemporary American politics, I feel I cannot see the wood for the trees. Too many details and minor issues. What I want are long views. I find something of this sort in articles by Bernard Fay, in the *Revue des Deux Mondes*. There is one in the May number, from which I have copied out the following paragraph :

L'Amérique peut, avec ses immenses richesses et sa population relativement faible, organiser son territoire en sorte que chaque Américain puisse réellement jouir d'un bien-etre considérable et d'avantages que nulle autre pays ne possède. Mais elle peut seulement le faire si elle procède avec grand soin, et si elle ne gaspille plus. . . . Cette refonte de la civilisation est impérieuse et urgente, à moins que ne survienne une guerre.

Strange to find a foreign author suggesting that another war might save the American economy from disaster, whereas the greater part of this country is pacifist to the core. Whether the government is as peace-loving as it makes itself out to be, is a matter on which I could not hazard an opinion. Before I left New York, a business man (from Chicago) said to me :

'Our government has built up enormous stocks of cotton, to help the southern planters. It has bought up wheat and silver, and has buried underground most of the gold in the world. What are we going to do with all this? Only if there is a war, would these things come in useful.

'THE MAYFLOWER'
WASHINGTON D.C., *September 1935*

I am on my way back to N.Y.C. and Margherita to Cape Cod. It is pouring with rain. Migone has lent Margherita a car. She drives about in it and gets lost. This morning she got stuck in a 'circle', coming out of 16th Street. Every now and then she put her face out of the window and hailed a passer-by, saying 'Kertukkety! Kertukkety!', which was the nearest she could remember to Connecticut Avenue. Seeing a policeman, who appeared to be off duty, she suggested he should get into the car and show her the way. He accepted with alacrity, and even proposed that they should do a little sightseeing together. When he heard she was a Countess, he was much impressed and took her to the White House. Margherita says he was a nice 'cop', but the rain off his waterproof cape ran down on the seat of the car, and wet her behind.

NEW YORK, *September 1935*

Having been asked, by Mr. William T. Dewart, to meet him at the offices of the *Sun* in Broadway, to go on with him to lunch at the Hardware Club, and Broadway being only a couple of blocks from here, I imagined, in my innocence, that I could stroll out of the hotel about half-past twelve and be on the spot at one o'clock. Luckily I met Monsieur Albous in the hall and asked him how long it would take to walk. He answered : 'About two hours, or more.' I jumped into a taxi and got there just in time. Broadway is about fifty miles long !

The N.B.C. people (National Broadcasting Company) asked me to give an address on the Ethiopian question, which I did last night. I was shown into a room with leaden doors, weighing a ton each, and had fourteen minutes and a half in which to speak. Broadcasting is useful in teaching one to avoid useless verbiage. If my 'time on the air' had been paid for (which it was not —neither was I !) it would have cost 8,000 dollars. No previous quarter of an hour of my life has ever been so costly !

Though I have not used it much hitherto, I now discover that the argument that seems to appeal most to the American mentality is the following :

"If you look up any international almanac (say the *Almanach de Gotha*) for the years 1890 to 1896, you will find that Ethiopia figures as an Italian dependency. When the Abyssinians refused to abide by the Treaty of Uccialli, signed in 1889, we lost our hold in an unsuccessful colonial war, just as the English lost their hold on the Sudan. They reconquered their former possession, and an Italian army protected the British advance, acting as a bulwark on their left flank. The reconquest of the Sudan is considered, by the British, as a national glory. Our move, to follow their example, is condemned as an international crime. They justify this discrepancy by claiming that they have created a new morality, dating from 1920."

NEW YORK, *October 1935*

There is an *Italo-American Society* here, which pursues, rather timidly, the laudable object of promoting good relations between the two countries. One of the people who run it is young Sorbello. He wanted to interview me for a magazine edited by the Society. I had no objection, but when he asked me for my ' impressions of America ', I jibbed. What can it matter to the American reader what some fool foreigner, just off the gangway and through the custom-house, thinks of American cooking and the American climate ? So I offered to give Sorbello my impressions about American dogs. I am sure there are more Scotties in Central Park than there are north of the Tweed.

> And in that town a dog was found
> As many dogs there be,
> Both mongrel, puppy, whelp and hound
> And curs of low degree.

When I arrive up at the Embassy in Washington, Tobia and Tobiola stand with their front paws on the railing of the outer gate, or prance round me in the entrance hall, suggesting that I should take them along Sixteenth Street to the public gardens. They have long since discovered how dog-ridden I am.

A week ago, Margherita and I went for a week end to Oyster Bay to stay with Colonel and Mrs. Theodore Roosevelt, Junr. An Alsatian, belonging to the household, insisted on taking walks with me. And all the dogs in the vicinity would join the party, so that, by the time I'd been out an hour, I was followed by a varied and obstreperous pack that, as O'Henry puts it, made the cats in that district grateful that prehensile claws had been given them.

After the walk was over, the dogs (all but the original nucleus) dispersed to their homes. What is the reason for such abnormal sociability of dogs in America ? Can it be that their masters don't walk any more ?

Sorbello wanted an illustration for my ' interview '. And just behind the St. Gaudens statue of Sherman we found a negro chauffeur with a kind of fox-terrier on the leash. We asked him what the dog's name was and he said : ' Husky.' We then asked if he would lend us Husky for a minute, as we wanted to photograph him. The chauffeur seemed much astonished, for Husky was certainly not a prize specimen, but he raised no objection. Husky and I posed, while Sorbello squatted on the grass near the pony-ride, with his pocket camera pressed against his cheek. He kept on shouting : ' Hold it, Husky ! ' like an operator to a film-star. Husky held it all right ; that is to say, he held his hind leg up against a low wooden pointer in the grass, with

CAFETERIA written on it. And thus we were immortalized together. I hope the members of the *Italo-American Society* will be impressed and that my interview, complete with illustration, will contribute to promote good relations between the two countries.

NEW YORK, *October 1935*

Margherita is in New York again. We are asked to stay with Rosso once more and shall be going to Washington in a few days. The idea is that Margherita should ride *Water Baby* in the horse show.

We have been to lunch with Mr. and Mrs. Frank Griswold. What impressed us both was the fact that we got out of our taxi and entered a hall-door that opened on the street. From there we passed into the entrance hall and walked up a carpeted stair to the first floor, where the drawing room and dining room were situated. This may not seem remarkable to you, for it happens quite often when we go out to lunch in Rome. But you must remember that the Griswold mansion is on Park Avenue, where most of the houses have thirty-five floors, or more. To waste such valuable ground-space on a house of only two or three floors is the height of extravagance.

Margherita found a kindred spirit in Frank Griswold (though I think he might have been her grandfather). He had hunted in Rome, when her father-in-law, Pompeo Campello, was M.F.H. They talked ' horses ' all the time they sat together at lunch.

I sat next to Mrs. Cornelius Vanderbilt. I don't know if there are two ladies of this name. If so, it was the elder one. She told me that, when she was a baby, King George V had pushed her in her pram. It was not clear to me whether the point of this story was the narrator's familiarity with the British royal family, or merely a question of age. . . . Perhaps I did not understand her rightly. Maybe it was she who had pushed him in his pram. . . .

Afterwards I went to see Doctor Nicholas Murray Butler, President of the Columbia University. His doings and writings and his academic titles occupy two pages of the American *Who's Who*. It is the fashion to poke fun at him. But I found him very pleasant, and he gave me an excellent piece of advice. I told him that I had been asked to speak on the radio, giving my opinion on the Neutrality Act and on President Roosevelt's policy. He said : ' Better not speak on the politics of the country you are in. It is bad taste. So it is to speak badly, when abroad, of the policies followed by your own government at home.'

It is a pity that so few people are wise enough to abstain from these two errors of *savoir faire*.

NEW YORK, *October, 1935*

People in the States seem to me to take an exaggerated view of the political situation abroad. Or perhaps it is that they prefer indignation to understanding. To hear them talk, you would think that we were at war with England.

Even the State Department in Washington seems to consider that this is so. I have been asked to speak to the officers of the General Staff, about our military operations in Abyssinia. But the State Department put its veto, and explained to our Ambassador that it would be unfair for me to speak, whereas there was no one to speak 'for England'. Rosso answered that he had understood it was Ethiopia we were at war with, not England !

Such being the case, and having been asked to speak again on the radio (this time from the WOR broadcasting station), I took it on myself to asure the Americans that a great part of the British public and public men, were perfectly fairminded and understanding towards our action in Abyssinia. There is also a section of the British Press that upholds the Italian point of view, in the conviction that it would be in the true interest of the British Empire, as of European peace, to maintain friendly relations with Italy, and come to some agreement with us on the matter of resuming the old position, as between 1889 and 1896, when Ethiopia was a dependency of ours. I have been told that Sir Samuel Hoare, himself, is of this opinion, but not being certain of the fact, of course I could not mention it.

Anyhow, I quoted Lord Rothermere :

' *White men and women can now travel unescorted and by motor-car throughout the whole length and breadth of Africa, with the exception of one solitary corner. That corner is Abyssinia, whose borders are still occupied by savage tribes, which require their young men to prove that they have killed and mutilated an adversary, before they are allowed to marry.*

' *All sound-thinking Britons will wish Italy well in the great undertaking to which she has set her hand. The day that Mussolini establishes Italian authority over the ancient but barbaric land of Ethiopia will complete the beneficial progress by which Europe has brought law, order and public health to a continent, which less than a century ago was plunged in primitive misery.*'

ITALIAN EMBASSY
WASHINGTON D.C., *October*

There is a large photograph of Margherita in the *Washington Times*, taking *Water Baby* over some hurdles.

Water Baby is a fine horse, but untrained for horse-shows. Margherita was schooling him over the more complicated jumps. He had never seen a ' cage ' before, and the result was that he fell and Margherita broke a finger. She went on for two days as if nothing had happened, but in the end had to give it up and retire to bed with fever.

I had arranged to run up to Boston for two days, which worried Rosso very much. He could not be left alone—so he said—with a pretty woman staying in the house with him. Margherita, on the other hand, refused to move. She said she was very comfortable where she was, and if she did not mind about *her* reputation, why should Rosso be so fussy about *his* ?

MARGHERITA

It ended by Margherita getting her own way, and sticking to her room and bed. But to save appearances, during my absence, Rosso asked Rebecca Wellington, who acts as his 'social secretary', to stay there too, and occupy the other bed in Margherita's room. And there I found them, when I got back.

In a few days we return to New York, and should sail for Europe on the *Conte di Savoia*, on the 2nd of November. By the tenth or eleventh, I may be with you, in Rome.

London during the Abyssinian Crisis

It is not Carnegie's millions, nor millions added to those millions, that can kill war and bring peace. It is a just weight and a just measure in international politics.

DAVID LUBIN (on the erection of the Peace Palace at the Hague).

WHILE in London, in the spring of '35, I promised, rather reluctantly, to give a lecture, next autumn, at Chatham House, otherwise the Royal Institute for Foreign Affairs, in St. James's Square. I am inclined to agree with Stephen Leacock that most of us tire of a lecture in ten minutes and that sensible people don't go to lectures at all. But apparently there are other people, who are not sensible, and they take to lectures as a duckling to a pond. Count Kayserling once spoke to me about his countrymen's mania for attending lectures. He said : ' Imagine a German walking up a stair, on the top of which is a landing with two doors. Over one door is the legend ENTRANCE TO PARADISE. Pinned to the other door is a notice that a lecture is about to be given there, about how Paradise is laid out and administered. The German would make for the lecture-room. Paradise itself might wait. . . . '

The subject of my lecture was to be ' British Foreign Policy Through Italian Eyes '. It was put off because I had gone to the States, and this might have offered an excuse for not giving it at all. British public opinion had been worked up into one of those moral rages that have something biblical about them, so that it would seem as if they could only be stilled by a casting out of devils. A mere lecture seemed utterly inadequate. On the other hand, the business of stepping out on a little platform, with a false air of a conjurer, and being introduced to the audience by somebody saying : ' We have with us tonight . . .' promised to be more exciting than such moments usually are. If it had not been so, I doubt if I would have crossed and re-crossed the Atlantic (I had not finished my business in U.S.A.), for an hour's talk in a lecture-room.

Italy's expansion overseas had represented, since my first youth, an *apologia pro vita mea* ; it was a form of rebellion against the conception of Italians as a picturesque people who will work in mines abroad, and in other people's colonies, for a few pence a day. But I was told that aspirations such as mine were obsolete. Mussolini's move into Abyssinia was denounced as ' a callous anachronism ', incompatible with contemporary ethics. It was time to stop it. The natural law of conflict and survival had been replaced by more modern methods. This had not been the case, even recently, as long as British interests, French interests, Spanish interests, Russian and Japanese interests (in Asia), had been at stake. The conquests of greater powers had been whitewashed. Only Italy might be condemned as ' an aggressor '. Here is the reasoning of the reformed criminal, eager to stick to the loot.

On my part, I considered as ' a callous anachronism ', the smug, selfish policy that denied to a hard-working, thrifty, sober people like the Italians, the possibility of earning their living in their own currency, under their own flag, in undeveloped lands beyond the seas. Pantaleoni was right : this was the philosophy of Scrooge in *Christmas Carol*.

The dispute had its comic side. I was much amused at a conversation between Lady Oxford (Margot Asquith) and Leonardo Vitetti, Councillor of the Italian Embassy. She maintained that, whereas the Italian advance in Abyssinia was morally indefensible, the campaigns that had founded the British Empire could not be criticized on moral grounds. Vitetti answered:

' My dear Lady Oxford, I am a catholic. As such, I believe in the Immaculate Conception. But I accept it as a dogma connected with the birth of Christ, not of the British Empire ! '

In those days Italians were repeatedly admonished to revert to the liberal, peaceful politics of Giuseppe Mazzini.

The austere and schoolmasterly remoteness of this rebuke was marred by ignorance of Mazzini's ideals.

In the year 1871, just after Rome had become the capital of United Italy, the principal newspaper in the Eternal City was the *Roma del Popolo*, and Mazzini used to write for it. In three successive articles (dated 22nd and 29th March, and 5th April) he claimed for Italy the right to contribute to the work of civilizing African regions, and he pointed out that, just as Morocco pertains to the Iberian peninsula, and Algeria to France, Tunis which is only twenty-five leagues from Sicily, obviously pertains to Italy. The prosperity of Tunisia was due, in great part, to Italian emigrants, who greatly outnumbered the foreign population of any other nation in the Regency.[1]

Except in such political seers as Mazzini himself, there was, in his day, no conscient ' colonial policy ' among Italians, no ' imperialism ' in the modern sense of the word. But the same urge that impelled American frontiersmen to press on beyond the ranges, impelled Italian peasants, during the nineteenth century, to set forth in feluccas with lateen sails, from the ports of the Grand Duchy of Tuscany, from the Kingdom of the Two Sicilies and the Kingdom of Sardinia, to seek a new home along the Northern coasts of Africa, the natural outlet for our exhuberant population. Our claim for colonies has ever been justified by the urgent want of the humbler classes, eager for opportunity to work. Oscar Wilde's jibe, that his countrymen carried the white man's burden only as far as the Stock Exchange, could never have been levelled against the Italians.

A century-old, spontaneous gravitation proves how we have need of Africa. For us, the desire for expansion overseas, the hunger for land, does not represent a policy, but an instinctive effort to preserve the life of the nation. Anyone who valued our friendship, should have taken this need into account. Our emigrants settled with their families in Tunisia, and developed the land. But the fruit of their industry was wrested from them, to be exploited by a foreign power

---

[1] Here are Mazzini's own words in the original Italian :

" Nel moto inevitabile che chiama l'Europa ad incivilire le regioni africane, come il Marocco spetta alla Penisola Iberica e l'Algeria alla Francia, Tunisi, chiave del Mediterraneo Centrale, connessa al sistema sardo-sìculo e lontana un venticinque leghe dalla Sicilia, spetta visibilmente all'Italia.

" E sulle cime dell'Atlante sventolò la bandiera di Roma, quando, rovesciata Cartagine, il Mediterraneo si chiamò Mare Nostrum. Fummo padroni, fino al V secolo di tutta quella regione.

" Oggi i Francesi l'adocchiano e l'avranno fra non molto se noi non l'abbiamo."

that faked a pretext to plant a ' protecting ' flag on the territory that had been fertilized by the labour of Italian peasants. British acquiescence was bought at the price of France's consent to the occupation of Cyprus, at the time of the Congress of Berlin. Thus Italians were taught the bitter lesson that expansion in its most peaceable form is not possible in a world full of political intrigue and greed.

The ever-recurring policy of those foreign powers that deny to Italians a right to colonize has sought to justify itself by many specious pleas. Even now, after the second world war, I read in an English publication called *The Price of Peace*, a condemnation of ' the greed of the Italians ', who ask for a return of their former colonies. Is there anything morally iniquitous in wanting a colony ? And does it behove an Englishman to say so ?

In Harold Nicholson's *Life* of his father, Lord Carnock, he mentions an occasion when some Foreign Office official was declaiming in righteous indignation against Italy's occupation of Tripoli. He was startled to find himself checked by a flash of sudden wrath in the blue eyes of his Chief. ' It is not for us,' said Arthur Nicholson, ' to cast that sort of stone.'

Had fewer of such stones been thrown at us, during the following decades, the traditional Anglo-Italian friendliness might have survived.[1]

*   *   *

One of the arguments put forward to deny us the right to colonize is that Italy is too poor. This thesis was brought forward, after the second world war, to justify taking away from the ' poor ' Italians the territories on which they had made a notable outlay of capital, which was thus rendered a total loss. Mr. James T. Byrnes uses this argument, in his *Speaking Frankly*. He adds that Italy's record of administering colonies was one ' of inefficiency and oppression '. Mr.

---

[1] I would like to quote, here, a remark made to me by Bettina, while we were together, in London, during the Abyssinian crisis. She said :

' The English never will understand that any policy of theirs can be provocative. They are always satisfied that anything *they* do is merely what every decent person would do under the circumstances, and they feel hurt when other people do not see things in the same light.'

We both noticed, Bettina and I, in after years, that the British resented our remembering sanctions, when they, themselves, had forgotten all about them.

Byrnes evidently does not speak from first-hand knowledge. It is not difficult to guess the source of his information. The same sources of information were placed at the disposal of the natives of Tripolitania and other African territories formerly governed by Italians. They were told that, in the ' Peace Treaty ', Italy had formally renounced all right to colonies. This being so, it was useless to ask for the return of an Italian administration. It was outside the alternatives of option, and this by the express wish of the Italians themselves. I do not think I have ever come across a meaner piece of lying propaganda.

Italians are, in some ways, better colonists than the British. In other ways, they cannot compare with them. One, or two, British officials can administer enormous territories of African territory, and keep order therein. I doubt if any Italian administrator could equal their efficiency. But Italians colonize in a different way. They work on the land, and they settle on the land as labourers, and get to love it because of their toil. Englishmen don't usually colonize in order to find opportunities for manual labour.

The merits of the Italians as colonizers was officially admitted and stressed, at the conclusion of the eighth International Congress of Tropical and Sub-Tropical Agriculture, which met in 1939. The United States, Great Britain, France, Belgium, Holland and fourteen other states were represented. At the close of this Congress, Professor Edmund Laplae, President of the International Scientific Association for the Agriculture of Hot Countries, made a speech in which he said :

The representatives of the colonial countries, which can boast the oldest traditions, cannot but recognize that Italy has accomplished in Libya a work that opens up new horizons to colonial activities, directing them not only on the lines which will promote the increase of production and the revival of land but also and above all the progress of the native population and the spread of civilization.

*   *   *

The subject of this chapter is one that I have very much at heart. The reader must forgive me if I dwell on it at length and recall some historical data, which are not known to the Man in the Street.

In 1906, an agreement was signed between Great Britain, France and Italy, defining the limits of their respective spheres of interest in Ethiopia, in view of the probability of that ramshackle empire falling to pieces. This Tripartite Agreement was renewed from time to time, but it might have been expected to lapse automatically after Ethiopia had been admitted into the League of Nations. Lord Curzon expressed the opinion that it had died a natural death. But it was obvious that the possibility of the empire disintegrating had not disappeared, simply because the Negus was now represented at Geneva. His suzerainty, in his own kingdom, was little more than nominal.

The admittance of Ethiopia into the League was the *fons et origo mali*, the original mistake, from which so many subsequent troubles inevitably arose. The responsibility for this error belongs to France.

The French author, Henri de Monfried, wrote in the *Nineteenth Century* of August 1935 :

In bringing Ethiopia into the League, France did her the worst service imaginable, since it involved both a perversion of truth and the foisting upon that unhappy country, in the fullness of innocence, of charges and obligations, which she could never hope to fulfil.

It is well-known that the Negus had to hide from his chieftains the commitments, which he had entered into at Geneva, and from Geneva the real conditions of his country, as described by Lady Simon, and in Henry Darley's book, *Slaves and Ivory*. That a country where slavery is not only tolerated but where taxes might be paid in slaves, should be a member of the League of Nations, on the same footing as Switzerland and Sweden, is one of those inconsistencies of contemporary politics, that are only possible as long as the general public does not understand the situation, and does not want to understand it.

In his work on Italy in Africa Christopher Hollis writes that the French move to admit Ethiopia into the League was " a proposal of cynicism and outrage against any true principles upon which the League professed to be built ". And he adds that it was " confessedly put forward in order to keep the Italians out ". I, myself, heard some

French diplomats put forward as their motive that of keeping the British out ! And they spoke of Sir Sidney Barton as having been appointed British Minister in Addis Ababa to prepare a virtual annexation of Abyssinia ! Some years later I lunched with Barton at the Travellers Club (I had known him well in China), and I asked him if the French suspicions were well founded. He seemed more amused than surprised, and said that his task of influencing the Negus had been much facilitated by the recall of the Italian Minister, Giuliano Cora : ' Cora had them all sitting in his lap ! ' As to the motives that inspired his own appointment to Ethiopia, Barton said that they might have been justified by the kindly desire, on the part of the Foreign Office, to give him a post where he should not be obliged to spend too much money !

The British Government strenuously opposed the admittance of Ethiopia into the League, and in this it showed itself foresighted and consistent. It would have been wiser on our part, if we Italians had followed the British lead. But at that time we were endeavouring to negotiate a Pact of Friendship with the Negus. This would have been utterly impossible if we had opposed his request for membership in the League.

Even after an Ethiopian delegate had been admitted to represent his country in the annual Assemblies of the League, the British Government continued to anticipate a possible dismemberment of that tottering empire, and though not seeking to hasten its demise, they apparently thought it prudent to be ready for it. In 1925, Sir Ronald Graham, British Ambassador in Rome, initiated a correspondence with our Ministero degli Affari Esteri, referring to the old Tripartite Agreement, as if it were still in force.

The French Quai d'Orsay was only informed later of this correspondence, and reacted with considerable resentment. Not to be surpassed in the gentle art of double-crossing their friends, the French informed the Negus that negotiations were going on behind his back. . . . Ras Tafari, justly incensed, essayed a protest, but his démarche came to nothing ; after which, the French, fearing that they might be left out in the cold, gave up their self-righteous attitude and renewed their agreement with the other two interested powers.

Such items of backstair history were of little use to me, in defending Italy's action, at Chatham House. But they gave rise to a doubt whether we could not have gained our point by demonstrating, at Geneva itself, that Ethiopia had not fulfilled, and could not fulfil, the conditions on which she had been admitted into the League. In proof of which, Great Britain herself had shown that she considered the question of a future dismemberment still open.

As so often happens, the international question was soon submerged by considerations of home politics. While I had been over in the States, Mr. Baldwin's government showed that its principal anxiety was to ensure votes in the coming parliamentary election. That pestilential organization, called the ' League of Nations Union ', animated by the zeal that Talleyrand deplored, organized a straw vote, in which the public was asked several garbled questions that practically amounted to the query : ' Do you prefer peace or war ? ' There could only be one answer. And it was this cheap little electioneering stunt that ultimately led to ' sanctions ' and to much that followed, even after the ill-feeling over Abyssinia had died down.

Let me add a comment of Monsieur André Tardieu's (quoted by the *Revue des Deux Mondes* of the 15th January 1936) : ' *Chaque fois qu'elle n'a pas cru ses propres intérêts engagées, l'Angleterre n'a pas cherché de fortifier la Société des Nations.*'

★   ★   ★

It is customary for a lecturer, at a meeting at Chatham House, to be the guest of some prominent member of the Institute. On the evening of the 19th of November, Bettina and I dined with Lord Howard of Penrith. As Sir Esme Howard, he had been British Ambassador in Washington. Lady Howard was Italian born (a Princess Giustiniani-Bandini).

At the lecture, an old friend was in the Chair : Sir Ronald Graham. He introduced me in a graceful, witty little speech, pulling my leg in the kindest way. He was glad I had come to England to speak about British foreign policy. He, himself, had been mixed up in British foreign politics during many years, but had never been able to make head or tail of them. He took them as a matter of faith. . . .

No need to give a resumé of my speech. Italy was being calumniated in those days, and the Italians were victims of every kind of abusive propaganda. The buttons were off the foils, and I struck back. I maintained that no more cruel insult had ever been levelled at a proud and sensitive nation than the assertion, repeatedly made by British statesmen, that the Ethiopian question offered ' a test case ' for the League. The British government thought that the time had come to test the efficiency of the Covenant, by making an experiment on the vile body of a friend. Italy was the rat for vivisection, the guinea-pig, on which to try the virus of sanctions ! To test the efficiency of the League, a black people were egged on to fight against a white. All the power and prestige of Great Britain were brought to bear against her ally in the Great War, and in favour of a people who mutilate their prisoners and sell small children in the slave-market.

I pointed out how the British moral indignation was selective. No action had been proposed, or taken, when the Polish general Zeligowski forcibly occupied Wilna, in defiance of the League. Nor was anything done when Japan occupied Manchuria. As Garvin wrote, in the *Observer* : "You do not come into court with clean hands, when you mete out one measure to an Eastern power that appears too formidable to be opposed, and another to an European power who you think might be weak enough to be cowed into submission."

You might think, when reading this page, that the tone of the meeting was heated and acrimonious. Far from it ! In verbal discussion much depends on the tone of the voice. Mine was gentle and slightly mocking, as if I were merely poking fun at my audience. And the audience itself was cordial and perfectly good-tempered. The British feel a chivalrous and sportsmanlike sympathy for anyone who stands up fearlessly for his own side. For this same reason, our Ambassador, Grandi, was personally very popular in London during the Abyssinian crisis.

When my lecture was over, a sort of general mêlée followed. Old Admiral Freemantle started to speak, and was obviously intending to be critical, but before he could get down to brass tacks, he got mixed up with another member, who shouted ' Malta ! ' There followed a row about Malta, though nobody seemed to know why, for nothing had been said about that island, one way or another. A gentleman named Victor Fisher, with a moustache and imperial, like the Frenchman in a detective story, came in on my side with an extraordinary speech, like the charge of the Light Brigade, in the course of which he said : ' Coming generations in this country will be able to say of *our* generation that England stood four square to all the winds of heaven, in favour of torture and emasculation.'

Another member—his name was given as Mr. G. Edinger—came out with the following :

' The sudden information that Italy must expand or explode has taken people in England by surprise. Italy has got on very well for many years without African colonies. She has free access to all the raw materials of the world at the same price as the British.'

If the necessity, in less than three decades, of sending abroad (and losing as Italian citizens) fourteen million emigrants, to earn the bread they could not find at home, can be described as ' getting on very well', Mr. G. Edinger was right. His argument about raw materials reminds me of a saying of Walter Bagehote's, that poverty always seems an anomaly to the rich. They find it difficult to make out why people who want dinner do not ring the bell. It is true that raw materials can be bought.[1] It has taken a second world war to show the British what a difference it makes to be able, or not, to buy in your own currency. John Quincy Adams was right when he said : ' No expedient ever devised could equal a debased currency for fertilizing the rich man's field with the sweat of the poor man's brow.'

*   *   *

" We pay our Bishops to shew us how to gain Heaven, not how to lose Singapore." This quotation, out of Sir Barry Domville's book, *From Admiral to Cabin Boy*, comes very apt, when describing the attitude of the Archbishops of Canterbury and of York during the Abyssinian crisis. The former certainly was never at a loss for the wrong word, and both were animated by the proverbial ferocity of non-combatants.

[1] In 1920, at the first Assembly of the League of Nations, the Italian Delegate, Tomaso Tittoni, attempted to submit the two major problems of our foreign policy : the pacific expansion of our population and the supply of raw materials. His plea was ruled out of order.

But, in spite of the lead given by its chiefs, the Anglican clergy was divided. Lord William Cecil, Bishop of Exeter, wrote a letter to the papers, in which he said :

There is a type of English individual who is a public danger. He loves either by pen or speech to express his opinions on the moral iniquities of other nations. If he would express it from the point of view of the fellow sinner, if he would point out that we English are much to blame by reserving great territories both in Australia and elsewhere, which we cannot pretend to cultivate, while Italy and other overcrowded nations cannot find room to expand, he might produce an atmosphere of peace. But, on the contrary, he will thank God that he is not as other men are. And from this high moral altitude he will administer rebukes that will cause the most profound irritation. When he does not rebuke, he will patronize. . . .

The League of Nations is quite on the right lines, but its weakness is that it does not go far enough. I believe that Italy ought not to have been allowed to feel the necessity of expansion. In peace time we should be trying to build up the prosperity of our neighbours. And we should find that that ended in our own prosperity.

Such were the views of those Englishmen who did not deliberately blind themselves to the truth that Italy's need of expansion had been made more urgent by the ruthless closing of outlets to our emigration, and the high tariff policies that raised everywhere a Great Wall of China against our produce. Our move into Abyssinia was not so much a war as the desperate sortie from a beleaguered city.

Austen Chamberlain, with whom I discussed the situation, was naturally unwilling to give away his nationals. But he said mildly : ' I would not have chosen to champion the Ethiopians. They are not good neighbours.' They were, indeed, such bad neighbours that their proximity cost the neighbouring British dependencies some £100,000 annually to repel the raids of savage tribes : those tribes that—as Lord Rothermere pointed out—required their young men to prove that they had killed and mutilated an adversary before they were allowed to marry ! Austen Chamberlain said to me that both Great Britain and Italy would have done well to invoke what was then called ' the Titulescu formula ', against a people that made a practice of invading their neighbour's territory.

Sir Austen's attitude was that of an expert in international affairs, who was also well up in modern history. What he most feared—

and he made no mystery of his anxiety—was that Italy be thrown into the arms of Germany, just as she had been in 1881, when the French faked a pretext to occupy Tunisia. On that occasion, Italy had been pushed into the Triple Alliance. Something similar might happen again.

Judging the situation from another standpoint, Sir John Maffey, one of the principal British experts in colonial matters, showed himself by no means hostile to the Italians. He was the author of ' the Maffey Report' (carefully hidden from the British public), which concluded that it might not be disadvantageous to Great Britain if the Italians occupied Ethiopia. The fact that these two men, Chamberlain and Maffey, expressing the views of experienced British politicians and officialdom, should both have taken such a moderate view of the situation, is a proof, in my opinion, of the following truism. As long as each nation limits itself (as, for example, the Swiss do) to defending its own national interests, there is not much difficulty, among reasonable people, in coming to an agreement over controversial questions. But when nations start crusades to attack, or to defend, an ideology, or an institution, such as Fascism, Communism, Democracy, or the League of Nations, the seeds of strife are sown over a broader field, and the danger of war is multiplied a thousandfold. It brings us back to the wars of religion, as in the Middle Ages.

Like Lord Palmerston, we may not attribute much value to ' friendship' between nations. Yet it is true that there was once what the Marchese Imperiali used to call ' a perfume' that hung about the relations between England and Italy. No amount of direct bickering between Whitehall and Palazzo Chigi could have destroyed that perfume. The ill-wind of sanctions blew it away.

During the Ethiopian crisis, if the Italian government remonstrated with the British government about their unexpectedly unfriendly attitude, they were assured that Great Britain was really their friend. If we remonstrated at Geneva concerning the exaggerated venom against us in the proceedings of the League of Nations, we were assured, by each single delegation, that it was England that had bribed or blackmailed them into following a policy which they deprecated. Mr. Anthony Eden was compared to Shere Khan, the lame tiger, going to the Council Rock, to ask that Mowgli be handed over to him. Valconcellos and Titulescu vied with one another for the part of Tabacqui, the jackal.

Could this have happened in the days of the old diplomacy?
The only one ultimately to benefit was Adolf Hitler.

Even 'sanctions' were nothing new to the Italians. Foreign nations had been imposing them for some time, with Exclusion Acts, Imperial Preference and other forms of economic hostility. Applied, as they were, half-heartedly, their only effect—as Winston Churchill points out in his War Memoirs—was to arouse 'the undying hatred of the Italians '.

*　　　*　　　*

Like myself, Alberto Pirelli went to London, during the Abyssinian crisis, at his own initiative. He invited Sir Arthur Salter, Walter Layton and Josiah Stamp to a small dinner, and did his best to induce them to stop the Press campaign in England. In his book, *Personality in Politics*, Salter admits that he was moved by Pirelli's plea, when he said :

' We can't go back. Everyone knows that we have sent an expedition. We thought we had your tacit acquiescence. We went to the Conference of Stresa expecting to learn England's real attitude. We had assured ourselves of Laval's acquiescence. We knew that you knew that our military stores were already going through the Suez Canal. We knew that you wanted us to be on your side in an issue with Hitler, and we thought it likely that you were prepared to acquiesce in our Abyssinian venture as the price. When your Ministers said nothing, we thought we could rely at least on being safe from active intervention.'

Sir Arthur Salter goes on to tell how he felt sufficiently disturbed to go privately to Ramsay MacDonald and to ask him whether it was in fact true that he had said nothing about Abyssinia. MacDonald replied that, on the contrary, Foreign Office experts had been taken out especially and had made contact with their opposite numbers. Sir Arthur insisted in his question : " I said that what Pirelli alleged was that no British *Minister* had said anything—on a question of obviously outstanding importance."

To this MacDonald replied that he, himself, was completely pre-occupied with the main problem, that of Germany. He did not know if Sir John Simon had raised the question of Abyssinia.

*　　　*　　　*

During the Abyssinian crisis, a British author, Mr. Wyndham Lewis, was writing *Left Wings Over Europe*, a book that was published (by Jonathan Cape) before the Italian conquest of Ethiopia was an accomplished fact. This work contains a very remarkable prediction. In describing, as a contemporary event, the cleavage that came about in international relations, in the years 1935–36, it points out that this cleavage foreshadows a far more serious split in Europe, between East and West. The distant origins of what was afterwards called ' The Iron Curtain ' go back to the days when the Russian Delegate at the Council of the League of Nations, Mr. Litvinov, found a heaven-sent opportunity for intrigue and mischief-making, while he posed among his colleagues at Geneva as the staunchest Covenanter of them all ! World war number two has since then given a geographical definition to what has long been a world-wide schism. Mr. Wyndham Lewis, writing in 1935, has a chapter called ' The great fissure that has appeared in European society in our time '.

We all know now how it came about that, some time after the U.S.A. and Great Britain had agreed, at Yalta, to hand over to Russian domination Poland, Czechoslovakia and Yugoslavia (including Albania and Italian cities on the Adriatic) there arose a sharp division between the extreme form of internationalism, which is best expressed by Moscow, and the other political trends that can be grouped under the general term of ' Fascist ', as misused by the gentlemen of the Left. We have heard this term ' Fascist ' applied to the U.S.A., by communist Ministers in Sofia and Belgrade.

There is nothing new in this. The phenomenon was evident, in the embryo stage, even during the Abyssinian crisis. To illustrate it, the author of *Left Wings Over Europe* mentions Sir Walter Citrine, who said to his followers at the Trade Union Congress at Brighton, in 1935 : ' Defend Abyssinia—by doing so, you will be defending Russia ! '

Mr. Lewis also quotes an article in the weekly, *Great Britain and the East*, published during the early days of the Abyssinian campaign :

There is a wider, more ominous, shadow, which people in this country may not fully realize, but which is weighing heavily with continental statesmen. This consists in nothing else than the possibility, should the war in Ethiopia endure for any considerable time, and should the accompanying economic sanctions endure for approximately the same length of time, that the particular issue between Italy and the League might be converted into a general issue between Fascism and its variations, and the Second or Third International and *its* variations.

Commenting on the above, Mr. Wyndham Lewis points out how, according to this classification, His Britannic Majesty's Government comes under the heading of one of 'the variations of the Third International'.

★   ★   ★

I do not believe that Pirelli, or I, cut much ice, when trying to influence people that were sitting in arm-chairs and reading the papers. But in Africa the facts themselves gained us the support of people on the spot. At one time, the American Foreign Correspondent, Webb Miller, shared the animosity that British propaganda so ably fostered against Italian expansion. What he saw for himself, while 'covering' the campaign in Ethiopia, diluted this ill-feeling. And he came to the conclusion that the Italian invasion was no less and no more reprehensible than the series of unprovoked aggressions and land-grabs, by which England, France, Belgium, Spain, Portugal and Germany gobbled up the continent of Africa.

What I myself had been trying to say I found expressed, better than I could have done, in the last chapter of Evelyn Waugh's *Waugh in Abyssinia*. This chapter is called 'The Road' and it describes the Italians, sturdy and indefatigable men, employed in hard manual labour, in the construction of motor-roads where, up till then, there had been nothing but rough bridle-paths for pack-mules. The idea of conquering a country in order to work there represented a new idea in Africa. Such a novel kind of conquest was rather shocking to the other imperial races, and quite incomprehensible to the Ethiopians, for whom the fruit of victory is leisure.

English colonization was the expansion of a ruling class, but the Italian occupation of African lands had a broader basis. Commenting upon our type of colonization, Evelyn Waugh writes :

It began with fighting, but it is not a military movement, like the French occupation of Morocco. It began with the annexation of potential sources of wealth, but it is not a capitalistic movement, like the occupation of the South African gold-fields. It is being attended by the spread of order and decency, education and medicine, in a disgraceful place.

He goes on to compare this advance to the great Western drive of the American peoples, dispossessing the Indian tribes, to establish new pastures and cities in a barren land.

Back in my Skyscraper

DURING my earlier stay in the U.S.A., I had declined to make a tour of lectures, as I was often asked to do. While on my way back to New York (where my book, *The Last Empress*, was in the throes of publication) I decided that I had better accept any similar offers that might be made to me. Judging by the success that my modest efforts had obtained so far, this was perhaps the best way to pull my weight.

So, when I got back, on Xmas Eve, to my skyscraper, I called up the Italian Embassy in Washington on the 'phone, to inform them that I was once again in the States, and that my services were at their disposal, if required. It was the Councillor, Rossi Longhi, who answered my call, and his advice was as follows.

' The best thing *you* can do,' he said, ' is to keep quiet. No radio talks, no speeches, no interviews, no articles in the papers. Show yourself around, answer questions if they ask any, but don't take the initiative. Just walk about and smile ! '

' That suits me all right. What's the bright idea ? '

' The English are doing our propaganda for us. That is to say, they are over-doing their own. Every journalist, every Bishop, every minor politician, thinks that the moment has come to make a lecture tour in the U.S.A., and to instruct the Americans as to what they should do. People here are fed up with them.'

I don't know whether it was a mere coincidence but just at that time, I read a novel by Wodehouse, called *The Girl on the Boat*, and this is what I found in it :

About this time, there was a good deal of suffering in the United States, for nearly every boat that arrived from England was bringing a fresh swarm of British lecturers to the country. Novelists, poets, scientists, philosophers and plain ordinary bores ; some herd instinct seemed to affect them all simul-taneously. . . . On this one point the intellectuals of Great Britain were single-minded : that there was easy money to be picked up on the lecture platforms of America, and that they might just as well grab it as the next person.

This being the case, I took things very leisurely, and went to stay once more with Rosso, at the Embassy. The following is an extract from a letter of mine to Bettina :

ITALIAN EMBASSY
WASHINGTON D.C. *2nd January 1936*

The Ambassador was out somewhere, and Rossi Longhi came and dined here to keep me company. He tells me that his little boy goes to a school where there are pupils of different nationalities, besides Americans. The American children boycott him, because he is Italian. The result is that his only playfellows are the Germans. Exactly the same thing is happening in the field of high international politics. We are being thrust into the arms of Hitler, whereas a little *savoir faire*, on the part of England and the states she influences, might hold Italy to the side of her former Allies in the world war.

I have met the Grand Old Man of American journalism, Frank H. Simonds, and he asked me to lunch with him. I had some difficulty in finding his house in P. Street, as the rain poured down on the wind-screen of my car (or rather Rosso's car) in such a torrential flood that it was almost impossible to see out.

I have jotted down some of the things that Simonds said to me :

' The economic nationalism of the richer powers may lead to another war.'

' When you Italians ask for " vital spaces ", you are only voicing a general plea, and the aspirations of the rich states as well as of the poor. World communications being what they now are, it is absurd to divide the world up into independent, self-contained estates. Some plan should be sought to do away with frontiers, at least in the field of economics. At present only the poorer states are reacting against a policy, which all the world will some day discover to be suicidal.'

' This economic nationalism, among the more prosperous powers, serves indirectly to foster Communism, or Fascism, within the borders of less fortunate states. To consider such ideologies merely as the outcome of human error or wickedness is childish. They are the consequence of weakness in the social order.'

Since lunching with Frank Simonds in Washington (it was just a month before his death) I have seen his *obiter dicta* quoted in many books, for example, in Sir Norman Angell's *The Steep Places*. Here, Frank Simonds's opinions, and those of Mr. Leland Stowe, as of the American Foreign Policy Association, not to mention Lindbergh and an un-named Judge of the American Supreme Court, are carefully selected to show that they are all based upon a fallacy. For Sir Norman Angell, the truth is simple and visible ; Britain does not own her Empire ; it is not her property. She has governed and governs a rapidly decreasing area of it. But she owns none of it. Nine-tenths of the arguments put forward by people like Frank Simonds, Mr. Leland Stowe (he might have added : by Daniele Varè) are due—so Norman Angell tells us—to a crude confusion between the meaning of the word ' own ' and ' govern '.

In describing as a myth the economic advantages possessed by the ' Have ' powers, over the ' Have not's ', Sir Norman Angell is guilty, himself, of a fallacy, or at least he shows himself sadly behind the times. It may be perfectly true, as he so persuasively maintains, that the causes of war are often psychological rather than economic. Indeed, if it were not so, why should countries like Italy and Jugoslavia be eternally quarrelling among themselves, when it would be to their mutual interest for each to furnish to the other what they respectively lack ? But the contention that a change of rulers makes no difference to the proprietors of the land, in a territory that passes from one sovereignty to another, may have been well-founded during the Napoleonic wars, when Goethe travelled in Lorraine, but it is certainly not true in our day.

Almost contemporaneously with the publication of Sir Norman Angell's *Steep Places*, the *Saturday Evening Post* published an article " The Swarming of the Slavs ", by Demaree Bess. It was illustrated with photographs, showing how Germans and Hungarians were expelled from Czechoslovakia and forced to abandon the territory where they had lived for generations, in order that the ' victors ' might create an exclusively Slav State.

I have watched the S.S. *Roma* drop anchor before ' le Zattere ' in Venice, to disembark Italian peasants, with their families and such poor goods and chattels as they could bring with them, so that the ' victorious ' Jugoslavs might possess themselves of the farms, the forests, the mineral resources of Istria. Refugees from Zara (a typically Italian town, with a typically Italian population) came to me, in my house in Rome, to describe atrocities which were much worse than the *dragonnades* that followed, in seventeenth-century

France, the Revocation of the Edict of Nantes, obliging the Huguenots to flee to England, Holland and Brandenburg. (Nowadays, we would have called them displaced persons.)

So again, after the French had hounded most of the poorer Italian residents out of Tunisia, I used to visit, in hospital, one of their number, an old woman of over seventy, who had tried to commit suicide by throwing herself out of a window. She had no one to turn to in the country of her origin, and what help the Italian authorities could give her was inadequate. She had not succeeded in killing herself; only in breaking both her legs. It is charitable to assume that a would-be suicide is of unsound mind, and the old woman had been taken to the provincial mental home of St. Elisabeth, on the top of Monte Mario, near Rome.

She had passed all her life in Tunisia, and having been forced to leave as soon as the war was over, she felt that she had no other home. When I saw her last, she still longed for death.

*　　*　　*

Frank Simonds was a better informed writer than most journalists and politicians. He was one of the few people I have met, who had ever heard of the Italian proposal for a ' triangular collaboration in colonial matters '. This project was submitted, as far back as 1925, by the Italian Delegate, de Michelis, to the *Bureau International du Travail*, in Geneva. Countries that were suffering from demographic pressure were to contribute labour ; countries with unexploited territories and raw materials were to contribute these ; countries with capital to invest were to finance the enterprise. Each of the three was to be entitled to a share of the produce. In this way, a consortium would have combined the different forms of production.

The idea was given favourable consideration by the *Comité d'Etudes pour une Union Européenne*, presided over by Briand, and later by Herriot. The former was personally favourable, but he could not forego a characteristic jibe. He said to Count Sforza, then our Ambassador in Paris : ' What you want is that we should contribute colonies, while you contribute a consortium ! '

Simonds had heard of the project through the *Institut de Hautes Études Internationales*, established in Geneva. He pointed out to me how the idea of a consortium had been insufficiently advertised. The general public, which is always on the side of the best publicity, never heard of it. Yet Albert Thomas, the French labour leader and Trade Unionist, had spoken at length and with a well-considered optimism of this proposal, in his last report, concluding the activities of the sixteenth Session of the International Labour Conference (1932). He compared it to the projects of Saint Simon, founder of French socialism, and follower of Lafayette.

Some such collaboration in the administration of African territories will have to be carried out in the interests of economic justice.

*　　　*　　　*

One of the first people I met, during my sojourn in the States, was Mrs. William Brown Meloney, who edited the weekly magazine of the *N.Y. Herald Tribune*. Her initial interest in me was based on a misunderstanding. We found ourselves seated next to one another at a dinner-party. She turned to me with a pleased expression and said : ' I know your name. You have written a religious book, haven't you ? '

' A religious book . . . Me ? No ! '

She had been in London and had seen various publishers, in order to find out if there were any book, recently published in England, that she might bring out in serial form, in her magazine. One of the books sent to her by Methuen had been discarded by her secretary, because—as she informed Mrs. Brown Meloney—it was a religious book. The title was *The Maker of Heavenly Trousers.*

The fact that she travelled to Europe with a Secretary (however inefficient) showed me that the lady I was sitting next to at dinner must be an important person, and I soon discovered that Mrs. William Brown Meloney was very influential indeed. Her power in the land lay in the fact that she was a woman. She told me this herself.

And she accused us Italians of not thinking enough about women. This astonished me, for I have heard people say that we think of nothing else. There was an old gentleman in Venice (a relation of mine) who, in his youth, had travelled round the world merely to find out what the women were like in different countries. But Mrs. Meloney regarded the question from a different angle. She told me that eighty per cent of the money spent in the U.S.A. is spent by women. Eight million women support their families. They represent, to a remarkable degree, the intellectual life of the nation.

Yet when Claudel was French Ambassador in Washington, he once declared that there *were* no women in America : ' *Elles sont des flappères. Et quand elles cessent d'etre des flappères, elles deviennent des Daughters of ze Revolution* ! '

It was through Mrs. Brown Meloney that I made the acquaintance of Professor James T. Shotwell, of Columbia University. I had heard a lot about him in Europe, as being one of those responsible for the Briand-Kellogg Pact to outlaw war.

As Professor Shotwell first suggested, this should have been a bilateral agreement, limited to France and to America. In such a form, it merely put into words what was a generally accepted fact, a point already gained in the progress of the world's history. No one could conceive a war breaking out between France and the United States.

The idea of extending the scope of the proposed pact to other states is due to Senator Borah, though it must have been obvious that any extension of the bilateral agreement, as originally proposed by Shotwell, must lend to making it less, and not more, efficacious. Senator Moses is quoted as having exclaimed : ' Let's extend it to all nations, and get rid of the dam' thing ! '

I once discussed the Briand-Kellogg Pact with Arthur Henderson, who had attended the ceremony of the signature in Paris, in the same Salle de l'Horloge, where the Covenant of the League of Nations had been signed, ten years before. He declared that it was dishonest and unfair to public opinion, to pretend that any such document could have practical value, in the dangerous atmosphere of international politics. Bernard Shaw described it as a step backward towards war, instead of a giant stride towards peace. And President Coolidge was sceptical.

My own feelings towards it were inspired by a certain resentment. While attempting the impossible, the Briand-Kellogg Pact renounced much that was necessary. (In this, it resembled proposals like total disarmament : perfectly safe to make, as they are certain to be rejected.) After the signing of the Pact, the powers gave up all the good work that was being done (at the initiative of the United States), to render illegal, in international law, the more inhuman and brutal methods of warfare, such as attacks by air on the civilian population. Negotiations already begun, to attain this object, were first suspended and then abandoned. The Briand-Kellogg Pact had outlawed war, therefore war itself could not be subjected to laws. To make new laws for warfare would have been equivalent to a breach of faith. So we returned to the mentality that preceded the Thirty Years War, before Grotius wrote *De Jure Belli ac Pacis*.

Professor Shotwell's innocent and practical suggestion, to outlaw war between two friendly nations, was destined to have some unexpected consequences.

More Letters from my Skyscraper

NEW YORK, *Thursday, 9th January 1936*

I arrived here yesterday evening by the 'Congressional' from Washington, and the first person I met, this morning, was a ghost: the ghost of an old gentleman, with a drooping moustache, bushy eyebrows and a corn-cob pipe. I had last met him in Rome in 1897. I mean the ghost of Mark Twain.

Blasts of icy wind, sweeping down Fifth Avenue, drove me in through the doors of the Public Library, where, on the ground floor, is housed the 'Mark Twain Centenary Exhibit'. Many of his relics were affectionately collected there, and among them I found the little poem by Owen Seaman, written after Mark Twain's death, and published in *Punch*:

> Pilot of many pilgrims since the shout
> 'Mark twain!' that serves you for a deathless sign,
> On Mississippi waterways rang out
> Over the plummet's line.
>
> Still where the countless ripples laugh above
> The blue of halcyon seas, long may you keep
> Your course unbroken, buoyed upon a love
> Ten thousand fathoms deep!

It was through a girl friend of mine, Elsa Grant, that I wangled an invitation to accompany her, her father, and Mr. Clemens in the family landau that trundled about the streets of Rome in a leisurely way and took us to the Vatican. In the Sistine Chapel, our American guest stared at the 'Day of Judgment' and remarked: 'The healthiest place to stay, in Michelangelo's time, must have been a tomb!' And indeed it is true that, in the huge fresco behind the altar, the reincarnated souls, emerging from their sepulchres, have the muscular figures of athletes and the brown limbs of bathers on summer beaches.

During tea in Mr. Grant's apartment in the Palazzo Salviati, I asked the author about the almost medieval feud, between the Grangefords and the Shepherdsons (in *Huckleberry Finn*), those two aristocratic families of a past Mississippi civilization. The story might have been transplanted from the banks of the river Adige, where Montacutes and Capulets waged war on one another, to the sorrow of Romeo and Juliet. Mark Twain assured us that such a feud, ' under the old code ', was just what he had described it to be, down to the shooting, from the river bank, of a wounded boy, who is trying to swim to safety. There is something Homeric about that story. Does Mark Twain's ghost now hob-nob, I wonder, with that of Homer κατ' ἀσφοδελὸν λειμῶνα?

NEW YORK, *Wednesday, 15th January 1936*

Sacha Jacovleff is here and came to see me. He has given up his studio in Paris and now teaches drawing in some Art Academy in Boston. He is up in New York for a few days, arranging for a ' one man show ' of his works at the Knoedler galleries. Jacovleff is doing well in the U.S.A. He passes most of his time, in New York, in the monkey house of the miniature Zoological Gardens at the Fifth Avenue entrance to Central Park. He is trying to do a portrait of a monkey called Woolly. But Woolly objects and spits at Jacovleff from the upper railings of his cage. At first he missed by a yard or so, but now he has got the range. Jacovleff cleans up his jacket with a pocket handkerchief and grumbles : ' *Ce cochon a appris à viser juste !* '

My sympathies are entirely with Woolly. It must be exasperating to be shut up in a small cage, to be stared at and painted. . . . And Jacovleff is doing a very good likeness. He has caught the almost human expression that yet is not quite human, and the angry sadness of the eyes !

Yesterday evening I dined, as I often do, at the Oyster Bar of the Grand Central. It has the advantage of being close by and nicely warmed. You can walk about there in comfort, even when there is a blizzard raging outside. I like to see the American youth returning from their winter sports, by the evening trains. There is snow on their caps and on the skis that they carry on their shoulders. The girls have red cheeks (and sometimes red noses) and very often they are limping from a fall.

I discovered that the waiters at the long tables with swivel-back chairs are mostly Spaniards. One of these worthies offered me a dish that sounded very indigestible and not very appetizing. I answered that I would not risk it : ' *Tengo miedo !* '

A woman who was sitting opposite promptly asked me if I were a Spaniard. I did not wish to enter into conversation, so I merely shook my head. But she insisted : ' French ? ' Again I made a sign in the negative.

'English?'
'No.'
'German?'
'I am Italian.'

She looked at me as though I had revealed some dire misfortune, and said :
'How pleased you must feel to be over here in a civilized country !'

The poor woman—I am sure—meant no offence. She probably thought she was being kind and tactful. And anyway she is spoon-fed by a propaganda that finds it convenient to put on the same level the countrymen of Dante, of Columbus, of Michelangelo and Leonardo, of Galileo and Volta and Marconi, with a conglomeration of African tribes—the only people that still practice slavery on a large scale and who emasculate their prisoners of war !

YALE

From rooms in a college in the
University (I don't know which)
17th January 1936

I am the guest here of Peter Belin and some fellow students, who have generously given up to me, to sleep in, a tiny room, chock-full of clothes, books and sporting trophies. My hosts asked me if I wanted to talk (meaning, I suppose, to give a lecture of sorts). On my answering, 'No !' they seemed much relieved. If I had been the guest of 'the faculty', I would have had to take myself seriously. But the learned Professors do not even know that I am here, which is all to the good. I attended a history class, just to see what they were teaching, and had some difficulty in recognizing the French Revolution names, translated into English. I have been given to understand that Yale is poor, when compared to Harvard. I wish we had some such poverty in the shadow of the two leaning towers, at the University of Bologna.

LAMSON HOUSE

SOUTH HAMILTON MASS., *18th January 1936*

Left New Haven in a blizzard, lunched at Boston and came down here in the evening. The countryside is deep in snow.

I passed the middle of the day, in Boston, with Jacovleff, who took me to his studio. He has found a lovely model here. There are drawings of her all over the place.

I am beginning to realize that my ideas of America are as out of date as the slang of the eighteen-eighties, or the legendary notice : 'Don't shoot the pianist. He's doing his best !' The telephone, the cinema, the radio, the dude-ranch and the frigidaire, have created a new America. Something of the older one is left here and there : the little town, all a-rustle in summer with elm-leaves, all white and glistening with snow in winter (as now) ; a place of home-staying people, who squirt their hoses on front lawns in the evening, and sit and gossip on a back-porch, and eat creamed chicken and waffles and soda-biscuits ; where ladies go a-marketing with a basket, and the young people eat molasses candy, even if they no longer sing part-songs.

Life today in the small towns that dot the asphalted roads is doubtless more pleasant than it used to be. And people are just as hospitable and friendly as the old folks one used to read about in books. But where is ' Main Street ' ? I have not come across it yet. Or perhaps it is that I find the same atmosphere as in English cathedral-towns, or in the Alban Hills. Main Street now runs round the world.

NEW YORK, *16th February 1936*

Very hard frost. A hydrant has burst not far from this hotel, and the frozen spout is about sixteen feet high ; it looks like a Xmas tree. The papers publish photos of ships coming into port, smothered in icicles. It is warmer in Central Park and out in the country than in the New York streets.

I have been out once more to see the Oyster Bay Roosevelts (Teddy and his wife). My hosts were just the same as ever, both talking nineteen to the dozen. Teddy with no waistcoat (in this cold !) ; his jacket standing well away from his collar and tie, and every now and then looking at his wife across the dinner-table, as if he were frightened of her. But he kept on telling stories, to poke fun at her. One of them was about the ' Preparedness Parade ' (just before America came into the war—some time in 1917). It was a gigantic procession up Fifth Avenue. Mrs. Roosevelt (Elinòr, as he calls her, with the accent on the o) was ' Marshal ' of ' The Patriotic Women of America '. There were to have been no less than 3,500 of them : Elinòr at the head of the procession, and Daisy Harriman behind her, carrying a large banner. But, owing to a sudden change of plans by the organizing committee, there was a hitch down the line. The band passed, playing hard. Then came Elinòr, stiff as a ram-rod, looking very military and wearing a broad white band across her chest, with ' Marshal ' written on it. Then came Daisy Harriman bearing the standard with ' Patriotic Women of America ' on it. And then . . . nothing at all ! Though unaware of the fact, they had got separated from their following ; there was no one on the asphalt road behind them. The ' Patriotic Women of America ' were reduced to two !

After lunch, Teddy gave me a definition of the difference between totalitarian and democratic régimes. He said : ' In totalitarian states, you cannot say, or do, what you like. In democratic states, you may say what you like, as long as you do what you're told.'

It was odd to see Oyster Bay again under deep snow, even the sea. The bay was frozen solid, and boulders of ice stuck out, here and there, from under the snow. The trees loomed through a grey mist, as in a Japanese print.

NEW YORK, *17th February 1936*

New York is indulging in a 'permanent (cold) wave'. Sleet, snow and rain. Then hard frost and an icy wind. Madison Avenue is as slippery as the 'Cresta Run' at St. Moritz.

Henry R. Luce and Laird S. Goldsborough came to lunch today. Luce is the founder of *Time*, and Goldsborough a foreign editor.

It was interesting to meet Luce (I knew Goldsborough already), but our lunch was not a success. We had a table in the corner of a small dining room, and waited an interminable time for what we had severally ordered. At last, our waiter came in with a tray, tripped over something at the door, and spread-eagled himself over the room, with all he carried. Another twenty minutes passed before we got anything to eat. By that time, we were all three so faint with hunger that we could hardly speak politely to one another. The smell of food from the other tables, all around, was tantalizing. I made some inane remark about the Americans not being 'military minded'. Luce said it would be a grave mistake to count on this, and he foresaw that, before many years were over, the Americans would be caught up and swept away by some powerful wave of emotionalism, that might carry them almost anywhere and in no predictable direction.

Another American super-journalist, whom I have met in these days, is the 'columnist', Brisbane. He owns the 'Ritz Tower', next door to this hotel. Also some land, I didn't understand where, that he wants to people with Italians, whom he considers good citizens (Al Capone notwithstanding).

He predicts that the war in Abyssinia will be over in a few months. On the other hand, President Roosevelt—so Brisbane says—predicts that it will last for years and fizzle out through inanition of the Italians.

I asked where President Roosevelt got his information, and Brisbane said : 'From the English General Staff. He would do better to take it from the American General Staff.'

NEW YORK, *18th February 1936*

I hear that the 'Universal Service' news agency is sending representatives to Europe, on the assumption that there will be war there in March.

Though I have known Nora Iasigi (that was) ever since we were in our teens, I had never met her husband, William Marshal Bullitt. He asked me to dine at the Union Club, a sumptuous repast in a private room, with caviare, bisque, roast quails, ice-cream and wonderful wines. I gathered that my host is a 'corporation lawyer'. And two of the other guests were high up in the legal profession.

One of them gave me news of Judge Bassett Moore, whom I met when he was the first U.S. member of the World Court at the Hague. Apparently he is still going strong, though seventy-five years old.

He was one of the shining lights in International Law, when I was a student at the University. I remember pouring over his monumental *Digest*, and enjoying his articles in *Harper's Magazine*. He wrote on such subjects as ' The Beginnings of American Diplomacy', and ' The United States as a World Power '. He seems to have been something of a pioneer, for in those days very few people in America seemed to think that they needed a diplomacy at all, unless it was to present their wives and daughters to the English Court. I hear that, as an authority on International Law, Judge Bassett Moore now disapproves of ' sanctions ' and expresses strong doubt as to their legal justification. Two years before the present trouble began, that is to say in 1933, he maintained that the new internationalism's efforts to guarantee peace would merely assure the world-wide scope of future wars.

One might say of Judge Bassett Moore what Talleyrand said of Alexander Hamilton : ' *Il avait deviné l'Europe.*'

NEW YORK, *29th February 1936*

Salvador Madariaga is here in New York. I had not seen him since we were both at the League of Nations in Geneva. Some Association of Women's Clubs has invited him to come over, paying his expenses and housing him on the thirty-fourth floor of the Sherry-Netherlands building, under (or above) the apartment for which Mary Pickford pays some fabulous rent. I accuse him of living ' in guilty splendour '.

If the women's clubs had known Madariaga as well as I do, I doubt they would have asked him to lecture to them. He is far too unbiassed in his opinions, and—like myself—does not take anything, not even high politics— very seriously. At the Disarmament Conference, he was considered rather an *enfant terrible*, especially when he ridiculed the Russian proposal for total disarmament all round. He compared Russia to a huge bear, suggesting that teeth and claws and talons should be abolished, and that all the animals should come together and give each other ' a good hug '.

Today we were comparing the English and the American mentalities. I remarked that both felt the necessity of assuming an attitude of moral superiority. ' Quite true,' said Madariaga, ' but the English get away with it. The Americans don't ! '

From this, we got on the subject of oligarchies. He said :

' All governments are oligarchies. You can appoint them by putting bits of paper in a ballot-box, or by giving your opponents castor-oil. It is not proved that the latter method is necessarily the worst. Personally I prefer Mussolini to Bill Thompson ! '

' Big Bill ' Thompson, Mayor of Chicago, became famous overnight by saying he wanted to give His Majesty King George ' a punch on the snoot '.

To explain such animosity, it was pointed out that in English school books, such as Schlesinger's *New View-points in American History*, George Washington is described as a rebel against the British Crown : a sure proof that such text-books are designed to poison the innocent minds of American children !

This is the story as generally told and accepted. But did the Mayor really mean King George V of England ?

I have heard quite another version of the story : namely that 'King George' was the nickname of a political boss in Chicago—and a priest withal !—against whom Big Bill Thompson has a grudge. Hence his remark about the punch in the snoot.

His words having been taken for a crime of *lèse majesté*, the Mayor was far too clever to clear up the misunderstanding and explain what he really meant. The story of a tiff with King George was excellent publicity. So he left it at that !

POST-CARD FROM NEWHAVEN, CONN., *3rd March 1936*

Came here to see our Consul, de Cicco. He took me to a meeting of the local Rotary Club. They asked me a lot of questions about Abyssinia and ended up by bursting into song :

> Oh, give me a home where the buffalo roam
> Where the deer and the antelope play,
> Where seldom is heard a discouraging word
> And the skies are not cloudy all day !

I believe this is what they call 'community singing !'

I hear there is a strike of elevator boys in New York. I am booked to dine with Mich Davenport (editor of *Fortune*). He lives on the fourteenth floor. I hope I will not have to walk upstairs !

NEW YORK, *7th March 1936*

Vecchiotti (our Consul General) took me to a meeting of the Foreign Policy Association at the Hotel Astoria, in Times Square. These meetings in which I have no obligation to put myself forward (I only answered a few questions) are quite enjoyable, and I learn a lot about public opinion in the U.S.A.

The best speech of the evening was made by a negro, who said he was an Abyssinian, but he spoke the language of Harlem. He brought forward an unanswerable argument, when he asked : 'What fault is it of ours that so many babies are born in Italy ?'

I went and congratulated him afterwards.

Anyway, Abyssinia is no longer in the news. There is trouble nearer home, since German troops have crossed the bridges over the Rhine and marched into the 'demilitarized' territory on the left bank. I seem to remember that this was foreseen by a journalist in Washington—Constantine Brown, (the foreign-editor of the *Washington Star*). He considered it inevitable that the Germans would take some advantage out of the sanctions racket which threatened to bring about a major war, in Europe, because we Italians had started a minor war in Africa.

American public opinion is much divided : for and against us. In spite of (or because of) the insistence of British propagandists to lead their Western cousins into the path of righteousness, there is here—as in France—a certain bias in our favour. It is perhaps an echo of their own ' frontier spirit ', which claimed (I am quoting J. T. Adams's *Epic of America*, page 67) that :

" . . . it was against the law of God and nature that so much land should be idle while so many Christians wanted it to labour on and raise bread.'

And this is perhaps the only answer we can make to the negro's argument, as quoted above, that it is really no fault of the Ethiopians if so many babies are born in Italy.

POSTED IN NEW YORK, *Sunday evening, 8th March 1936*

I am writing to you in the train between Baltimore and New York. Our Consul at Baltimore was very pressing in an invitation to me to come and give a talk at the meeting of an ' Open Forum '. But, being new to Baltimore he had made a bad mistake. There is, I believe, quite an important institution there, which calls itself a Forum, but it was not the one I was taken to this afternoon.

We found ourselves in a slovenly suburban hall, very dingy and squalid, opening out on a street with cars clanging down it. A ragged individual at the door was selling communist pamphlets. The Secretary was an elderly woman, showing—as Oscar Wilde would say—the remains of a truly remarkable ugliness. Halfway through the meeting, someone went round with a hat, collecting money for the hire of the hall.

In this unexpected atmosphere I thoroughly enjoyed myself, but the audience took no interest in me whatever ; they were all busy abusing President Roosevelt.

What little was said about foreign politics was the sort of thing you might expect from the politicians in a comic novel by Leacock. A little man, who represented—so I was told—the Carnegie Endowment, took Europe to task for not following the example of the various States that make up the Union, here in America. He told us how these states have many divergent interests in the matter of transport, water, forestry, hygiene, etc. But they don't go to war about them. (Yet I seem to remember that they *did* go to war about slavery !)

This self-righteous ' Professor ' was evidently unconscious of the fact that the various races and nations and countries of Europe have different languages and possess a historical background, in which you may watch the Past acting on the Present. To quote one example, our frontiers are the result of historical events that go far back in history. They are often the result of an unjust peace, and therefore a cause of friction and unrest. History has a momentum, like that of a railway train in motion. You must take it into account, if you want to prevent accidents.

NEW YORK, *Tuesday, 10th March 1936*

This letter ought to catch the *Aquitania*. As soon as it is finished I will drop it in the tube that has an opening near my bedroom door and corresponds with the letter-box in the hall downstairs. I have the remains of a sore throat and will pass the afternoon at home, that is to say in my hotel sitting-room. Except to have tea, there will be nothing to do but write to you. So this letter is likely to be a long one.

I had lunch with Colonel William E. Donovan, a wealthy republican, who is just back from Abyssinia, where he toured all over the place and saw Badoglio, Castellani and all sorts of people. He is enthusiastic over the efficiency of the Italians and their morale. He has also been to Geneva, to Berlin and to Paris ; he has talked with Vansittart and various personalities . . . He says that the best way to persuade American public opinion that we have right on our side, will be to succeed in conquering Abyssinia. Most people judge the rights and wrongs of a question merely by its outcome. It is the victor by whom history is written, and defeat is the proof of wrong-doing. So it has always been and so it will always be.

Strange to say, the most interesting conversation I have had here in these last days has been with an elderly lady, whom I have known for years and who lives quite close to us in Rome ! I mean the Signora Olivia Agresti Rossetti.

She was first here in an official capacity just after the War, in 1920, or thereabouts, for the meeting of the International Labour Conference. This was called under the Treaty of Versailles though it so happened that when the Conference actually met, the Treaty of Versailles had been rejected by the Senate. The Conference founded the International Labour Office, which afterwards took up its duties in Geneva.

The Signora Agresti worked with the Italian delegate, Baldesi, a socialist and trade union representative. At her suggestion, he took up the question of raw materials and ocean freights : in the sense that the supply of raw materials and the cost of freight affect the standard of living (that is to say of employment), in the importing countries. Baldesi suggested some form of international supervision. He got the support of workmen's delegations, of employers' delegations and of several governments. But the whole British Empire (the governments, the employers and the trades unions) were dead against anything in the form of an international understanding on the subject. They formed a compact block against any threat to their national monopolies.

Today, the Signora Agresti is once more in America, preaching the same sermons against national monopolies, and once more her adversaries are the

British and the British Colonials, who form a solid block in favour of a selfish policy that opposes any attempt of the Italians to obtain room for their growing population and free access to raw materials. This is what is at the bottom of the Abyssinian venture. And it is on this, exclusively economic side of the question, that the Signora Agresti has been lecturing in the United States. It is the most legitimate form of propaganda : that which stands up for the living wage—the standard of living—of the working classes in a country that is as poor as Italy.

The fact that the Signora Agresti is a niece of Dante Gabriele Rosetti confers on her a halo of inherited celebrity, even among people who have only the foggiest notion of who Dante Gabriele Rossetti was. A Chicago girl came up to her after a lecture and asked her to sign a copy of the *Divine Comedy*, under the impression that she was a niece of Dante Alighieri !

NEW YORK, *19th March 1936*

The following item of news appeared yesterday in the first (morning) edition of the *New York Herald Tribune*, but was omitted in the subsequent editions, presumably by request of the British diplomatic and consular authorities :

BRITISH WAR FILM CENSORED

Scenes Showing Natives Mowed Down in Africa Deleted

(*From the 'Herald Tribune' Bureau*)

" LONDON, March 17.—Scenes showing British machine-gunners mowing down Matabele natives in the film *Rhodes of Africa* were obligingly deleted today by Gaumont-British pictures, as a result of a suggestion from the Foreign Office.

" The scenes were not protested on the ground that they were untrue but that they were 'unfortunate' at this time, in view of the Italo-Abyssinian war.

" The Foreign Office evidently does not want to hear an Italian taunt that the Fascists are only following the example set them by the British to be borne out so graphically by one of their own films."[1]

---

[1] The judgment expressed by the *Herald Tribune* is confirmed by G. K. Chesterton, in his own weekly newspaper (28th May 1936) :
" That ignorant insularity . . . is not content to make the Englishman the hero of every drama ; it makes him the old-fashioned hero of melodrama. And it makes every foreigner in turn not only a villain, but exactly the same villain in the same melodrama. . . .
" At the very moment when Mussolini is made a monster for annexing a small African state, our precious patriotic picture-makers produced a preposterous version of Cecil Rhodes and the annexation of the Boer State, in which the Kimberley millionaire is gazing at a vision in the manner of Sir Galahad."

Home-coming (1936)

ALTHOUGH I had enjoyed my stay in New York, it was pleasant, on a sunny morning in March, to find myself speeding down West Street towards the Chelsea Piers, to embark on the *Conte di Savoia*.

There were the usual crowds to see people off, and parting gifts being taken into luggage-strewn cabins and state-rooms : bouquets of roses, boxes of chocolates, books, telegrams, kisses, tears. Elsie Torlonia gave me some cigarettes to take to her son. I warned her he was unlikely to get them (he didn't). I don't smoke, myself, but my daughters do.

During our passage home, Passerini, the Purser, with one eye partially obscured by a drooping eyelid, entertained the more privileged passengers with cocktail parties. The ' smart set ' included Elsa Maxwell, Grace Moore and Colonel and Madame Balsàn (*née* Consuelo Vanderbilt, formerly Duchess of Marlborough).

The facilities offered by modern science on luxury liners permitted me to hear Bettina's voice in Rome, through the telephone installed on the Captain's deck, near the radio station. And a pretty Italian girl conversed with a boy-friend, in camp, somewhere in Abyssinia. He confirmed the good news of the campaign's progress. Italy would soon have her colonial empire, the Promised Land I had always dreamt of. There would be room for her sons to work overseas, under their own flag.

We sailed into the Bay of Naples on a lovely April morning, between the violet valleys and the orange-groves, sloping down on every side. Bettina was waiting for me on the new pier. She had taken rooms at the Excelsior, and we motored out for lunch at Pompeii.

That spring-time arrival from abroad remains as one of the happiest memories of my life. The approaches to Italy are all beautiful, but the gates of heaven are from the Mediterranean : a blue robe, starred with white cities.

We drank white wine from a volcanic soil and ate home-made spaghetti, under whispering pines, within the sound of little waves breaking along the shore. Behind us rose the mountain under which, as tradition tells us, burn the fires of Phlegathon. Vineyards covered its fertile slopes, and wistaria cascaded over the ruined walls of the long-dead city, whose fate is an eternal warning of the transient nature of our joys and sorrows.

On getting back to the hotel, we met Pirandello in the entrance-hall. Even he seemed to have lost his habitual melancholy. How could it be otherwise, coming back to all the sunshine?

★   ★   ★

To my sorrow, I cannot close my Memoirs at this point! Only in fiction can we write a protecting *Finis*, to end a story before dis-illusion casts a shadow on the page. In real life, it must go on.

Like my father before me, I have known the bitter-sweet torment that goes with the harvesting of a dream. But he was more fortunate than I, for his dream was never shattered. Good fortune and the willing support of his countrymen helped Mussolini to conquer the Land of Canaan. Unfortunately, he failed to realize that a statesman's duty is not only to acquire, but also to preserve. By reason of his subsequent errors, the Italians remained in the Promised Land just long enough to show what they might have done there.

PART III

SHADOWS

London during the Spanish Crisis

ONE morning in March 1937, when coming out of Aragno's in the Corso, I met Roger Boppe, of the French Embassy, and he stopped to congratulate me because—so he had been told—I was going to London 'on an important mission'. I answered truthfully that this was the first I had heard of it.

When I got home, I was called up on the telephone by a lady who wanted to tell me how pleased she was that her daughter was to go to London with me. Again I answered that I knew nothing about it. But later on I received a message from the Ministero, asking if I would be in London by Thursday. I answered that, as it was then Wednesday, it was unlikely. Also I had no particular reason for going to London just then. I gathered from the papers that it was snowing there, whereas, in Rome, the wistaria was in blossom in the garden underneath my study window.

Subsequently it transpired that they wanted me to go to London for ' Non-Intervention in Spain'. In discussing the matter between themselves, the government offices concerned had forgotten to get in touch with me. In the play-bill of *Hamlet*, they had left out the Prince.

However, in due course, I arrived up at Claridge's, and next morning went round to Three Kings Court, and picked up Guido Crolla at the Embassy. He took me to Whitehall, to interview those that sat in the seats of the mighty. But their arm-chairs were mostly empty, for everyone was leaving town for Easter. The lifts appeared to be out of order, and no one was making any effort to mend them till after Bank Holiday. The only signs of official activity was the presence of a group of young girls (typists probably) playing hockey on a patch of grass between the office buildings and the Thames embankment. While we sat waiting in the office of Francis Hemming, the Non-Intervention Secretary, Crolla asked me for the latest news from Rome.

Crolla is tall and pale and lantern-jawed, with a look of expecting the worst. This is the right physique for a diplomat nowadays.

The plump, swarthy, cheery look of old de Soveral, as I remember him at Goodwood, does not go with the times. Nor do foreign diplomats in London make the tour of the clubs, before dining at Court, in order to pick up some amusing stories to tell the King, and keep him in a good humour.

There was a large red book on Hemming's table, written by him : a treatise on Entomology, from which I deduced that his hobby was butterflies (*farfalle sotto l'Arco di Tito*). It is good for a government official to have a hobby, to keep him sane. The butterfly mania is a pleasant one. Indeed, there is one butterfly that should figure in the coat-of-arms of every diplomat. I mean the mountain ringlet (*Erebia epiphron*). It is not unknown in England, in the Lake District, above a certain altitude. In colour it is chocolate brown, with dotted orange bands on the wings. I have often seen these butter-flies in the High Alps, flying over the turfy hollows, above the limit of the trees. They can only live near the summits, where—as Goethe says—there is peace (*Ueber allen Gipfeln ist Ruh*).

★　　　★　　　★

During the next two years, you might have met me, most days, going in and out of the Savile. Brook Street is an old haunt of mine, and I had some animal friends in the vicinity. There was Rory, the black poodle with the green collar, who watched the passing show from the top of the area steps at No. 73, and there were the ponies of the ' United Dairies ' : Pansy, and Tom, and Jim. Tom used to beg for lumps of sugar, standing in the shafts, with his forefeet on the pavement in Gilbert Street, while his master distributed milk in the neighbourhood.

The upstair library of the Savile Club, with a southern exposure, is a good place to work in. Its bow-window takes in all the sun there is, and from it one gets a bird's eye view of back-stair diplomacy. For it looks down on Three Kings Yard, behind the houses in Grosvenor Square. There, on a fine morning, one might see the *Cancelliere* of the Italian Embassy, excercising his Peke, by throwing an india-rubber ball for it to run after. Other people would join in the fun : pretty little typists from the American Embassy next door, and good-looking young chauffeurs, who were supposed to be cleaning their cars. The dog and its ball furnished them with an excuse for entering into conversation.

Both the Italian and the American Embassies are occupying new premises, since the day when the Marchese Imperiali represented Italy at No. 22, and Mr. Walter Hines Page represented the United States, at No. 6 Grosvenor Square. No. 22 and neighbouring houses have been knocked down, to make room for a mammoth building in concrete and steel, faced with pink brick and divided into apartments, where hundreds of families eat and sleep and bathe in perfect symmetry, one on top of the other. The American Embassy, at the corner of Grosvenor Street, is also faced with pink brick and surmounted with a hideous green roof. In Berkeley Square and Bruton Street, twenty of Mayfair's best-known houses have been knocked down to make room for a giant, modernistic construction.

I can't honestly say that I recall the days when ' the nightingale sang in Berkeley Square ', but I do remember the house in Bruton Street that belonged to Lord Strathmore, where the present Queen of England lived with her parents, and where the Princess Elizabeth was born. Also Lansdowne House, with its huge dining-room, where the naked statues so shocked the American family, to whom the house was once let, that they fig-leaved them all ! (Since those days, the furnishing of many modern apartments appears to have been given over to what I have heard called ' the inferior decorator '.)

With my recollections of London, I feel like Monsieur Bergeret, when modern ' improvements ' demolished the old Paris of his youth : " . . . *voici que tout ce qui me plaisait dans cette ville, sa grâce et sa beauté, ses antiques élégances, son noble paysage historique, est emporté violemment* ". And I can sympathize with Monsieur Bergeret's dog, Riquet, when they were going to live in a new apartment, and heavy-footed *porteurs* began to carry away the furniture of his old home. For me, the old houses, as for Riquet the old armchair and his master's slippers, were like minor divinities, with a soul of their own. The modern cliff-dwellings, mere *machines à habiter*, have no sentimental appeal ; they merely prove that, after a prolonged struggle, the English—as Osbert Lancaster puts it—have at last become flat minded.

The following is an extract from my Diary, for the first day of my stay in London:

The Club staff at the Savile appears to be much the same as in 1935. Lawrence, the hall-porter, still wages incessant warfare with the page-boys in buttons. And in the corridor on the second floor, I met Old Louie. She is a superannuated housemaid, and even when I was here last, the Club Secretary admitted that he would have liked to get rid of her, but lacked courage to do so.

Old Louie is a little morsel of a woman, who by virtue of some imaginary Statute of Limitations, claims proprietary rights in the upstair rooms and guest-rooms, and she upholds these rights against the world. She has untidy hair, and is often grimy, after polishing the grates. Nevertheless, I have noticed occasionally a certain ill-advised gaiety in her raiment. Anyway, her heart (though lacking the initial *h*) is in the right place. She is continually moving small articles of furniture from one guest-room to another, in the hope of pleasing the occupants. But she is subject to fits of absent-mindedness. On one occasion, when I was staying in a guest-room, I found, on going to bed, instead of a hot-water bottle between the sheets, one of those steel instruments that, lacking a self-starter, are used for cranking up motor-cars. Why Old Louie should have had such an instrument in her possession is a mystery, like those of the Eleusians.

Having exchanged civilities with Old Louie, I went down to the dining-room. It being Good Friday, there were only two people there, besides myself: Gerald Horner, who runs some medical magazine, and H. G. Wells. I noticed that the latter was greeted by Frank (the wine-waiter) with great cordiality. Apparently Wells has just 're-joined' after an interval of twenty-eight years. Thirty years ago, he wrote a book called *Ann Veronica*, which was the beginning of his fame as an author. But both he and Ann's father were members of the Savile, and this led to unpleasantness. So H. G. Wells resigned. Now Ann Veronica's father has died, and the author of the 'Scientific Novels' has come back to the fold. And Frank remembered what he used to drink!

Wells and I sat for some time over our coffee, after lunch, and we got on to the subject of religions. I quoted to him (as typical of a new attitude in the Vatican) Monsignor Costantini's remarks about the gradual fading out of the principal Oriental religions, that once were so powerful in the Far East. In China, for example, Buddhism is on the wane, and many Taoist temples are deserted. Costantini said to me: 'We are the first to deplore this, for every great religion is a manifestation of God, and to see it disappear is mourning for the soul' (*un lutto per l'anima*). H. G. Wells admitted the spiritual value of such tolerance. But he is slightly—or perhaps not so slightly—anti-catholic. Talking with me today, he upheld the theory that the various denominations in England should uphold Communism. 'The eternal discontent in man should be the rock on which to build a church.' But why mix up our belief in God with the various 'isms that afflict the world today ? On the whole, I get on less well with H. G. Wells than with Old Louie, despite her cockney accent and dislocated aspirates. She—I am sure—has none of the communist sympathies that are now so fashionable among British intellectuals and the pink-international members of Gollancz's 'Left Book Club'! Hers is all the traditional British veneration for wealth and rank and titles.

*　　　*　　　*

While living in London, life for me centred round my office and the Clubs ; not only the Savile, but the Athenaeum and the Travellers, to which I was kindly invited. But I missed the old friend who had first introduced me to the Clubland of London. George Street had gone to join the *Ghosts of Piccadilly*, of whom he wrote so delightfully. It was sad not to be able to sit next to him any more, at the end of the long table at the Savile, where he once presided, like the hero of the *Pickwick Papers*, among his devoted fellow-members. He was a typical Englishman, though one of the élite, and most exquisitely civilized. His conversation was scholarly, racy, kindly and lucid, with a flavour of the very best dry sherry. I never heard him say anything dull or ill-natured, or unbalanced. And his wisdom was not complicated by enthusiasms.

I was told that, during most of his lifetime, George Street had very little money. But he lived comfortably enough, for besides his pay as King's Reader of Plays (acting for the Lord Chamberlain), he had his little suite of rooms in St. James's Palace. And he told me, the last time I saw him, that he had inherited a considerable sum from a relative. This must have given him pleasure, for he could leave the money to someone he was fond of.

Of all the similes that are used to define our life on earth (and they are innumerable), one of those I like best is that which compares it to a Roman road, bordered with tombs. For me, the memory of George Street is like one of those stately tombs that, near Rome, stand on either side of the old Appian Way. When I look back, I see it outlined against the sky.

While I was in London, people often asked me what 'Non-Intervention in Spain' really meant. It was not easy to answer, and I generally got out of the difficulty by quoting a remark of my German colleague :

" Non-Intervention is like a bed. The principal powers are quarrelling about Spain. When things begin to look serious—that is to say, when some statesman feels that he had gone too far—he jumps into the Non-Intervention bed, and pulls the bed-clothes over his head. After a bit, he peeps out and looks around. If things are brighter, he jumps out of bed and begins quarrelling with the others again."

Among the ' Humours of Non-Intervention ', I might also mention that in April 1937 there were four masters of British merchantmen, all unwillingly delayed in the harbour of St. Jean de Luz, because they could not force the Spanish blockade of Bilbao. All four mariners boasted the good old name of Jones. They found themselves in the centre of the international stage, under *noms de guerre*, culled from the cargoes that they carried. Hence we had Potato Jones, Corn-cob Jones, and Ham-and-Egg Jones. These sobriquets were not romantic. Potatoes cannot compare with the wealth of the Indies, ivory, apes and peacocks. But they were worth their weight in gold to a beleaguered city.

The more people laughed at Non-Intervention, the better I was pleased. In the opinion of the public at large, it was nothing but an elaborate futility. But an old diplomat like myself could look for realities underneath appearances. Without that seemingly ineffective scheme for international supervision of imports into Spain, Italian troops and French troops might have been fighting on Spanish territory, *under their national flags*. This did not happen. Non-Intervention may have been a fiction and a farce, but it staved off a world conflagration, thanks to our pretending to believe that the fighting forces in Spain, on one side or the other, were made up of ' volunteers '.

It is true that we could not stop any ship that was not flying the flag of a power that was signatory to the Non-Intervention Agreement. We could not stop a Spanish ship, nor a ship flying the flag of the Republic of Panama (and it was extraordinary what a huge mercantile fleet that diminutive state managed to put on the water). But all this was beside the point. What mattered was that, although the civil war in Spain contained the germ of a far larger conflict, we found an expedient that led away from that conflict. What we set up, in London, may have been a sham. Better a sham than war.

My own private opinion of the whole business brought me, at one moment into sharp disagreement with Ciano. I held that we Italians ought to have held aloof, even though we were perfectly justified in opposing the capture, by Communism, of a Mediterranean state. At that time it would have been prudent to avoid stirring up any more ill-feeling against ourselves, among the foreign powers who had opposed our conquest of Abyssinia. I was not alone in expressing these views ; most of the Italian Ambassadors *en poste* abroad thought as I did, and our opinion was shared by the higher naval and military authorities. Activities connected with Spain were more costly to our Navy than the war in Abyssinia had been. We lost no ships, but we consumed a lot of valuable material through what the officers called *logoramento* (deterioration through prolonged use). On land, thousands of young lives were sacrificed for a cause that could not justify the loss. And our support of Franco cost us four billion lire, at a time when the lira was not devalued. For all this we got nothing in return except the ill-will of other nations whose battles—had they only realized it—we were fighting. Even the Spaniards on Franco's side disliked us, being jealous of our power in the Mediterranean.

It was a fact that we were supporting the class of Spaniards that was traditionally most friendly to England, against a communist-ridden class, which both England and France had good reason to fear.

A large section of the British public had been bamboozled into supporting the ' Reds ' in Spain, in the illusion that this meant supporting ' democracy '. They wanted Franco to be beaten, imagining —despite much evidence to the contrary—that the alternative régime was a tolerant, fair-minded one, in which everyone could have his say and count on the protection of the law. This was about as untrue in Spain, in 1937, as it was in Czechoslovakia, in 1948, at the time when Jan Masaryk committed suicide, rather than serve the Eastern form of ' democracy '. Yet, for almost two years, the British government, egged on by its pink internationalists, attitudinized as an opponent of the Falangists, even though Great Britain's economic interests in Spain would not really allow her to antagonize the probable victor. While talking about Right being on their side, they took care to have the Left on their side.

England's foreign policy had suffered many set-backs, and these left behind them a feeling of bitterness that broke out in the form of an anti-Fascist phobia, wherever opportunity offered. The result was that British public opinion was guilty of using two weights and two measures. They abused Mussolini for being a dictator, while they tolerated Stalin. They held up Matteotti as a martyr, because he was murdered by the Fascists, but they would shrug their shoulders if I mentioned Calvo Sotelo, who was murdered by the Spanish Reds, just as Matteotti was, after he had made an inconvenient speech in Parliament. German prosecution of the Jews produced a violent outcry—which was quite right, as far as it went—but hardly any disapproval was shown when hundreds and thousands of defenceless women and children (not to mention thirteen catholic bishops) were dragged from their homes and deliberately slaughtered by the adherents of the 'legitimate' government in Spain. Atrocity stories were accepted when the victims belonged to the tribes of Israel ; they were rejected or ignored, when the victims were catholic priests and nuns. I found it strange (and so did the former Spanish Ambassador in London, Merry del Val) that the British should sympathize with militant atheism, directed from Moscow.

The British public has always been an adept at not seeing what it does not want to see. Like Nelson, the English put the telescope to the blind eye. Few people would believe me, when I said that the Russians had been fomenting a revolution in Spain as far back as 1934, when they were admitted to the League of Nations. Yet the *Revue des Deux Mondes* stated this, in its number of 1st October of that year :

La loi de la Societé des Nations veut que les Etats ne se melent en rien de la politique intérieure de leurs voisins ; or la loi communiste est de fomenter partout des revolutions sociales aboutissant à une dictature du prolétariat. L'Espagne, à l'heure actuelle, n'en est-elle pas menacée ? Des bateaux mistérieux, des agents secrèts, n'y apportent-ils pas des armes, des explosifs, tout l'outillage d'une revolution et d'une guerre civile ?

Here, in an article published in Paris three years before I went to London for Non-Intervention, was an accurate and detailed description of the Moscow-organized preparations for the local disturbance that later gave rise to an international quarrel.

The Times, in a leading article (20th April 1937) described Non-Intervention as ' a novel as well as an important experiment in international co-operation'. The author concluded optimistically that we might be preparing ' a phase of pacification, which should embrace more than Spain itself'. These were Lord Plymouth's views ; it may be that he inspired the article.

But we had our hectic moments. . . . Every now and then it looked as if the French would force our hands by sending a couple of divisions across the Pyrenees. This was suggested, in Paris, several times. But the French Chief of Staff, General Gamelin, would consent to do so only if, at the same time, the army were mobilized on the Alps and on the Rhine. So nothing came of it.

In view of the political situation that arose ten years later, after the second world war, the following prophecy (taken from one of the leftist publications during the Spanish crisis) is not without interest : " We have come to the end of a period of national wars. There will never again be a united nation, fighting against another united nation. War from now on will involve civil war." This production was falsified in 1939 and following years. But some day it may still come true.

The following letter, written by me at that time to Bettina in Rome, is not without interest, even after so many years :

CLARIDGE'S
LONDON, *20th April 1937*

I talked with Grandi, after lunch, about the feeling towards us Italians here in England. He says that the hostility towards us is perhaps greater than it was during the Ethiopian crisis, but the tension is not so acute. He, himself, is less anxious, but finds it more tiring : '*Allora si camminava sulla lama d'un coltello.*' Quite true. In 1935–36 we were walking on the razor-blade summit of a mountain, with deep precipices on either side. Now we are drifting hopelessly on an almost irresistible stream and must go where it takes us. The prolonged tension is producing a fatalistic apathy.

In Downing Street, they want their own way, coupled with a quiet life. These sentiments figure, in their speeches, as ' a profound love of peace '.

It is true that they want peace. But they want it cheap, and they have no ideas of their own. I have met one exception : a Labour Peer, Lord Allen of Churtwood. He says that England should take the initiative in a general settlement, and give up hectic attempts to settle, first one crisis and then another, as they arise. It would be of no use whatever if the initiative came from Germany. Whenever *they* make a proposal (and Lord Allen considered Hitler's offer to rejoin the League of Nations on an equality of status as perfectly reasonable), they are immediately dubbed 'liars' by the B.B.C., and by the French. The British refusal to put forward any positive policy, coupled with abuse and a passive acceptance of German action, is leading us nowhere.

When in conversation with Lord Allen, I quoted a student song that I had learnt in Heidelberg, when Mother and I went there to visit Agnès in her farm. It ran :

> *Und willst du nicht mein Bruder sein,*
> *So schlag' ich dir den Schädel ein !* [1]

This represents the usual attitude of the Germans towards those that will not agree with them. Allen agreed with me that it might be so. German diplomacy is clumsy and heavy-handed. It is a pity that short-sighted governments should remain irreconcilable, for history is there to prove that there are no incompatible nations.

In British military circles, they talk of the next war, as of a receding horizon. It is always to come 'in ten years' time'. The Foreign Office is more pessimistic. They speak of 1939. It is a bad sign when diplomats are oppressed by a pessimistic fatalism, while politicians (those that are in power) have nothing constructive to offer.

There is a red-faced squire at the Savile, rather like Colonel Blimp, who every now and then, while reading the paper, loses patience and exclaims : 'It would be a good thing if we *did* have another war, to be followed by a really democratic peace.' I could not remember the exact words, or I might have quoted Abraham Lincoln, who once said that you cannot fight always, and when, after much loss to both sides, you cease fighting, the identical old questions are again upon you. A similar idea is expressed in a book I am now reading : *Left Wings over Europe*, by Wyndham Lewis. He writes : "The slump after Great War number two, if that comes to pass, will be an all-in slump. The Marxist will have got his savagery and his wilderness—his *tabula rasa*—by the time the last gun has received its 'cease fire'." Wyndham Lewis does not share the belief that once Germany is destroyed, we shall all live happily ever after. And he asks : 'If the Russian steam-roller reaches our frontier, the Rhine . . . what then ?'

Meanwhile, a French diplomat who works with me at the office, Etienne

---

[1] If you won't be my brother, I'll bash in your skull !

de Felcourt, suggests that he and I should sample all the best restaurants in London. *Et apres nous le déluge !* A really sound, practical idea !

* * *

While Non-Intervention was holding the lists in a cockpit, where the major powers fought out their quarrels by proxy, friends of mine from distant lands would write letters to me, which showed that I was considered as the hero in a novel by John Buchan : a modest individual, but deep in international intrigues, from which, after incredible adventures and hairbreadth escapes, he clasps the girl of his heart to his bosom, and saves the peace of Europe. The girl, in my case, did not materialize, nor did I save the peace of Europe. I suppose I was too old.

Meanwhile, a side-issue of the Spanish conflict gave rise to a controversy in which I could take no part. The same humanitarian feelings that, in my youth, had urged me to champion the cause of Italian children in French glass-factories, would have drawn me to do my best for Spanish children during the civil war. I knew what they had suffered during the retreat from Malaga. The tragedy of that six days march, under shell-fire, was heart-breaking to anyone whose sensibilities were not blunted by political passion. This being so, I was much astonished at the criticisms levelled against the charitable people who organized a camp near Southampton, where the Basque children might find a refuge. On the other hand I was not surprised to hear that the philanthropic English guardians, who perhaps were unused to dealing with southern children, had a lively time looking after them, and considered them perfect little devils. Some of my sympathies were due also to the Duke of Alva, and his young collaborator, Prince Pio Falcò. For these two kind men, the Basque children created a real hornet's nest.

* * *

During the time when I was busy with Non-Intervention, the family was much scattered. But communications were so easy that we saw a lot of each other, and I was continually getting messages suggesting that we should foregather in Paris (where Diana was studying dancing, with the Russian ballet), or else warning me to expect an invasion of daughters in London.

One day a huge young man arrived up at the Savile and addressed me in French. After a moment's doubt, I recognized the Baron Antoine Allard, a friend of Diana's, whom she had first met at the Lido. He said that his wife was arriving in London next day, and that Diana might be coming too, with the idea of staying with me. They had all been together at Regenboog, in Flanders, where he had a cottage. He added that he had been painting and that Diana had posed for him part of the time.

I wanted a portrait of Diana, and as she failed to turn up in London, I wrote to her, to ask if she thought Antoine Allard would let me have the picture of her, that he had painted at Regenboog. She answered promptly to say that the picture in question could hardly be described as a portrait of her. She had posed as Jesus Christ ! Not all the time, but alternately with a Dutch sailor, who was too muscular to serve as a good model for Our Lord. So I had to look elsewhere for a portrait of Diana. In the end, I got one. But again, she posed as a member of the opposite sex ! This time as Hamlet, in a costume she had worn at a fancy-dress ball at the German Embassy in Rome. The artist was Uberto Pallastrelli, who was then the fashion in London, and who painted portraits of the Duke of Westminster, and other notabilities. He did a fine picture of Diana, in black and grey and white, with only one touch of colour, in the lips.

★   ★   ★

Bettina and our youngest daughter, Gianmarina, came over twice to see me in London. The first time was when I had been suddenly taken ill, and was lying in hospital at St. John's Wood.

Gianmarina's obvious delight at the sudden journey, that took her away from school, reminded me of a joke that appeared in the *Journal Amusant*, at the time when the Institut Pasteur was first opened in Paris. A young French girl, somewhere in the provinces, rushes excitedly into the room where her sisters are busy sewing : ' Marie ! Juliette ! Such a piece of luck ! Papà has been bitten by a mad dog, and we are all going to Paris ! '

The following letter of mine to Margherita was written during convalescence, from the Beresford Hotel, at Birchington :

Your mother and Gianmarina have brought me down to the seaside, to recuperate. I miss our own hot sands, on which to lie all day under a real sun, but this is very pleasant, and the Kentish gardens look as if they were loved (there is a great difference between a garden that is loved and one that is merely kept).

Our rooms on the ground floor have glass doors that open straight out on grass-covered cliffs. We get out of bed in the morning and stroll to the edge, and look down on the sea, while mendicant gulls fawn round us, with white wings curving. At night, distant lights flash on the horizon : light-houses and light-ships, and beacons, marking the traffic-route from the North Foreland up into the mouth of the Thames.

Gianmarina has learnt to play croquet and makes me help her build castles on the sands, which the incoming tide promptly wipes out : a symbol of my achievements in other spheres. She has also discovered an earthly Paradise, which one can go to by motor-bus, and is called Margate. You hire little motor boats there, built expressly for children, and padded all round with old motor-tyres. She has already spent innumerable sixpences, navigating these vessels during successive laps of ten minutes each.

We have also been to Canterbury, and Gianmarina suggests that I should be buried in the Cathedral, along with the Black Prince and Thomas à Becket. She may not be wrong. If I am to stay in England till conditions in Europe settle down peaceably, it might be a good idea to look about for a cemetery.

Filippo Doria has a cottage here, but he is in Rome at present. And there is a bungalow where Dante Gabriele Rossetti died in 1882. Literary memoirs will hardly interest you, but you would like the characteristic British village, with its typical country station and array of little shops down the High Street ; the chime of Sabbath bells on a summer morning, and the ' little golden bells ' (as the Chinese would say) which are the larks. Also the wafts of clover from the meadows, mingling with a smell of sea-weed in the breeze.

The countryside is very unlike ours. Agriculture (in the shape of ploughed fields and vineyards) does not come right up to your door. A British nobleman's country-seat must have its park. These mani-cured acres remind me of a beautiful lady who does not want to have children.

Gianmarina's English is fluent, but peculiar. She calls the Marble Arch ' il *Mabelaccio* ', and she has come to the conclusion that England is a very Fascist country, much more so than Italy. She saw a notice on some trees : BIRD-NESTING STRICTLY PROHIBITED. Her comment was : ' Even

the birds here are not allowed to build their nests where they want to ! '
Love from us all to yourself and to the children. . . .

My next letter to Margherita was written from London, after our
return there. For her edification, I recounted a small episode that
occurred before the Coronation decorations had been taken down
in Oxford Street. This is what I wrote :

I had been to buy two straps for Gianmarina to wear with her johdpur
breeches, and was coming out of the saddler's shop in North Audley Street,
when I noticed a group of children on the opposite side of the road, playing
in the porch of the little church of St. Mark's. There were six children, four
boys and two girls. When I first noticed them they were all standing stock-
still in rather constrained attitudes, and the boy in the foreground had taken
his right arm out of his jacket and had pinned the loose sleeve across his chest.
After one brief moment, the group broke up like a flight of sparrows and the
children ran off.

I walked on to post a letter in the Air-mail pillar box at the corner of Orchard
Street, and was walking back, the way I came, when I saw the same group of
children scampering on ahead of me. To my surprise, they turned in once
more to the porch of St. Mark's, and after some arguing among themselves
remained for a few seconds silent and motionless. The boy who had worn
his empty sleeve pinned across his chest, now appeared to be riding an imaginary
horse, and he held his cap at arm's length in front of him. The other children
were lined up in the background, in two rows. . . .

And then it dawned upon me what it was all about ! The children were
acting, for their own edification and pleasure, the historical scenes that were
depicted in bas-relief on Selfridge's Coronation panels. There are eighteen
of these scenes, framed among the pilasters of that monumental shopping
centre, and they are silvered over, though the silver is beginning to look a bit
dingy.

When I first saw the children from over the way, they were representing
Nelson at Trafalgar. In the second of their *tableaux vivants*, they were imper-
sonating Wellington at Waterloo. The little boy with the cap might have
been saying : ' Up, Guards, and at them ! '

Once more the children scattered. I waited a few minutes, but they
did not come back. So I strolled up the steps into the porch, and began
to read a mural tablet, that is let into the wall, to the right as you enter the
church.

Sacred to the Memory of

LIEUTENANT GENERAL SIR HUDSON LOWE, K.C.B., G.C.M.G.

Knight of the Red Eagle and Military Order of Merit of Prussia
St. George of Russia and Crescent of Turkey
Colonel of the 50th Queen's Own Regiment

After having served his country uninterruptedly from 1787 to 1815 including active
service in Corsica, Egypt, defence of Capri, capture of Ionian Islands, and the
campaigns of 1813–1814 with the Allied Army under Marshal Blucher, he was
selected for the onerous task of Governor of St. Helena
during the captivity of

NAPOLEON

His obedience to the orders of Government in the fulfilment of this harrassing duty
earned for him the approbation of his sovereign
But exposed him ever afterwards to persecution and calumny and more than once
his life to be endangered

History will do justice to a brave man and zealous officer and an upright and faithful
servant of his country

Born 28th July 1769 — Died 10th January 1844

Strange—is it not?—that the children should have chosen to impersonate Nelson and Wellington, just above that grave.

As the Shadows Lengthen

THE summer of 1938 was drawing to its close, and I had taken Bettina and Gianmarina to Baveno. But meanwhile the political situation had become so tense that I thought it better to return to London. If war had broken out, it would have been up to me to get the foreign personnel of 'Non-Intervention' safely home.

Here below are some extracts from my Diary during that hectic time.

THE 'DAYS OF MUNICH'

Saturday, 24th September—(Claridge's, London). I came back here in a hurry, two days ago, and last night I slept badly, owing to the news on the 'ticker' downstairs. It read as if Chamberlain were coming back from Berchtesgarten, having received a rebuff, and that negotiations were broken off. This morning, things looked a little better, but nothing to be pleased about. People who hold quite reasonable views are beginning to lose patience, and to say that war might be a solution after all. The utterly abnormal heat and stuffiness seem to accentuate the feeling of anxiety. I do nothing but perspire.

Monday, 26th September. Lunched yesterday at the Belgian Embassy. There was a painted, tedious woman sitting opposite me. She said that, if there came to be a war, she would have to shut up her London house, which cost her nine thousand a year and gave her no satisfaction. She seemed to think that this economy would justify another war.

I walked home through the Park with Mary, Lady Howe (this seems to be the right way to call her. She is the best-looking woman I have met for some time). The soap-box orators were in great force, telling us what should be done. 'Stop Hitler and act for peace.' Quite easy, of course !

Wishing to go to High Street, Kensington, I took a No. 30 bus in Park Lane, and discussed with the conductor where I should get out. A lady leaned across and asked me : ' Do you mind a short war ? '

An odd thing to ask a perfect stranger, but I answered : ' Oh, dear no.' ' Because, if you did, No. 24 bus would be better.'

She had said ' walk ', not ' war '. But we all have war on the brain.

The Italian waiters at Claridge's tell me that they are on tenterhooks (' *Siamo tutti sulle spine !* '). So is Grandi, for that matter. And so am I. So are my German colleagues in London. They tell me that nobody in Germany wants war with England, or any war at all. Unfortunately their masters in Berlin belong to that type of statesman whose ambitions thrive on tension.

I gave old Frank, the wine-waiter at the Savile, a copy of *Laughing Diplomat*, for I had mentioned him in it. He thanked me and said :

' Have you seen Mr. Compton Mackenzie's book, Sir ? He also mentions me.'

He paused and then added : ' *That's* an eighteen-shilling book, Sir ! '
I am not quite up to Frank's standard.

Wednesday, 28th September. The atmosphere yesterday in the House of Commons was very similar—so they tell me—to that of August 1914, when Sir Edward Grey was speaking. I listened in from the library of the House of Lords, where they had installed an amplifier, connected with a microphone that was placed in front of Mr. Chamberlain. He paid tribute to Mussolini's intervention, to which was due the postponement of German mobilization for 24 hours. Applause in the House interrupted the speech for some minutes, and during this pause came an aside that, thanks to the microphone, *we* heard but the House itself did not. A type-written sheet was handed in, and passed from Lord Dunglass (parliamentary secretary to the Prime Minister) to Sir John Simon, and from him to Mr. Chamberlain. The latter asked the question : ' Shall I tell them now ? ' Sir John Simon answered : ' Yes '.

Thus encouraged, Chamberlain told the House of the invitation, extended to himself and to Monsieur Daladier, to meet the Duce and the Führer in Munich. The conclusion of his speech was to have been a further appeal for peace. But this was left out.

Yesterday evening, we heard, here in London, that an agreement had been reached. Last night I could not sleep, through sheer relief.

Thursday, 29th September. I lunched with H. G. Wells today and we talked about the city's preparations for war, that were reminiscent of the ' handling machines ' he describes in *The War of the Worlds*. There are some strange erections in St. James's Park, called, I believe, ' mechanical navvies '. A huge steel hand-shaped scoop is held by a crane at the end of steel ropes, and jerks about angrily, like a savage dog on the leash. Its steel fingers, or prongs, tear up the soft green turf and the damp earth, collecting them as in the palm of a hand. Then they drop them on a mound near-by. It was horrid to see the grass torn up in that way. Is it true, I wonder, that the lovely clump of trees that crowns Primrose Hill in Hampstead has been cut down ? The big anti-aircraft guns have been roped off in the Park.

All this may have been done, in part, to impress people, and not only people at home. Including ' stand by ' orders to the armed forces, it has cost 40 million pounds in less than a week. As somebody said to me at the Atheneum : ' We've had a dam' good dress-rehearsal ! '

There has been a sort of ' Exodus ' from London. Crowded trains, thronged departure-platforms, piles of trunks and perambulators, hurrying porters, harrassed officials, mothers and nurses carrying babies, husbands bidding farewell to wives and children ; dogs on leads, cats in baskets, canaries and parrots in cages.

George Morrow, just back from Paris, tells me that opinions were divided, but mostly against war ; one aged mother, who had lost three sons in the last war, watching a regiment depart for an unknown destination, while her last remaining son was called up for the reserve . . . A very smart, aristocratic young officer, declaring that all this had been engineered by the Jews and the bourgeoisie. He, for his part, admired the Prussians ; if there had been three million Frenchmen under foreign domination, in some ' Sudeten ' province, would not the world hear a lot about it . . . ; or three million Englishmen ?

Not every one is pleased at the solution. Many people say that Chamberlain has been to Canossa. And the German and Austrian refugees in London are much disappointed. Someone asked a German Jew if he were going home in the event of war. He answered : ' No ! ' He means to sit tight in a comfortable concentration camp in England.

Friday, 30th September. *The Times* has an editorial in which it points out that the nickname of ' The Big Four ', given to the statesmen gathered in

Munich, stirs a chord of significant memory. It recalls the negotiation in Paris in 1919.

This time, however, there is no American Delegate, and Russia also is absent, as she was then. *The Times* seems to think that this is all to the good. It implies that not to have admitted Germany, on a par with the others, during the negotiations for the Peace of Versailles, was a mistake and 'responsible for the fact that Germany had been left to press revision on the rest. If the present negotiations can be regarded as at least a step towards substituting an agreed peace for an imposed peace, then they yet come to be regarded as heralding the emergence of a more normally stabilized Europe.'

So we hear again the opinion that it was the presence of the Americans among the belligerents that led to an 'imposed', instead of a 'negotiated' peace. Consequently it is now hoped that the Americans and the Russians will keep out of European politics and mind their own business.

Needless to say, if war *had* broken out in these days, *The Times* editorials would have declared the opposite, and told everybody that the democratic states (Russia included !) must stand or fall together !

Tuesday, 11th October. A short time ago, I happened to go in to the Athenæum for lunch, very early, on a Saturday. I sat at a little table against the wall, between two windows. The place is always pretty empty on a Saturday, and at that hour (before one) I was quite alone in the dining-room.

A distinguished-looking, rosy-cheeked old Bishop came in. He wore spectacles, of which one of the glasses was darkened. He chose to sit at a table close to mine. Encouraged by his benevolent expression, I ventured on a remark. I said : 'We seem to have the place to ourselves !'

He did not answer in words, but smiled courteously and pointed to a table near us, where the chairs had been placed, leaning forward, showing that that table was reserved. Nothing more was said.

After a bit, owing to some awkward movement, my neighbour upset his little carafe of white wine. Now, at least, I said to myself, I shall hear his voice. But no. He said nothing. Only when a waiter passed by, he pointed at the table-cloth. And the mess was cleaned up.

In the hermitage of Camaldoli, there is an Englishman who has not spoken to anybody for thirty years. Evidently a former member of the Athenæum.

Now I come to the point of this story. During the recent crisis, the political tension in London has been so acute that an old gentleman in the Athenæum actually spoke to me ! He asked if the Club was preparing an anti-aircraft shelter. I answered : 'Yes. In the billiard-room, down in the basement, and in the corridor where the bound collection of *The Times* is kept.'

Today I lunched at Lady Howe's, and sat opposite the picture of her by Laszlö. I had my eyes on it all the time, and could hardly attend to the conversation. There were two ambassadors at table—France and Belgium—

Corbin and Cartier. Corbin was looking very glum, but cheered up a little, when I reminded him of the days when we used to play tennis in Rome, with Bettina and the two de Martinos. He resumed his dolorous expression, when discussing with Hore-Belisha the sad business of Flandin having telegraphed congratulations to Hitler, over the happy solution of the crisis.

We spoke of the impending horror that had oppressed us all, last week. Our hostess said to Cartier : ' Do you know ? When Varè and I came out from your luncheon party two Sundays ago, we walked in the Park together, and we both felt a little sick.'

Cartier answered gravely : ' I always tell the cook not to put so much butter in the French beans ! '

A TRIP TO PARIS

It cannot be long before everyone travels by air, and a description of a journey, by train or ocean-liner, will read like the descriptions of journeys by coach and diligence, such as Mother took in her youth.

Even I look back with a certain nostalgia to the old second-class railway carriages, lit by a hooded lamp with a trembling flame and a residue of oil slopping about in the concave glass beneath it. And the early-morning start from a country railway-station, in November : the rain beating on the carriage-windows ; the click of the guard's puncheon as he clips the cardboard ticket ; the doleful clang of a steel hammer, testing couplings and axles. And a white face against the darkness of the compartment, as the train moves off . . .

One may recapture something of the old feeling (as described in a poem of Carducci's and by Max Beerbohm in *Ichabod*) in the departure of the night express from Victoria, when the porter slaps a label on the luggage, indicating a destination that lies not only in the distance, but in the future. With the pasting of that label, part of one's soul is already wafted to Paris.

Not many of us now taste the joy of morning hours, after a cup of steaming coffee and crisp rolls at Dieppe, when one enters the dun-coloured coupé, with Chemins de Fer de l'Ouest, perforated on the antimacassars.

Max Beerbohm scorns the sleeping-car, but I was delighted to discover the Ferry-Train from London to Paris and back. Let hurried financiers take the plane to Le Bourget, and go and come between breakfast and tea-time. I love the long platform, the burnished rails, and the big, blue carriages, with my bed already made and waiting. No need to hurry through the wicket-gate, long before the time scheduled for departure. I can linger at the bookstall, or stroll along to look at the engine, with steam hissing round its cylinders and twin lamps sending bars of light into the gloom, under the iron bridge.

And when the train has started, and is moving warily out among interlocked points and signals, how pleasant to prop the bed-cushions up against the metal partition, and look out on the lights of London : garlands of stars, yellow, blueish and sea-green, like incandescent aquamarines.

And again, how pleasant, on waking, to look out over the French countryside, the fen around Amiens, with its tiny lakes and its peat-cutters ; the silver poplars at Chantilly, and the brown woods of Creil !

There is a long entry in my Diary, written on the Ferry-Train, during the return journey, after a trip to Paris. I had been over to see Diana, who had taken a studio in the Rue Lota, near the Étoile, to practice her dancing in.

> (Ferry Train, 8 a.m.—after breakfast
> in the restaurant-car)
> *Thursday, 17th November 1938*

We should be in London in little more than an hour. I imagine that what I see out of the windows is the Weald of Kent. I caught a glimpse of labourers heaping apples into a cart (cider-apples probably), and of gentlemen in sporting attire popping off their guns at something : partridge, or perhaps pheasants.

Diana had a lovely studio in Paris ; one huge downstair room, like a small cathedral. You go down some steps to it from the front door (passing a tiny kitchen, on your right) ; a spiral wooden staircase in the opposite corner leads up to bedroom and bathroom. And that's all. But the windows are huge, and the heating excellent. The mantelpiece covered with photographs of Serge Lifar and other shining lights of the Ballets Russes, not to mention Diana herself.

The domestic staff consists of Victorine (a maid, from Luxembourg), who comes in and sews, and mends, and irons ; and a Russian colonel, who also comes in with a broom and a Basque cap, and goes about humming to himself, but looking inexpressibly sad. I spoke to him, but he took no notice. Diana says he never does, but he helps her paint the unvarnished deal cupboards, chairs and tables, that she has bought at the Printemps and at the Magazin du Louvre. She is painting them in modernistic style, to match her crétonne curtains.

Diana says that the Russian colonel goes out on service to escape from his wife, who makes life a burden to him at home. She (Diana) first met him at Chialiapine's house, in company with the Grand Duke André. On religious festivals, they all foregather in the Russian church, and eat cake, and hold lighted candles, and kiss each other on the left shoulder, grand-dukes, dancers, chauffeurs and retired colonels.

It seemed to me that everybody took a hand in cleaning Diana's studio for her : Victorine, and Victorine's husband and their seven children, besides the colonel and sometimes the colonel's wife. Then there is a boy from the dairy near-by, who is in love with Diana, and brings her more milk than she's entitled to. Her dog, Aras, is no longer there. She left him in Italy, the last time she went home.

Walking under the arcades of the Rue de Rivoli, I met Camille Barrère. His reddish beard is almost grey. We hailed each other with that enthusiasm that is characteristic of former diplomats, when on the shelf. And we crossed into the Tuileries Gardens and sat on a bench in the sun, talking over old times, when he was Ambassador in Rome, and we rode together in the campagna, or made music in the Palazzo Farnese. Barrère possesses a Stradivarius that makes me break the tenth commandment, every time I think of it.

Barrère was too good a representative of France to be also a good friend of ours, while we were part of the Triple Alliance, but he knows his Italy well. And naturally, we talked shop. We agreed that only recently—that is to say, in 1935—had there been signs of a real *rapprochement* between our two countries, and that had been spoilt by England's insisting on imposing ' sanctions ' on us, during the Ethiopian conflict. The French had fallen into line, but most unwillingly and with rancorous abuse of the English.

Barrère has not a high opinion of either British or Italian politicians. He maintains that the former are short-sighted : ' *Parmi les dons que la destinée a repartis à la nation anglaise, elle en a omis un, pour fixer les bornes de sa puissance : celui de prévoir.*' On the other hand, speaking of Italo-French relations, he mentioned that, during all the long years he was in Rome, he had always found himself up against *une sorte d'ineptitude franco-italienne à degager les points sur lesquels on peut s'accorder, pour en faire des bases d'une politique commune.*

The nations should begin by seeking out the points on which they can agree, and should build upon them a common policy that, in time, and in favourable circumstances, could be enlarged till it covers more and more ground. Here is the very essence of patient, constructive, foreign politics. Instead of which, what do we see, all around us ? Nothing but long-distance bombardments of mutual abuse on the radio ; press-campaigns of hatred and suspicion ; economic aggression that is nothing but war in masquerade.

It is a relief, occasionally, to talk to a real diplomat, and not to people whose main object in life would seem to be to find ' news-value ' in foreign events, and whose judgment is often blurred by the assumption that foreign statesmen are all extremely clever and extremely wicked. We Italians, of course, are sinister people, brought up on Machiavelli's *Principe*. We are regarded, especially in Anglo-Saxon countries, much as the Italian followers of Catherine and Maria de Medicis were regarded by the jealous courtiers at the Court of France. And people resent, in us, the one quality, for which perhaps we *do* resemble Machiavelli : a certain intellectual honesty about political dishonesty. French diplomats possess this quality even more than we do. There is a certain frankness in Barrère's conversation—at least with me—that would astonish people whose profession consists in distorting the news ! It is true, however, that, when on active service, he was more reserved.

Last night, before I came away, Diana and I partook of *fillets de sole* at the Grill of the Hôtel Crillon, and then she came to see me off at the Gare du Nord. We were surprised to find that the outer platform, where the taxi-cabs draw up, was smothered in flowers. The body of von Rath, the German Embassy official who has been assassinated by some fanatical Jewish boy, was being taken back to Germany. The police feared a riot, and were out in great force. On closer inspection, we found that there were machine-guns under the flowers.

Waiting for the railway-guard to shout *En voiture !* Diana and I admired the Whistler-like effects of the foggy darkness and the red lights in couples, repeated in the distance ; the white arc-lamps high up under the station roof ; the huge engine of my train, puffing black smoke and white steam. I looked around for a drinking fountain, for I felt thirsty. Diana remarked : ' Do you imagine that, in Paris, you can get a glass of water *for nothing*? '

Meanwhile, here are the suburbs of London. We are nearing the river. There are the twin chimney-stacks of the Battersea electric plant. . . .

ISRAEL IN ITALY

. . . Mussolini's reply was :

' There are no pure races left ; not even the Jews have kept their blood unmingled. Successful crossings have often promoted the energy and the beauty of a nation. Race ! It is a feeling, not a reality ; or at least, 95 per cent of it is a feeling. . . . National pride has no need of the delirium of race. Anti-semitism does not exist in Italy. Italians of Jewish birth have shown themselves good citizens, and they fought bravely in the war. Many of them occupy leading positions in the Universities, in the Army, in the Banks. Quite a number of them are Generals. Modena, the Commandant in Sardinia, is a general of artillery, and he is a Jew.

EMIL LUDWIG, *Talks with Mussolini* (1932).

The English papers seized upon the publication of my *Laughing Diplomat*, in the autumn of 1938, to point out that the policy of the

Italian Government did not meet with the approval of the author, at least in one particular ; that is to say in the Jewish Question. I can only confirm that these papers were perfectly right, even though what happened to the Jews in Italy cannot compare with what went on in Germany and Austria. Mussolini's consent to harden his heart, like Pharaoh, against the Children of Israel, convinced me that he was no longer the man I had known when he first came into power. I had positive proof that he was acting against his own former convictions ; which could only mean that he was falling under the ill-omened influence of Hitler.

I never made a secret of my own opinions, and it was only natural that the British Press should comment on the antithesis between what I wrote and what was being said, officially, in Italy. *The Times* of the 27th September published an article called ' Italian Diplomat ', in which it quoted a conversation of mine with Lord Balfour, during the meeting of the ' Supreme Council ' at San Remo, in the early spring of 1920. While strolling on the terrace of the Villa Devachan, we had talked about the project of a Jewish National Home. I said that there was no Jewish question in Italy, and that Italians did not consider the Jew as an ' eternal alien ', as people did elsewhere. Twelve years later, Mussolini said much the same thing to Emil Ludwig.

But when refugees from Germany began to flow into other countries, they created a Jewish question where such problems, until then, had been unknown. The numerical factor is one of the greatest importance. In his book, *The Hapsburg Monarchy*, Wickham Steed dedicated some forty pages to the problem as it once existed in Austria-Hungary, and he summarizes it all in the words of a Jewish shop-keeper : " When there are two or three families of Jews in a village, things go well and there is a living for everybody. But when others come, there is competition, and the peasants hate us."

In Italy, the policy of the open door was maintained under the Fascist régime, even after the influx of Jews had begun to cause some uneasiness.

Count Cesare Majoni, our Ambassador in Warsaw, told me that he had been disagreeably impressed by the great number of visas conceded by our Consular Authorities in Poland to Jewish students, going to study in Italian universities. He suspected that many of these might be communist agents of propaganda, and he advised his subordinates to be careful. A month of two later, he received a despatch from Rome, telling him that the ' Rector Magnificus ' of the University of Padua had protested against the curtailing of the inflow of Jewish students from Poland. The Government also supported the view that the ancient Italian universities should remain, as they had always been, free to all.

The same Count Majoni represented Italy in the International Commission that was instituted for the purpose of coming to the aid of refugees from Germany. This Commission held its initial meetings at Geneva, but later moved to London. The Chairman was an American ; the British representative was Lord Robert Cecil. The idea was mooted of using certain buildings that had once belonged to the Customs and had remained empty after the removal elsewhere of the old Austro-Italian frontier. A centre for chemical works was to have been created there, under Jewish direction and with Jewish personnel, recruited from among the refugees out of Germany. No objection was made to their entry into Italy, as long as they did not belong to a class of labourers that might come into competition with Italian labourers of the same class. It was also proposed that young Jewish refugees should be educated for the sea, in training-ships at Livorno.

In the early spring of 1933, soon after Hitler's ' proclamation ' that started the anti-Jewish campaign in Germany, Doctor Chaim Weizmann, Chief of the Zionist Executive, came to Rome to see Mussolini and possibly to enlist his help. It so happened that I went to see Mussolini the same day, and when I arrived at the Palazzo Venezia, Weizmann was closeted with the Duce. I conversed for a while with the Jewish Rabbi in Rome, who was waiting in the little antechamber. I knew Weizmann slightly, and when he came out, I took the opportunity of exchanging a few words with him. While we talked, a batch of English school-girls were ushered into Mussolini's presence, shepherded by a nun. I put no questions to Weizmann, but he volunteered that he had been cordially received.

This did not surprise me, for I happened to know that, only three weeks before, Mussolini had advised Hitler to go no further with his campaign against the Jews in Germany, pointing out that it would arouse antagonism all the world over. Certain precautions—so Mussolini said—might be taken to limit the activities of the Jews, but they should be *semplici misure di difesa* (' mere measures of defence ') and need not be based on a question of ' race '. Italy had been the object of unfriendly campaigns, engineered by the Jews abroad. She had met them by answering calumny with an exposition of the truth, or by an attitude of indifference.

I may add that Mussolini's advice to Hitler, to revoke his ' proclamation against the Jews ', was contained in a telegram, dated 31st March 1933, to our Ambassador in Berlin, Vittorio Cerruti, who, himself, had suggested to the Duce that a word of warning from him might have the effect of obtaining the withdrawal of the order. This order had been inspired by the editor of *Der Stuermer*, that is to say by Streicher, who had persuaded Hitler to authorize the boycotting of all shops owned by Jews, as well as the exclusion of the latter from schools, libraries, theatres, cafès, etc.

Mussolini immediately accepted Cerruti's suggestion, and gave him instructions to go in person, to see Hitler, and to give him a friendly warning against his ill-advised policy.

Before the interview with Hitler, Cerruti spoke with von Papen and von Neurath. They told him that Marshal von Hindenburg had attempted, during an interview that had lasted over one hour, to induce Hitler to desist from the action proposed. The Marshal had even mentioned the 12,000 Jews that had died for the Fatherland during the first world war. But the Führer was obdurate. He would not listen to reason. It might be that a word of caution from a friendly foreign source might succeed, where others had failed, and obtain the recall of the ill-omened instructions.[1]

Hitler had put off a Council of Ministers, to receive the Italian Ambassador, and he greeted Cerruti with great cordiality. He listened in silence up till the point, in Mussolini's message, where the Duce suggested moderate measures in dealing with the Jewish problem. Then he interrupted to declare indignantly that no excesses had been committed in Germany against the Jews. He gave as a reason for

---

[1] Former Ambassador, Vittorio Cerruti, published an article concerning his interview with Hitler, on the Jewish question, in the *Stampa* of Turin, and the *Tempo* of Rome (15th September 1945).

his boycotting the German Jews the fact that the Jews abroad had unjustly boycotted Germany and the Germans. It was his mission to rid Central Europe from the pest of Bolshevism, and it was the Jews who carried the contagion with them. The boycott, already initiated in Germany, would not necessarily last more than a few days. By then it would obtain the desired effect of silencing the calumnies of Jews abroad.

Cerruti went on reading Mussolini's message to the end, while the Führer showed signs of a growing irritation. Finally he broke out in a furious diatribe, affirming that, with all the admiration and sympathy he felt for Mussolini, he must point out that Italy was perhaps fortunate in having very few Jews, and for this reason the Duce evidently did not understand the situation at all. 'You are to be congratulated on your immunity from the contagion, but it is quite clear that you do not perceive the danger represented by the connection between Hebraism and Bolshevism. I possess precise and recent information, that proves how even the United States of America will soon have to face this grave problem, in order to free themselves from the Marxist peril. They will be obliged, in America, to have recourse to methods that will be far more energetic than those adopted by me.'

Statesmen will sometimes uphold one thesis in their official correspondence, and its opposite in private conversation. Mussolini himself was often guilty of this double-mindedness. But, in the year 1933, he confirmed, in conversation, the ideas that he had instructed Cerruti to put before the Führer. That same spring (I don't remember the date), von Papen and his wife came to Italy for a holiday at Sorrento. When passing through Rome, they were asked to dinner by Mussolini, who spoke to Madame von Papen about the Jewish question. They conversed in French (she came from Alsace-Lorraine), and they both deplored the anti-Jewish campaign in Germany. With extraordinary frankness, Mussolini admitted that he, himself, had Jewish connections in his wife's family. Probably he was alluding to an aunt of Donna Rachele, who lived in Alessandria, in Piedmont. She was a Jewess, and in former days, when Mussolini was working out a sentence of three months imprisonment, his wife and children took refuge with this aunt.

The Jewish question is like Pandora's box ; when you open it, all sorts of things fly out, till nothing is left but hope. All through my diplomatic career, this question cropped up to bother me, in one form or another.

When travelling abroad—a thing I was always doing—I had frequent occasions to observe, and sometimes to resent, the hostility shown by Jewish financiers towards my country. At the bottom of it was a question of money and of investments.

All nations possess the right (as long as they can exercise it) of keeping out of debt to the foreigner. But if everybody kept out of debt, where would the money-lender come in ? The Jews, in Great Britain and in America, were, in my time, the great money-lenders of the world. Now, the profession seems to have been adopted also by Gentile financiers, but the trouble remains.

The internal indebtedness of a country leads to a redistribution of wealth as between its own citizens ; it is no drain on the wealth of the nation. But when a debt is a foreign one, the interest on the loans, bonds or direct investments, flows out of the country into the coffers of the foreign banks and capitalists, and the wealth of the debtor is slowly but steadily transferred to the creditor country.

It was in the years 1920, '21, '22, that, in the intention of certain international financiers, Italy was to be reduced to the status of a proletarian state, working to enrich the foreigner. Excluded from a just share in the African colonial empire, which France and England reserved for their exclusive benefit, and from other colonial territories rich in the raw materials she lacks, Italy was to pay interest on the international loans she would be forced to accept, when anti-immigration laws and prohibitive preferential tariffs deprived her of the possibility of exporting goods and services to the extent required to pay for her essential imports.

In the early twenties, the invasion of Italy by foreign capital had begun in earnest ; loans were being made to Italian municipalities, bonds were being floated in London and New York markets to finance her leading industries, there was serious danger that her hydroelectric plants, her telephones, her subsidiary railways would become mortgaged to foreign bondholders. This campaign was conducted on the specious plea that the intention was to help Italy after the war. What could be more plausible than the claim that a timely loan of money would be beneficial to the recipient?

> 'Will you walk into my parlour?' said a Spider to a Fly;
> ''Tis the prettiest little parlour that ever you did spy.'

Italy's plight, after the first world war, was in no way comparable to her condition after the second. And Mussolini's government saw the danger. Timely preventive measures were taken. A law was enacted requiring government consent for foreign loans, a consent which was not granted, and the securities which had been issued abroad were gradually repurchased and repatriated. But not without provoking the spiteful animosity of those financial circles which had been thwarted. The policy of protecting Italy against inroads of foreign usury, the insistence on freedom from foreign debt, was one of the leading causes of the Press and propaganda campaign conducted in the British Empire and in the United States against Fascist Italy.

And for this, certain Jewish communities abroad were largely responsible. The Jews in Italy were the first victims.

On my return to Rome, after a long journey abroad, I went to see the old Senator Teodoro Mayer, whom I had first met in the house of Ernesto Nathan. Mayer was a true patriot, if ever there was one, and I thought it my duty to warn him of the danger that any undeserved hostility, shown to us by the Jews in foreign countries, might provoke a reaction in Italy, a reaction from which many worthy Italian citizens of Jewish persuasion would inevitably suffer. Mayer told me that a Jewish paper, published in Paris, had already given an identical warning (I have forgotten the name of the paper he mentioned, but I think it was *L'Univers*).

*   *   *

Mussolini's change of policy and his decision to follow Hitler's example in persecuting the Jews deprived Italy of one of the world's leading scientists : the Nobel Prize winner in physics, Enrico Fermi. He had a strain of Jewish blood in his veins. So did Germany lose by the expatriation of Lise Meitner, a woman who might be compared to Madame Curie. The studies of these two expatriates were continued in America and led to a crowning success in atomic research.

The fatal miscalculation that induced Mussolini to follow in Hitler's footsteps put an end to the project of offering to the Jews of the contemporary διασπορά, a new Land of Canaan in our recently acquired Ethiopian Empire. *The Times* announced what might have been the solution of a world problem, in a telegram from Rome, dated 7th September 1938, with the heading " Italian Home for Jews " :

The omission of Italian East Africa from the Italian territories from which foreign Jews are to be expelled appears after all to have been no oversight. It is now stated, on good authority, that the area has been fixed, and that it possesses agricultural and industrial resources, sufficient to support a considerable population. Foreign Jews will be allowed to emigrate there, after applying for permission, which will be granted without undue difficulty. Italian Jews will be allowed to emigrate there, after applying for permission.

Here we have a new and different aspect of what true Zionists used to call ' the Uganda heresy ', a plan by which the Jews were to be offered, and to accept, hospitality in a foreign colony, rather than insist on making for themselves a national home in Palestine. In his book, *Trial and Error*, Weizmann recalls a conversation on this subject between himself and Lord Balfour. The latter could not understand, at that time, why the Jews should reject the Uganda project. Weizmann said to him :

' Mr. Balfour, supposing I were to offer you Paris instead of London, would you accept it ? '

' But, Dr. Weizmann, we have London.'

' That is true, but we had Jerusalem, when London was a marsh.'

What the Zionists dreamt of was the rebirth of a nation, not merely a haven of refuge.

*　　　*　　　*

In the rivalry between Israel and Ishmael, both Mussolini and Ciano sympathized with the Arabs, and Ciano would have offered to the Jews a refuge, not in the Holy Land, but in Ethiopia. Ciano's convictions, however, were superficial, and he did not often have the opportunity, or the will-power, to carry his point. When the American Ambassador in Rome went to him, to ask that Italy should be represented on an International Commission, to succour and to distribute the refugees that were again pouring out of Germany (mostly Jews), Ciano refused, even though three years before our Ambassador, Majoni, had collaborated in just such a way.

If I remember rightly, Weizmann's original idea of a national home for the Jews in Palestine would have limited their number to one Jew for every two Arabs. This was reasonable. Italians could not but sympathize with the Jewish peasant class that was transforming the arid lands of Palestine into a garden, with that same tenacity that was shown by Italian peasants, in cultivating the waterless lands of Cyrenaica.

*   *   *

The friendly attitude of the Italians, even under Fascist rule (except in as far as we were constrained, for a time, to follow unwillingly the example set by the Führer) became evident once more, after Italy had entered the war. Wherever the Italian army occupied foreign territory, in France, in Jugoslavia and in Greece, the Jewish community was protected, despite the irate protests of the Germans and of Ribbentrop himself.

This humanitarian conduct of our soldiers is described in a booklet by General Ottavio Zoppi, with special reference to the eight Départements in France (Alpes Maritimes—Var—Hautes Alpes—Basses Alpes —Isère—Drome—Savoie—Haute Savoie) occupied by our IVth Army Corps, from the 11th November 1942 to August 1943. The Author quotes L. Poliakov's ' *La condition des Juifs en France sous l'occupation italienne* ' :

A une époque ou, dans sa presque totalité l'Europe se trouvait sous la botte alle-mande, ou de Brest jusqu'au Caucase, les polices de tous les pays étaient mobilisées pour la chasse au Juif, huit départements français se transformèrent comme par enchante-ment en une ' zone-refuge' pour les Israelites. Ce furent les huit départements du sud-est de la France, occupés par les troupes italiennes.

*   *   *

Fortunately for the gaiety of nations, even the Jewish question has a comic side. When I was a junior official at the Consulta, in Rome, the Minister for Foreign Affairs was the Marchese di San Giuliano, and Luigi Luzzatti (a Jew) was at the Treasury.

One day, a personal letter arrived from Luzzatti to San Giuliano suggesting that an Italian decoration be given to a gentleman called Saul Blumenthal, who lived in Munich. The reason was that

180

'Gigione' (as Luzzatti was generally called) had written a book, and Herr Blumenthal had reviewed it in laudatory terms. The author's heart was touched, and he wished to reward the reviewer (at no cost to himself) by conferring on him the Cross of *Cavaliere della Corona d'Italia*.

San Giuliano told his secretary to write to our Consul in Munich, to ask for information concerning Herr Blumenthal. Was he worthy of a decoration?

In due course, the answer came back, saying that the journalist in question was very small fry indeed, ' a little Jew with no social position or wealth' (*con scarsi mezzi di fortuna*). It was not advisable that the Cross of Cavaliere be bestowed upon him.

San Giuliano, rather maliciously, passed this message on to his Jewish colleague in the Cabinet. Upon which, Luzzatti took up his pen and wrote : " What your Consul says may be true. But remember that nineteen centuries ago, a little Jew of no social position and *con scarsi mezzi di fortuna* founded a religion that changed the face of the world."

San Giuliano read this answer and smiled. Then he too took up his pen and indited the following :

What you say, my dear Gigione, is certainly true. But remember : Jesus Christ did not want the Cross. It was the Jewish community that insisted. . . . For this they were much blamed. And we have been vexed by a Jewish question ever since !

After which, the correspondence ceased.

'AMERICANS, HAIL!'

> . . . You are come to us
> Full of the strong wine of your Western air,
> Full of the marrow and the sap of life,
> Full of the tingle of youth and maiden valour,
>
> . . . .
>
> And not more beautiful upon the mountains
> Were ever yet the feet of him that brought
> Glad tidings, than your prows upon the sea !
>
> SIR WILLIAM WATSON, *American Hail!* (1918).

Soon after my return to London at the beginning of March 1939 I lunched at the United Services Club, with some old colleagues of the days when I was a member of the Political Section of the Secretariat of the League of Nations in Geneva. There was Colban, Norwegian Minister in London, and ' Tiger ', otherwise Miss Howard, who used to be Drummond's secretary. In former days, it was she who ran the League of Nations, like Begonia Brown, in Bernard Shaw's *Geneva*. Since she had come back to London, she had been and still was running a Cripple's Home, somewhere in Darkest London. Our host and hostess had left the Secretariat of the League much later than the rest of us. They were Gerald Abraham and his wife, an American by birth.

I talked with her about the extreme ill-humour, very noticeable at that time, between the English and the Americans ; not a political tension, as between governments, but sheer bad-temper and mutual dislike, utterly at variance with that cordiality which should have existed between the two peoples. I think that Mrs. Abraham was inclined to put the fault on the British side. She said that, after a tour through most of the countries in Western Europe, she had come to the conclusion that the English were disliked everywhere, except perhaps in Italy ! Not having been in the States for some time, she could not tell what the Man in the Street, over there, felt about it.

As they had been living, up till a short time before, at Geneva, I asked our hosts if they had met there an American journalist, whose articles in the *Saturday Evening Post*—dated from Geneva—interested me. Gerald told me that he *had* met the author, Demaree Bess : a white-haired old gentleman, blessed with considerable wisdom. He had long been the correspondent of the *Christian Science Monitor*. As an authority in international politics, he might replace Frank H. Simonds, who died shortly after I last saw him in Washington, in 1936.

I was first attracted to Demaree Bess's writings by an article called ' Uncle Sam Scares Europe ' (25th February 1939), in which the author maintained that people in Europe were more apprehensive about the foreign policy of the American Government than about the aggressiveness of Hitler's Germany. This corresponded to what I myself noticed, in Paris and in London. People, especially in government circles, were offering up thanks because, after the agreement reached at Munich by the four powers, England, France, Germany and Italy, American influence, and Russian influence had been liquidated from Europe.

What amused me in Demaree Bess's article was the story of an acquaintance of his, who visited his aged grandmother in a small Kansas town : the sort of place where, ten years ago, people hardly knew that Europe existed. Through the radio and the newsreel, the old lady had discovered Europe and was much wrought up about it. But whereas most other Kansans in her home-town were busy hating Hitler, she had picked on Mussolini as her pet hate, and wished to start a crusade to save the poor Italians. She said : ' I don't like that man, Mussolini. I don't like the way he talks on the radio, and I don't like the way he acts on the newsreels. I get mad every time I see his picture. . . . ' That Mussolini should have become a pet aversion of people on Main Street was quite understandable. I noticed myself, when in the U.S.A., that the radio and the newsreel carefully selected the speeches and the photographs that were most likely to make Mussolini unpopular with people who might never have heard of him at all if these mechanical inventions had not come to stir them up.

I know nothing about old women in Kansas, but I dined one night with Lady Barlow at the Sport's Club in Upper Grosvenor Street. A former Governor of Minnesota (or perhaps it was Winconsin) was there with his wife. She was boiling over with indignation over events in Europe—which were—so she assured me—much worse than any war could ever be ! Here you have the characteristic mentality of belligerent peacemaker. No wonder the English, and the French, wanted to be left to settle their own affairs in their own way, without American interference. I mentioned this conversation, next day, to Hemming, when I saw him at the ' Non-Intervention ' offices. He remarked : ' The moral and righteous indignation, which the Americans inject into European politics, are really of no help to anybody.'

Which may be true. But not so long before some Americans had been saying much the same things about the moral and righteous indignation that the English injected into African politics, at the time that we Italians occupied Abyssinia ! The pot is always willing to call the kettle black. As to me I reserved my disapproval for people nearer home. For example, I thoroughly disapproved of Mussolini's policy towards America. Why refuse to let Henry Ford set up a huge factory near Trieste, for the repairs and the assembling of his cars in Europe? Italian cars might have been cheaper for the Italians, and our own factories might have concentrated on motors for aviation, or for the army. Trieste would have benefited enormously by the added business and industrial activity.

Again, take the following little episode, which was told me by Augusto Rosso, after he had ceased to be our Ambassador in the U.S.A. :

Just before his departure from Washington, Rosso expressed the desire to pay the customary visit of farewell to President Roosevelt. The latter asked him to tea, and during the ensuing conversation, mentioned his intention of going on a sea-cruise, to rest from his labours.

'It might be useful,' the President went on to say, 'if I and your boss could meet somewhere. There are many questions we could profitably talk over. A sea-cruise would probably do *him* good too. I was thinking of a trip to the Azores. We might come across each other, in those waters. . . .'

This was not a formal proposal to the Chief of the Italian government. Nevertheless, it came direct from the President himself, speaking to the Italian Ambassador. But the latter, on his return to Rome (and before his departure to take up his new post, in Moscow), was not received by Mussolini, and thus was never given the opportunity of speaking to him directly on this or on any other subject (Mussolini, in his last phase, kept the career diplomats at arm's length). Rosso spoke to Suvich of President Roosevelt's suggestion, and we may presume that it was brought to the Duce's ears. We must therefore hold Mussolini responsible for an error of omission that had (so I believe) the gravest consequences in the following years.

Italo-American relations are not to be compared with those between Great Britain and the U.S.A. These alternate between music-hall appeals to 'stand or fall together' and mutual recriminations; but community of interests render it almost impossible to maintain a long estrangement. So also, in the U.S.A., a pendulum-like oscillation alternates between a Pilgrim Father policy of aloofness and its opposite number, which the Soviets accuse of being mere ' economic-imperialism '. Compare Sir William Watson's verses, quoted in the heading of this chapter, to the following fragment of a speech by Winston Churchill (as quoted in the *Washington Star* of the 31st December 1940, and again by the *Catholic Digest* of February 1941) :

America's entry into the war was disastrous not only for your country but for the Allies as well, because, had you stayed at home and minded your own business, we would have made peace with the Central Powers in the spring of 1917, and then there would have been no collapse of Russia, followed by Communism ; no breakdown in Italy, followed by Fascism, and Nazism would not be at present enthroned in Germany. If America had stayed out of the war and minded her own business, none of these ' isms ' would today be sweeping the continent of Europe and breaking down parliamentary government.

From the same *Catholic Digest* of February 1941, I re-quote the following quotation, which is even more explicit. It is taken from an address by John A. O'Brien (16th December 1940) :

' If you Americans had kept out of the world war,' said a clear-thinking Oxford Don to me, ' we would never have been able to impose on Germany the monstrous terms of the Versailles agreement. We would have had a fair Treaty of Peace. You Americans tipped the scales so greatly in our favour that we sank the fangs of our hatred into Germany and sought to cripple her permanently. *This* explosion is traceable to that Versailles Powder Magazine. Thus you Americans, by rushing in, are responsible for this war.'

And so the music goes round and round !

DIARY OF A CHRISTMAS HOLIDAY

22nd December 1938 (In the train, between Paris and Rome). I stopped a day in Paris on my way south, to see Diana. Her apartment in the Rue de Lota is now quite attractive. The rooms upstairs prettily furnished, and the big studio downstairs practically empty, except for a big divan, a bookcase, a gramophone and a few Chinese silks brought from Rome. The atmosphere is distinctly Bohemian, which is what she likes.

Her numerous retainers might be described with the word ' casual ', as applied to persons who receive temporary shelter in a workhouse ; they come in and do a spot of work, when they think of it. A new one, since I was in Paris last, is a muscular Swedish girl, who aspires to become a dancer. In exchange for permission to come and practice in Diana's studio (which she does in a state of almost complete nudity and absorption in her own affairs), she is willing to be sent out to do commissions. Diana threw a party some days ago and sent this girl to buy the ingredients for some cocktails. She came back carrying six large bottles of milk !

Friday, 30th December (Rome). Constantine Brown turned up here on Xmas Day, talking, as usual, nineteen to the dozen. He is still ' Foreign Editor ' of the *Washington Star* and tells me that Government circles in the U.S.A. are beginning to discover that three totalitarian states to disapprove of are too many. They think it might be a good idea to improve relations with Italy. President Roosevelt makes this difficult by sending too many admonitory messages to the dictators in general.

Tuesday, 3rd January 1939. I heard yesterday, during lunch at MacClure's, that the programme of Chamberlain's coming visit to Rome is so heavily overcharged that it will hardly be possible to get through it all in a few days. Chamberlain was here last in 1921, and did a lot of very thorough sight-seeing. As former Mayor of Birmingham, he takes considerable interest in town and country planning, and would like to visit Littoria, to see the results of the reclamation of the Pontine Marshes.

I talked with Alberto Theodoli about taking Lord Halifax to Tor di Quinto, and I asked Margherita to go and see Ciano about it, also Forquet, who is now in command of the school. Forquet is delighted with the idea, but says he must have instructions from the War Office to make everything ready.

The Pope is very ill with asthma. I hear that the one thing that gives him relief is garlic. The smell of it in his study is enough to knock you down. Will he receive the British Prime Minister there, I wonder ?

Wednesday, 4th January. I have lived, and still live, so much abroad, that I lose touch with events and policies in my own country. On the other hand, on the occasions when I come home, I perceive the changes of atmosphere that sometimes escape those who stay quietly by their own fireside.

There is a change in the atmosphere here, and I don't like it : a wholesale importation of laws, methods and manners from Germany. Why it should be so, I can't think. When they first met, at Strà, Mussolini and Hitler could hardly be normally polite to each other. Ciano dislikes Ribbentrop, and the feeling is mutual. We are under no obligation to Germany. It may be in part thanks to them that we were able to conquer Ethiopia, without British interference. But it is also true that, in consequence of that crisis, the Germans were able to re-occupy the de-militarized Rhenish provinces. So we are quits.

The trouble began, so I am told, when Mussolini visited Germany rather more than a year ago, and was shown the wonderful new armaments that are the pride of Krupp's factories at Essen. And Ciano's wife, Edda, is supposed to be thoroughly pro-German. Like her father, she has been impressed by the heavy, masculine atmosphere of Berlin.

And now Italy is suffering from an exaggerated degree of organization and discipline that destroys for the Italians the very savour of life, so that they lose interest in the world and in themselves. And this is a result of importations from Germany. Our diplomacy is becoming heavy-handed and without *souplesse*, and losing both the dignity and the wisdom of its ancient traditions. In the old days we were sometimes too timid. Nowadays we are short-sighted and imprudent.

Also in 'home' politics, there is a change that is not for the better. The new constitution, embodying the 'Corporate State' was to have been Europe's latest experiment in government philosophy. There was nothing totalitarian about it. 'Vocational representation' might be adopted, with advantage, by the most democratic state. Such impartial observers as Walter Elliot, British Minister for Agriculture, saw in it a possible development of the old parliamentary system, which cannot be said to work well, at least not in Latin countries.

But the new Italian 'Chamber of Corporations' is not allowed to function freely and has become a mere rubber-stamp parliament. Its members are 'yes-men', resembling those little Chinese toys, a Mandarin sitting on the ground and waggling his head backwards and forwards.

Apart from the constitution of the Corporate State, there are the rules and regulations of the Fascist Party. Thanks to these, all the power is practically concentrated in the hands of the Secretary of the Party, who is almost more powerful than Mussolini. His consent has to be obtained even for the choice of members for a parliamentary commission ! And this key position within the state, this supreme, regulating office in the administration of the country, is deliberately entrusted to insignificant personalities, without culture, experience or intelligence. The present incumbent is Achille Starace, a typical example of Fascist presumption and intolerance, alternating a bullying attitude towards all and sundry, with an abject servility towards the Duce himself. Personally, I don't dislike the man. He is always very respectful and cordial to me. The reason for this is not that he knows I am a friend of Ciano's and that Mussolini rather likes me. The reason is that Starace admires my daughters, especially Margherita, for her exceptional knowledge of horses and all that concerns them. She often gets annoyed with him, and doesn't she let him know it ! And he takes it all meekly. I wish she could persuade him to keep out of the way during Neville Chamberlain's visit to Rome. He wants to take the British Prime Minister to see some autarchic exhibition of metals ! I can imagine nothing that could interest him less !

Monday, 9th January. Some day, I may write a magazine article, or a pamphlet, on the subject of diplomat's dogs. They have certain characteristics of their own, due, no doubt, to travelling so much round the world, sampling the smells of different nations.

In London, I made friends with Bärchen, Ribbentrop's dog, but not with Ribbentrop himself. Bärchen might be seen most days, in company with two policemen, at the top of the stairway that leads down from Carlton House Terrace, to the Mall. When he saw me, he would turn over on his back suggestively. This was an invitation to rub his chest.

I met 'Jeremy', the cairn, in Washington, before I knew his master, d'Arcy Osborne, who was Councillor of the British Embassy. He is now in Rome, at the Legation to the Holy See. I met him this morning in the Villa Borghese, with Osborne, and we talked—at least Osborne and I did—about the possibility of taking Lord Halifax to Tor di Quinto. It has all been arranged, but he may have to go, instead, to visit the English College.

Passing along the Via Po, I went in to see the Blancs. Alberto was one of the pillars of Fascism in its first days. He and his wife, Maria, would not hear anything against it. Today they are far from satisfied with the way things are going. Alberto says that the lack of any opposition results in the Duce being kept in the dark of many evils that should be known and remedied. Small local bosses (they call them 'ras' as if they were Abyssinian chiefs !) take advantage of a virtual impunity and bring discredit on the whole system.

Italian Fascism is degenerating into what its enemies abroad say it is, but which, in its best years, it was not. Friends of mine, rich, independent men, who took up some office or social work and served without self-interest, have now been thrust aside, to make room for a very different class of public servant ; a class that is out to make money, and do not care how they do so.

The Blanc's family come from Savoy, so they are naturally interested in our relations with France. These are so bad, at present, that Chamberlain is criticized in Paris for condescending to come to Rome. The papers say that it is an unfriendly gesture to France.

There is some idea that Chamberlain and his Foreign Minister might be persuaded to mediate between us and the French, so that we may take up again the threads of the Pact stipulated with Laval, in 1935. This would indeed be the moment for the British Government to inaugurate some such constructive policy as Lord Allen of Churtwood still hopes for, and others like him (including myself !). But it would require stronger and more dynamic personalities than Chamberlain and Halifax, to take such an initiative. They represent nothing more than a policy of negotiation *jusqu'au bout*, to the bitter end ! An excellent policy in itself, but not always sufficient to dissipate the danger that lurks in an international controversy.

Meanwhile Starace's followers are pushing matters to extremes. Ciano is not a strong character, but I wonder how even he could put up with having a very moderate speech of his, in the Chamber, interrupted by cries of ' Corsica !

Gibuti ! Tunisi !' All that can be said in favour of such vulgarity is that it may have what is called 'a nuisance value'.

Friday, 13th (an ill-omened date ?) January. Last night, at the British Embassy, Mr. Chamberlain addressed me as ' The Maker of Heavenly Trousers '. As this book of mine is dedicated to his sister-in-law, it is natural that he should know me by that designation. I retaliated by calling him the ' Umbrella Man '. His precious umbrella now figures in cartoons, press-notices and telegrams. I asked him why it should have become such a feature in the Chanceries of Europe. He did not seem to see anything strange in this. He is very much attached to that particular umbrella. It was given him by his wife, forty years ago. It has been four times re-covered, and he had it with him when he came to Rome, in 1921. Today, all the peace-parties in Europe are sheltering under it !

The Embassy party was quite pleasant, and I was glad to see Drummond again. He tells me that everybody is ragging him about a story I put in *Laughing Diplomat*, about my staring at a pretty girl, in the restaurant of the Hôtel Lotti, in Paris, and his objecting, because he had his back to her and couldn't do likewise.

Isa Chigi was there, and Pace (her youngest daughter). Pace is engaged to young Misciatelli. They were introduced to Chamberlain, who said he liked Pace's christian name and was glad that marriage would not change it. She was born just when peace had been signed, after the world war. If it had been a boy, I suppose they would have called him Armistizio !

Bettina and I came away early. I heard afterwards that one of the last to leave was Starace. He drank a lot of whisky, and tried to dance the Lambeth Walk. If he would limit his activities to this sort of thing, it would be the better for everybody !

Tuesday, 17th January. There is a poisonous article in the *Tevere*, abusing the French in the coarsest language. I went to the Palazzo Chigi, to protest, and saw Guarnaschelli. He pointed out that we are only paying the French back in their own coin. Attacks on us, in the French papers, have been almost as scurrilous as they were against England during the Boer War. This is all very well. But insults are like bad coins. A gentleman does not try to pass them on.

Somehow or other, Ciano heard that I was in the Ministero, and sent for me to come and speak to him on a very important matter ! When I heard what he wanted, I couldn't help laughing. . . . He is getting much too fat, and asked me to get him the prescription of a diet that Bettina followed for some weeks when she thought her weight was going up too much. She had mentioned this to Ciano, who kept the idea in his mind. . . . I promised to copy out the prescription and to send it to him.

Then I mentioned the question of our relations with France. Ciano astonished me by saying that the cries of ' Tunisi ! Corsica ! Gibuti !'

in the Chamber of Corporations, after his speech, came as a complete surprise to him, no less than to the French Ambassador, François-Poncet, who was upstairs in the strangers' gallery.

It was certainly a put-up job, but entirely due to Starace's misplaced zeal (That man is a real pest !). How can Ciano hope, now, to *riallacciare buone relazioni con la Francia* ? (to get our relations with France back on a cordial footing). And this happens just as Ribbentrop goes to Paris, to sign an agreement with the French ! Ciano did not say so, but I had the impression that he thought Ribbentrop was at the bottom of it all. Starace is not without patriotism. He would never take foreign gold for such a purpose. But he might be induced, by flattery, to stir the pot which has already too many cooks spoiling the broth.

Ciano tells me that at one of the various receptions (I did not gather which) Chamberlain said to Arlotta, speaking of Mussolini : ' He certainly is a very great man ! '

But, except for the cordiality of his reception by the people of Rome, Chamberlain's visit has left things much as they were before he came.

THE WAR-CLOUDS DISPERSE OVER SPAIN AND GATHER OVER POLAND

> So once again the soul-destroying horde
> That first with Attila its frenzy roared
> And now the living world has overrun,
> Has howled and fled before the Christian sword
> Of Spain. . . .
>
> ROY CAMPBELL, *Flowering Rifle*.

Civil war in Spain faded out, and the nationalist victory over the Reds was celebrated by Roy Campbell, the South African poet. A more convinced anti-communist it would be difficult to find, or a British subject that could bring a more savage satire over the ' International Brigade ' and its Left-Wing sympathizers.

But meanwhile trouble was brewing in Eastern Europe.

I was in London when I heard about Ciano's official visit to Warsaw, in February 1939. It was not a success, even though the Italian Foreign Minister and his wife were given a right royal welcome. Prime Minister Beck would have liked to have enlisted Ciano's sympathies in his struggle against the pressure brought to bear on him by Ribbentrop, who had also been to Warsaw a short time before. But Ciano was mortally afraid of compromising himself, and did not respond.

Meanwhile, the humble populace of the capital, watching from a distance the festivities organized to do honour to the distinguished guests, stood outside the princely palace, while strains of music, warmth and scent and dazzle, were flung out into the frozen street for a beggar's portion.

After cheering optimistically under the windows of the Italian Embassy, the crowd went and made a hostile demonstration under those of the German one. It was all very embarrassing for Ciano !

In my youth I shared the romantic ideas and ideals of Polish independence. Only when I had to deal personally with some of the questions regarding that distressful country was the gilt rubbed off the gingerbread. Very often I felt inclined to agree with H. G. Wells, who, in *The Shape of Things to Come*, expressed himself as follows :

Poland was restored, but instead of a fine-spirited and generous people emerging from those 120 years of subjugation and justifying the sympathy and hopes of liberalism throughout the world, they appeared a narrowly patriotic government, which presently developed into an aggressive, vindictive and pitiless dictatorship, and set itself at once to the zestful persecution of the unfortunate ethic minorities (about one-third of the entire population) caught in the net of its all too ample boundaries.

As the years go by, my sympathies oscillate between sorrow for the Poles, overrun by their enemies and betrayed by their friends, and a corresponding pity for the unfortunate people who are sometimes delivered up to them to rule over. Both the former and the latter are fated to be alternately sold down the Volga. Wars break out and drag on. Documents are signed, under the illusion that they bring peace. And ever there remains a ' Polish Question ', to furnish the occasion for another conflict. To realize the difficulties of the situation, you have only to stop and think of the character of Poland's neighbours.

I was horrified at the blank cheque given to Poland, at the end of March 1939, by Mr. Chamberlain's ' guarantee ', and could not help comparing it with the declaration made by Ramsay MacDonald in 1935, when he assured us, at the Stresa Conference, that it was impossible to ask the British people to interfere on the Continent of Europe, in matters in which British interests were not involved. If a British guarantee could save Europe, it was a pity it had not been considered possible to give one after the murder of Dollfuss, when Italy had shown willingness to come to the aid of Austria and to mobilize against the rising strength of the Nazis.

The Poles were urged to accept military aid from the Soviets. Upon which, they pertinently asked : ' Is the British guarantee to end in our country being overrun by the hordes of Voroschiloff ? '

In 1914 Sir Edward Grey was accused of not having made known, in time, the intentions of the British Government, in the event of the invasion of Belgium. . . . In March 1939, the British Government did make known that she would consider the invasion of Poland as a *casus belli*. Both policies were well-intentioned, yet both ended in war.

LAST DAYS IN LONDON

I forget the date, but not long before I left London, there was a musical evening at our Embassy, and Montesano and the Toti dal Monte sang to us. I noticed an empty chair near the Countess Ahlefeldt (a *chère collègue* of other days) and with some difficulty, for there was a fine crush, I pushed my way through and sat down beside her. Then I found that I was facing the first row in the audience, which was reserved for royalties and the higher social lights of London. Just at that moment, there pealed out the first notes of the duet

> *Là ci darem la mano,*
> *Là mi dirai di si . . .*

It was strange, and a little touching, to see those elderly faces : so well-bred, so distinguished, and so tired, suddenly become spell-bound by a beauty and a yearning, that made them young again. It was as if the lilt of the song had found an echo in the gentle, falling cadences of life itself. *Air doux et tendre, jadis aimé . . .*

So it was, a few days later, when I gave a reading, in a little room of the Anglo-Italian Society, of Carducci's *Fonti del Clitunno*. There were a lot of old ladies there, who evidently felt pleasure in the sound of the Italian endecasyllables.

I also gave a lecture (my second) at Chatham House, and I was astonished, some ten days later, to hear from Bettina, in Rome, that

Lord Phillimore had written her what almost appeared as an apology for the manners of his countrymen *a mon égard*. She quoted his own words :

> . . . we have now reached a crisis in world affairs that has long been hanging over Europe, and the work done by you and your husband takes on an even greater importance.
>
> Your husband is a very patient man. I was ashamed to the depths of my being of the way in which he was treated at Chatham House, and only regret that the assistance I was able to give him was so feeble.

Lord Phillimore need not have been apologetic. I thoroughly enjoyed myself ! Indeed, during the ' debate ' that followed my lecture, when the Chairman was trying, ineffectually, to get various people (including Miss Frida White) to stick to the point, I deliberately added to the confusion by contributing the following remarks :

' Ladies and Gentlemen ! Either this discussion, or I, or both, are getting very mixed. It reminds me of a conversation between two tourists from the wilder and woollier parts of America, who were being rowed in a gondola up the Grand Canal, in my native Venice. The gondolier pointed out a house and said : " *Quella è la casa di Desdemona.*"

' One of the two tourists asked the other : " What is the son of a . . . saying now ? "

' " He says : ' That is the House of Desdemona.' "

' " And who is Desdemona anyway ? "

' " She comes in an English book, called *The Merchant of Venice*. It's about a man, who smothers his wife, because he suspicioned she was carrying on with a black man. And for this he was condemned to lose a pound of his flesh. But his wife dressed up like a man, and came . . ."

' " What are you telling me now ? You said he had smothered his wife ! "

' " Yes. He smothered the first one, to marry this one. And she acted as Council for the defence, and got him off."

' " Gee ! That must be a cute book. I must buy it at once ! " '

It is not I who could take two plays of Shakespeare and make one story out of them, a story that could be told in a few words. Yet

I have a feeling that, in the matter of international politics, people attempt feats like that all the time. They take the most complex problems, problems that go back for decades and centuries, and have the impetus of history behind them, and they reduce them to the proportions of a newspaper ' story ' that can be told in a few paragraphs, in time for the evening edition. . . . On the basis of these ' stories ', the public is asked to make up its mind on world issues, to applaud its own leaders, to condemn all foreigners (except those who are likely to fight on their side), and to impeach foreign nations wholesale.

I concluded my lecture at Chatham House, by asking my audience not to commit the error of trusting to any new ideology, to any ' world movement ', to arrest national movements. People who maintain that the world, in its wisdom and new-born piety, has passed beyond such things, are no true prophets, though they may be suffering from a messianic complex. It is mere vanity that makes us seek out new forms of salvation, new symbols, and ignore the old. Let me give an example.

A certain philosopher went to see Voltaire at Ferney, and said to him : ' I want to found a new religion. How shall I set about it ? '

And Voltaire answered : ' Get yourself crucified, and then rise again from the dead.'

*   *   *

I left London on the 20th of April, and stopped, as usual, to see Diana in Paris. She and I lunched at our Embassy, with Guariglia (the Ambassador) and his wife.

They gave me the news, as seen through the eyes of the diplomats in Paris. I asked Guariglia if war was coming. He answered : ' *Non verrà, perchè non deve venire* ' (' It will not come, because it *must* not come ! ').

We forget that it is just the things that should not occur, that make up the greater part of history. Let me quote Voltaire again : in his *Essai des Mœurs*, he writes :

" *L'histoire des grands évènements de ce monde n'est guère que l'histoire des crimes.*"

PART IV
THE DREAM SHATTERED

Fourth of September 1939

GUIDO CROLLA was Italian Chargé d'Affaires in London in the late summer of 1939. Towards the end of August, he dined *tête-à-tête*, at the Carlton Hotel restaurant, with Dr. E. Kordt, who was acting as Chargé d'Affaires for Germany during the absence of the Ambassador, von Dirksen. Neither the German nor the Italian Embassies were kept informed by their governments of the course of events. As zero hour drew near, a few items reached them through the British Foreign Office. The only thing that was clear to them (and perhaps not to the British public) was that the French Government was struggling frantically not to be dragged into the war, at least not from its first outbreak.

During dinner at the Carlton, Kordt pointed out the adjacent long dining-room where, at the outbreak of war in 1914, the German Ambassador, Prince Lichnowsky, had been entertained, with chivalrous cordiality, by his numerous friends in London. ' Nothing of the sort will happen to me,' said Kordt. ' You will see. I will be turned out like a dog, *wie ein Hund* ! '

He was not far wrong. None of the customary courtesies were extended to the departing staff of the German Embassy, when they left London, by special train, on the evening of the 4th of September. The Brazilian Ambassador, Doyen of the Diplomatic Body, stayed out of London for an extended week-end. The neutral Ambassadors and ministers made themselves scarce. Only Crolla and the Vice-Marshal of the Diplomatic Body, representing the Foreign Office, showed up on the platform of a neglected siding, where the long sombre train waited for the station clocks to mark half-past seven. Then it moved off into the shadows under the iron causeway.

' You are lucky to be staying on in London ! ' said Dr. Kordt to Crolla, as they parted.

' My turn may come next.'

' Not likely ! The Italians are too intelligent to make such mistakes.'

This might be true. But our fate, like that of the Germans, was in the hands of one whom the Gods were determined to destroy. It was partly our own fault. As in Ecclesiasticus iv. 30 : " Make not thyself an underling to a foolish man, neither accept the person of the mighty.'

Diary of a Non-Belligerent (1940)

MY Diary for the year 1940 begins gaily enough. The war was stagnating like a sluggish stream ; no one seemed to take it seriously. And anyway, we Italians were not mixed up in it !

Monday, 1st January. This morning at the Club, Pepito de la Gandara told me that the Queen of Spain wanted my trousers ! When I got home, I sent them to her. That is to say, I sent her my book : *The Maker of Heavenly Trousers.*

I am beginning this year's Diary, seated with my back to the Xmas Tree that, during the afternoon, did its duty by my grandchildren and their guests. Now, the toys have been distributed, the lights put out, and the tree stands despoiled of its glory, ready to be thrown into a cold attic and used next year as firewood. It's a shame to fell so beautiful a thing as a young tree for one brief hour's enjoyment.

Father Xmas attended the party. He knocked at the outer door to be let in, hobbled through the rooms, carrying his sack, and sat down to distribute presents. He was a well-known cinema actor. He told me that he had never suffered from stage-fright before, but then he had never before acted before an audience who believed him to be real. . . . For days, he had been rehearsing his part and muttering to himself : ' Good day, children . . .' When it was all over, Bona Boncompagni's little boy asked Margherita : ' How do you invite Father Christmas ? Where does he live ? ' Margherita had to promise to pass on any message that might be sent him. The same little boy went tearing round the house in a big toy motor, knocked off a mudguard, smashed a lamp, and then complained that there was too much furniture in our rooms.

Although the papers don't say anything about it, we Italians are sending help to the Finns. I have always had a friendly feeling for Finland, since I tried to help the Finnish representative at the League of Nations (Monsieur Enkel) to get the question of Carelia placed on the *ordre du jour* of a meeting of the Council at Geneva. I did not succeed in doing this, but I *did* manage to obtain some authoritative opinions, by a rather silly expedient. There was a very improper play on, in Paris, in those days, called *Occupe toi d'Amélie !* So I put the file in front of Monsieur Briand's chair, after having written *Occupe toi de Carélie !* on the outside of the dosier. . . .

It appears that Daladier wants to send an expeditionary corps to the help of Finland, if only to break the somnolent spell of this *drôle de guerre*, in which —so far—huge armies face each other in almost complete inactivity. If ever an unprovoked attack on a neighbouring state could be defined as ' a war of aggression ', this Russian attack on Finland corresponds to that definition. But I miss that orgy of emotionalism that was provoked by British propaganda in the case of our war in Ethiopia. *Superior erat lupus ?* In the United States, however, the Finns can count on support from Jews and Catholics, Rabbi Wise and Father Coughlin. The Russians figure as ' godless atheists ', while the Finns are described as dropping Bibles on Petrograd.

Friday, 5th January. Ward Price is in Rome, and dropped in after dinner for a talk. He is one of the few foreign journalists who can always count on being received by Mussolini, and who might have, I think, some influence over him, if only because he shows some sympathy and understanding for Italian political problems. The more foreign journalists Mussolini sees the better. Some personal contacts with foreign press-men might bring him down to earth and dispel the vertigo of omnipotence.

When last in London, I tried to arrange for Mussolini to receive Philip Jordan of the *News Chronicle*. I spoke to Grandi about it, but the latter would not take the responsibility. . . . Philip Jordan told me afterwards that he was not surprised.

Saturday, 6th January. Several people to lunch. I had Mrs. Stuart-Wortley on my right. She is surprised at finding the Italian papers so ' neutral ' in tone. She had expected they would be more ' pro-German '. I was amused at an account she gave me of the evenings at Doorn, where she has been staying as a guest of the ex-Kaiser. She says that he reads aloud to the family. While she was there, he read them *Alice in Wonderland*. I wonder if some day the present war-lord of Germany will find himself a refugee in Holland and read aloud to his family and guests. Hitler doesn't speak English, or he might read *Uncle Remus* :

> " Good-bye, Brer Fox, take keer yo' cloze,
> For dis is de way de worril goes ;
> Some goes up and some goes down
> You'll git ter de bottom all safe en soun'.' "

       ★   ★   ★

As Themistocles sailed along the coasts, wherever he saw places at which the enemy must necessarily put in for shelter and supplies, he inscribed conspicuous writings on stones. . . . In these writings he solemnly enjoined upon the Ionians, if it were possible, to come over to the side of the Athenians, who were risking all on behalf of their freedom. . . .

I owe the above quotation from *Plutarch's Lives* to R. H. Bruce Lockhart, whose book, *Comes the Reckoning*, is an expert's analysis of British war propaganda. It is a pity there was no such British expert in ' the mechanization of thought' in Italy, during the winter of 1939-40. He might have done something to counteract the pressure brought to bear on Italian public opinion by the other side. The latter's task was the easier of the two, for they could make capital out of the various successive press and propaganda campaigns, which had been directed against Italy in Great Britain during the past few years. These had been efficient enough. But when it came to pleading their own cause, British propaganda took a year, or more, to get under way, and its methods were as rudimentary as those of Themistocles.

After the war broke out in September 1939, I made no mystery of where my sympathies lay. I had abused British policies, when speaking to Englishmen in England (as at Chatham House), which was a thing not many Italians would have had the ability or the courage to do. But I defended English policies, if I thought them just, when addressing my own countrymen, in Italy, in Italian. In this way, I made myself unpopular in both countries ! (Such is the fate of those who see both sides of a question.)

Thanks to Francis Toye, I was offered the opportunity of giving a lecture at the British Institute in Florence. I was nearly prevented doing so by a painful attack of neuralgia, but managed to start for Florence on the morning of the 12th of January (my birthday). As I could not sit up, I took a compartment in the sleeping-car, though the journey only lasted three hours, from nine to twelve in the morning.

On arrival, Bettina and I got down from our railway carriage, which rocked on its springs, as an icy wind off the Mugello swept the station platforms, covered with drifting snow. Our railway porter remarked : ' It's lucky I've got your suit-cases to weigh me down, or this breeze would waft me to Arezzo ! '

Foreigners have a fond illusion that Italy is a warm country, because the winters are short and you get frequent fine days. But oh, the cold, when it *is* cold !

A few minutes after our arrival at the Hotel Baglioni, Francis Toye found me lying on my bed, in the room he had reserved for me. By four-thirty I was feeling better and my lecture went off all right. The subject was 'Literature and Diplomacy', and I brought in, as an example of these two things, Nevile Henderson's *Failure of a Mission*, which was then a best seller.

The audience was mostly of Italians, headed by Carlo Placci. An Edwardian touch was given to our dinner by the presence of Mrs. George Keppel. She wore a lovely dress of dark velvet in various shades of violet, brown and blue, shading imperceptibly one into another.

That the French, like myself, were contemptuous of British propaganda, we gathered from the comments of the Ambassador, François-Poncet. The British Embassy sponsored a film, which was put on the screen at the Quirinetta. It was called 'The Lion has Wings'. Only England was pictured as fighting Germany. François-Poncet remarked that it was a great relief and pleasure to him to discover from the film that France was not at war !

Bettina was even more severe in her comments. The antithesis between the King of England in a kilt, singing comic songs with children, and Hitler reviewing troops, might have passed muster, even though as war propaganda it was feeble, to say the least. The shots representing rows of workmen's houses, recently built in England, as a contrast to Germany's bellicose preparations, may have seemed convincing to the lower middle classes in dreary English suburbs, but anyone who had seen anything of what had been done in this branch of social work in the totalitarian states (including Russia), knew perfectly well that in 1940 Great Britain was far behind them in every way.[1]

There is a special brand of obtuseness that is found more often in diplomacy than anywhere else. This was shown by the British Embassy's attitude towards a modest institution called the Peritalia, which might have done something, in 1939-40, to make known the English point of view to the Italians, as in the past it had made known the Italian point of view to the British and the Americans.

[1] Inevitably the best film with a pro-British appeal was not shown in Italy till the war was over. This was 'Mrs. Miniver'. One could not come out, after seeing that film, without feeling sympathy for Great Britain. The difference between 'The Lion has Wings' and 'Mrs. Miniver' lay in the fact that the latter appealed to sentiments of humanity and did not make a vain display of any vaunted British superiority.

This ' Association ', as it called itself, was founded in Rome, in November 1935, when both Bettina and I were abroad. Its founder was a British subject, an Australian, Doctor Herbert Moran.

I don't know when or why Doctor Moran first came to Italy. I think he had been in Ethiopia before arriving in Rome. He certainly was there at one time or another, during the Italo-Abyssinian war. And he was horrified to discover that the information given out in Australia, by British government agencies, on the Ethiopian crisis, was pure fiction. Reports, such as that Italy was on the brink of revolution and utterly incapable of conducting even a colonial war, appeared to him—when he had ascertained the real facts—so dangerously misleading, that he felt impelled to do his best to counteract this erroneous impression. It was easy for him to enlist the sympathies and to secure the co-operation of many Anglo-Saxon residents in Italy, and of many English and American ladies, married to Italians.

When the Association came to life, a person who took great interest in it was Mrs. Eugenia Strong, the well-known archæologist. But this lady, though interesting and pleasant to meet in society, was not easy to get on with. She soon quarrelled with everybody all round. When Bettina got back to Rome, the Presidency—during Doctor Moran's absence—was passed over to her.

I and my daughters regarded the Peritalia with scepticism and resented so much of Bettina's time being taken up with the dam' thing. We nicknamed her ' Mrs. Jelliby ' and made unkind remarks about the geese that saved the Capitol. But she paid no attention . . .

The ' sanctions ' period passed, but the Peritalia continued to exist with the object of procuring reliable information and of improving the relations between Italy and the English-speaking peoples. Never, in any way, was it financed by the Italian Government, or any Italian group or institution. Indeed, it was never financed at all, but led a hand-to-mouth existence, with voluntary workers, in borrowed offices. It was never anti-British, as a glance at the list of members might have shown to anyone. But Doctor Herbert Moran's original crime of having contradicted official British propaganda, at the time of the Abyssinian crisis, left a stigma on his offspring, at least in the slow-witted mind of some minor civil servant, unknown to fame. The attitude of the British Embassy was expressed in the phrase : ' It's an obnoxious little institute. Don't put your foot in it.' Not even when Mr. Neville Chamberlain was enthusiastically welcomed, on his ' peace mission ' in January 1940, and the Peritalia presented him with an illuminated parchment representing the Ara Pacis, did the British Embassy see light. The American Embassy, on the contrary, was most friendly, and the Ambassadress, Mrs. Phillips, used to attend the Peritalia lectures, in the Palazzo Salviati. And Lord Lloyd of Dolobran, when passing through Rome, spoke to me with admiration of Bettina's, and the other ladies' work, at the Peritalia. The Association was dissolved on the day that Italy entered the second world war.

The Peritalia is mentioned incidentally in my Diary for January 18 :

Diana went to see Ciano this afternoon, at the Palazzo Chigi, and found him wearing a hair-net and his hair all plastered down with that lotion, made out of a root, that Bettina's amah in Peking used to put on her own hair. Ciano now gets someone to send him this root from China. Now that he is Minister for Foreign Affairs, he continues to see my daughters, and to chatter away with them by the hour (when he should be doing some work) just as they used to play about together, in Gianmarina's nursery, at the Legation in Peking, or on the sand at Shan-hai-kwan. There is a certain boy-and-girl *camaraderie* between them, that is in sharp contrast to his habitual familiarity with young women, and yet in a way more pleasantly intimate, as if they strove to recapture something of the old irresponsibility.

Ciano said to Diana that Italy's part in this war need not be a heroic one. . . We should stand aside and make money, while the other powers tear each other to pieces. This corresponds to what Mussolini himself said to Bettina, when she took the members of her precious ' Peritalia ' to see him (a good move, both as pro-British and pro-Italian propaganda). The Duce pointed out that no country has such a real need of peace as Italy today. And he went on to enumerate the reasons for this . . . dwelling on the Herculean tasks that await us in Ethiopia, a huge country still in the pack-and-mule stage, where the hygienic conditions of the natives are appalling !

*   *   *

During those last months, when Italy was still at peace, my two eldest daughters made hay while the sun shone. They travelled all the time, whenever and wherever possible. The air mail of the 19th of January brought me a letter from Margherita, with messages from Balbo. It was written in the Sahara, and was the last letter I ever received from an Italian colonial possession. So I should like to quote it :

GHADÀMES, *15th January 1940*

DEAREST PÀ,

I am writing to you from a most delightful hotel—clean, fresh, cool, with excellent food, wonderful wines, nice rooms, good service : you could not find better in Paris !

Though there is no postal service, as far as I can make out, this letter should reach you in a very short time, for I will give it to Colonel Reale, who flies to Tripoli tomorrow morning ; he will forward it from there by air-mail.

This is a lovely spot. When approaching it by car, as we did two days ago, you do not realize that there is an oasis anywhere near, till you are right on top of it. In this way, it reminds me of the hamlets we saw in Mongolia : the arid plain seems to stretch away on every side, and then suddenly, in a hollow among the sand-dunes, you come upon human habitations. But here, it is quite a large town that lies hidden, and all around it is a forest of date-palms. Land for cultivation is so precious that they waste as little as possible on roads and paths and streets. Two people can hardly pass each other in the narrow, dark alleys between the houses.

And the houses themselves are very low—only one floor—and the roofs are reserved for the women, who can pass easily from one roof to another, so that Ghadàmes would seem to have been built in two stories, one above and the other below. The one above, like some compartments in the trains in France, is *pour dames seules*.

There is plenty of water here, gushing out of the sandy soil, and some of it is warm. The place may become fashionable, some day, as a spa. I must suggest this to Balbo.

We had an entirely unexpected picnic, four days ago, with Balbo, in the middle of the desert. Our party had just left Nalùt, which is a tiny oasis between here and Sinauen (which again is an oasis), when we saw an aeroplane circling above us, with only one motor working. It appeared to be in difficulties. So, having watched it land, we drove up and asked if we could be of any use. The plane was piloted by Colonel Reale, whom I know quite well. And he had a passenger with him, whom I had met years ago in New York ! An American journalist, called Weigand.

Their plane had a radio apparatus with which they could transmit messages. So Reale sent off two telegrams : one to Tripoli for another plane, and another to Balbo, who was shooting somewhere not far off, to tell him of their forced landing. Apparently they had left him not long before, as they had been together shooting, but had had to leave. In this second telegram, Colonel Reale mentioned that I was there too.

The answer from Balbo came almost immediately. He said he would come and lunch with us. Another telegram came through from Tripoli, saying that a plane was being sent off to Colonel Reale's assistance.

Less than an hour later, there we all were, Balbo included, sitting on the sand ; and around us the three planes ; the original one, the rescue plane, and Balbo's. Also two cars ; our own truck and a car belonging to the carabinieri at Nalùt. They had intercepted the wireless messages and came to see if they could be of any help.

Gèa barked a welcome to Balbo, and wagged her tail, as he came walking towards us across the sand. And she sat in the circle with us, while we had lunch, with her tongue lolling out and smiling a doggy smile. It's a pity Pucky was not there too. He would have enjoyed digging holes and sending the sand over us and over the food !

Balbo sends the usual messages to you, saying that if you come out here, you will find plenty to write about and some beautiful horses to ride. Gasolene is getting scarce (you would not think so, the way he flies about !) and everyone may soon have to resort again to the old means of locomotion, the Arab horse and the camels. . . .

I was much amused by a story Balbo told me about his little girl (she must be about nine years old). For some reason or other, an order came from Rome that the schools should carry on through Xmas, without any Xmas holidays. Naturally the schoolchildren in Tripoli, as elsewhere, were much disgusted, and they appealed to their companion in misfortune, the Governor's daughter, to intervene in their favour with her Pà. This she did, explaining to him that unless he helped her, *she* would lose face with her school chums.

He promised to do something, but went off next day to Rome and forgot all about the matter, though Xmas was only a week off !

He was in the air, flying over the sea, when suddenly he remembered his promise about the holidays. . . .

As he was piloting the plane himself, he explained the situation to his wireless operator, and told him to send an order to Tripoli, saying that the schoolchildren should be given three days' holiday.

When he got home, his little girl was profuse in thanks, but he answered : ' Don't thank me. Thank the wireless operator ! '

Upon which, Balbo's little girl went to the major-domo and demanded three bottles of champagne *of the best*. Having obtained these, she collected her school chums and together (all unbeknown to their parents), they went out to the market and bought a large, fat turkey. And they took it—the whole group of them—with the champagne, to the house of the wireless operator, where they found him with his wife and children. They presented their gifts, as an expression of gratitude, so that the family might have a grand Xmas dinner !

I forgot to say that all this happened in the very early morning, between half-past four and half-past six, when the parents of the donors were all asleep. Balbo's little girl began by waking up the major-domo, then she woke up her school friends, went out with them on bicycles to the market (which opens at half-past five a.m.) and finally woke up the wireless operator and his family, to make the presentation at half-past six ! !

She has all her father's energy and force of character. Isn't all this typical of Balbo himself? He's always in a hurry. Always making promises, *which he keeps*, but only remembers at the last moment, so that as often as not, it is his wireless operator who has to see about it !

Balbo himself confesses that his wireless operator is worthy of a monument, for all the situations which he has saved, *just in time* . . . I don't know if the wireless operator would appreciate a monument. But he must have enjoyed the turkey and the champagne !

My Diary for the 25th January 1940 contains two reminders of the days when I was a young Attaché at our Embassy in Vienna :

Eddy Czernin telephoned that two Hoyos girls were in Rome and wanted to see me. I imagine that, not knowing how to entertain them, he himself suggested getting hold of me, *faute de mieux*. . . . I asked them to lunch at the Club with Margherita, Diana and a couple of young men. It must have been an uncle of these girls, whom I used to meet in the *Kaiserstadt*. He had the terrible duty of coming back from Mayerling, to tell the Empress Elisabeth (who in her turn had to tell the Emperor) of their son—the Archduke Rudolph's —death.

One of the girls said she now draws and paints advertisements. The *Comtessen* did not do that in my time. They have escaped from the hot-houses of convention.

We sat under the fresco, in the ceiling, of Paolina Borghese, in the costume that she had her portrait done in by Canova. The Hoyos family is related to the Borgheses. Paolina's house in Paris is now the British Embassy. While we stared up at the undraped portrait, someone told a story of the Ambassador, Lord Tyrrell, finding himself next to a glum looking lady, at some dinner-party. Feeling he ought to make conversation, he said : '*Vous savez, Madame, que j'habite la maison de Pauline Borghese et que je couche dans son lit !* ' The lady answered icily : ' *Votre vie privée ne m'intéresse pas !* '

When the others had gone home, I strolled into the reading-room of the Club, and found old Senator Rota, snoozing in an arm-chair. He opened one eye and said : ' There's an old lady in Rome, who would like to see you again.' I asked who it was, and he answered : ' The Princess Stephanie, now Countess Loniay. She is seventy-one years old.'

Strange to think that, when first married (in May 1881) to the Archduke

Rudolph, this little old lady, now staying in a small hotel in Rome and forgotten by the world, expected to become Empress of Austria !

I felt that I had been transported back, in time and space, to where the Stephansdom soars up into the sky, like a song by Schubert.

*   *   *

I hardly like to read over the pages of my Diary for those last months when we were at peace with the world. Fluctuating hopes alternated with gnawing fears. The vintage that on a Monday bubbled in our glasses, on Tuesday would come up flat from the cellar.

Could we keep from being caught up in the maelstrom ? Thankfulness welled over when a lull seemed to indicate that it might pass by, like a cyclone that swerves from its course. There were moments of gaiety, as days passed and nothing happened. Then a sudden rush of reports showed how our world was crumbling.

My conflicting emotions filled the blank pages of the *Agenda* as they got written over, each under its own date, with the name of a saint, a religious festival, anniversaries, phases of the moon, and eclipses. . . .

Our morning's mail was spread on the lacquer table in the entrance-hall. Letters from England and from France . . . How much longer would they continue to arrive ? Some of those letters were full of the zest of life, as if war, after all, was not the end of everything. . . .

After a few weeks with no entries whatever, my Diary starts off again at an ominous date.

March 13th (The Ides of March). For the last week, despite remonstrances of the family, I have been sitting in an arm-chair, day and night, wrapped in rugs. I have been pretty bad, with influenza. But when unwell I am nervous of going to bed. So many people die there.

Kind people have brought me illustrated papers, and I have been reading Shakespeare. In a French comic paper, *Match*, I find a drawing of two *poilus* sheltering from enemy fire behind some trees. One of them protests indignantly : ' *Ma foi ! Ils tirent sur nous !* ' It is unheard of (in this war) that opposing armies should shoot at one another. On another page, a glamorous lady is depicted taking up the telephone, to say : ' *Donnez moi la Ligne Maginot.*'

In Shakespeare, I find the grim foreboding :

> " *Caesar :* The Ides of March have passed.
> *Soothsayer :* Ay, Caesar ; but not gone. "

207

THE DREAM SHATTERED

I don't think I am going to succumb to the inauspicious date (not this time). But while I was ill, Ribbentrop has been in Rome, ostensibly for an official visit to the Pope. This is good for propaganda purposes among the German catholics, and serves to counteract the persecution they are subjected to, in various devious ways. Ribbentrop considers himself well suited to decide religious questions, as, while being a believer (*Gottgläubig*), he is not a practising protestant. He says that this makes him impartial. But I cannot imagine any background less suited to Ribbentrop than the Holy See, and no diplomacy less congenial to him than Vatican diplomacy : all subtlety, patience, ancient worldly wisdom and *finesse*, robed in the majesty of an immemorial tradition.

I am told that people here are gaping with astonishment at the luxury of the special train Ribbentrop and his staff travelled in. Bathroom, study, reception-room, and chancery-offices all complete. But Ribbentrop is unpopular even with the subordinates he travels with. He is meticulous, exacting, inconsiderate, and never seems to relax, not even with his intimates ; perhaps not with himself. He is *tutto d'un pezzo*, as they say here (all of one piece, like an image cut out of wood). He has not even the saving grace of giving due support to his official subordinates, when they are criticized. Like Friedrich von Holstein in a former generation, Ribbentrop has again lost Germany the greater part of her friends.

I have known many Germans of the arrogant, domineering type that is so apt to get itself disliked (Ambassador Monts, Baron Marschall, Hans Guido von Bülow, pianist and conductor). They were formidable men. Ribbentrop does not fall into their category. He is a misfit. But I look back with pleasure to my acquaintance with his dog, Bärchen. We used to exchange civilities, when I came out of the Athenæum and walked down the Duke of York's steps, into the Mall. Bärchen would sit there, in company with the two policemen, who kept guard on the German Embassy, in Carlton House Terrace.

Like his master, Bärchen was rather haughty and distant in manner, but he would show real feeling when a little German boy, with a satchel of school books under one arm, passed in and out of the area entrance.

I am forgetting the news of the day. After 104 days of war, there is peace between Russia and Finland. The Finnish collapse has lowered the prestige of the Allies, who expressed sympathy but remained inert. In America, people find it hard to believe that propaganda is not enough, and that the Russians could let it go by default. God has been, as usual, on the side of the big battalions, and not on that of the more numerous typewriters.

Like us, the Finns once had a Fascist reaction against communism. They called it the 'Lapua Movement' : a march of 12,000 peasants who drove the Reds out of Lapua, and across the frontier into Russia. It was an article by J. T. Marcosson, in the *Saturday Evening Post* (2nd May 1936), that pointed out the similarity with Mussolini's 'march on Rome' in 1922.

March 24th (Easter Sunday). Low has a cartoon in the *Evening Standard*, representing Mussolini as Ulysses, being rowed past the rock where the Syrenes are singing : these sea-nymphs being represented by Ribbentrop and Molotov. It is called ' Mussulysses tempted '. Will the Duce be as wise as the wanderer in the *Odysseus* ? That is what we are asking ourselves and each other. Bettina went up to a garden-party at the American Academy on the Gianicolo, and everybody crowded round her to ask what she thought. And so it is everywhere. We may be gossiping gaily and lightheartedly, but soon the talk drifts toward the question that haunts us, even on the lovely spring days of a Roman Easter. It is like a shadow that broods over the sunlit scene—the apprehension of some inescapable doom, darkening our hopes.

We keep our eyes fixed on Mussolini, to guess his thoughts and his reactions to events. The lure of the German and Russian syrenes has a refrain which is particularly dangerous : it promises that Italian intervention on the side of Germany would bring the war quickly to an end. But behind the Lorelei-melody that enchants its victim with sheer sweetness, there is a hidden threat. If Germany is victorious without our help, Italy will be made to pay for her defection. The Germans would like nothing better than an excuse to invade the Valley of the Po.

The Duce, himself, is most reassuring. For example :

' They are trying to drag me into this war by the hairs of the head.' And then the smiling conclusion : ' Fortunately, I have no hairs left on my head ! '

And again—this in a letter to Hitler : ' The Italo-German friendship is a flower of too recent growth to survive a storm. We must let it grow and strengthen on its stalk, before exposing it to inclement weather.'

The Countess Daisy Robilant, like Bettina, runs some institution (I think a Woman's League of sorts), which is working for peace. She asked Mussolini, point-blank, if it were any use she and the Signora Varè going on with their work, in view of the situation. He answered : ' Certainly. Do your best ! ' (I don't see, myself, how he could have answered otherwise. He could hardly have told Daisy that he meant to go to war, as soon as the moment appeared propitious, even if this may be so.)

Fabrizio Colonna tells me that his sister-in-law, the wife of Piero, who is Governor of Rome, asked Mussolini, during some official dinner-party, whether it were true that we must go to war on the side of the Germans. To which he answered : ' Do you think it likely that I would send our young men to fight by the side of a people against whom their fathers fought at Monte Grappa ? '

The trouble is that Mussolini's conduct does not conform to his reasoning. And he can no longer control his nerves. At one moment he will be admitting that we are unprepared for war. The next, he will be losing his temper because some foreign journalist has presumed to say just that !

March 27th. English and French interference with our shipping—even more than the blocking of coal sent to us by sea from neutral countries—is causing great irritation here, and playing into the hands of German propagandists. At Whitehall, Bastianini is given the most cordial assurances, but in the Mediterranean, every naval officer of a small British, or French, unit seems to think this a heaven-sent opportunity to show the Italians where they get off. The same Italian merchantman is made to go 600 miles out of its way, to Malta, and when at last it is set free, the French make it go another 600 miles, to Casablanca, or to Dakar. And this, despite the fact that a visit on the high-seas would generally be amply sufficient for the purpose. All of which is exasperating to the most anglophil Italian. And the financial loss is enormous.

Can it be possible that the English and French General Staffs *want* us to come into this war against them ? Mention is made of a French General Fayalde, who is (or was) in command of the 16th Army Corps, in Savoy. He appears to have complained that Italy's neutrality prevented the Allies creating a second front by invading the Valley of the Po, at the moment when the Germans invaded Poland.[1]

March 31st. It is not long since Gianmarina (now aged fifteen) has been considered old enough to hear the chimes at midnight. Last night she went to a dance in a long evening frock of white tulle, the sort of thing young girls danced in, when I was young myself. Needless to say, GM. is thoroughly pleased with herself. Diana asked her : ' *Est-ce-que quelqu'un t'a fait la cour ?* ' Gianmarina answered : ' *Non. Seulment quatre ou cinq.* '

I wonder what the number should have been, to have justified her answering : ' *Oui !* '

Another inmate of our household, who was out last night, was Buster. He is a Persian cat, belonging to Margherita, and he has great success with the

---

[1] For confirmation of these rumours, see the article by Jules Romains, ' The Mystery of Gamelin ', in the *Saturday Evening Post* of 28th September 1940.

In this article, the proposal is discussed to ' put Mussolini on the spot ', asking him to give guarantees that his ' non-belligerence ' should not end in a declaration of war. The proposal was submitted to Gamelin, who answered : ' All I need is a fortnight to complete my mobilization in peace. Even if Italy starts to attack immediately after the first fortnight, I'd rather that than have her jump on us right away.'

Coulondre, who was acting Minister at the Quai d'Orsai, was quite satisfied with Mussolini's ' non-belligerence '. This was because, at that time, Italy had promised France to provide her with Caproni bombing-planes, to be paid for in olive-oil and phosphates from Tunisia.

The same information reached me later from another source. On June the 13th (after our ' non-belligerence ' had ceased, and the dogs of war had been let loose), I was told by the Marchese Alberto Theodoli of a rumour then current in the Senate, to the effect that we had been asked to declare war, by the French General Staff itself, in order to justify their inevitable surrender, and in order that the Southern provinces of France be occupied by Italian, in preference to German, troops.

ladies in spite of a broken tail. Buster came home about the same time as Gianmarina, with a crumpled ear, a face all covered with scars, and a ' morning after the night before' expression that is a disgrace to the neighbourhood.

Even the dogs did not recognize him, and started to chase him. When they discovered it was nobody but old Buster, they pulled up hurriedly and apologized.

While the rest of the family were out on the spree, Bettina, Margherita and I dined quietly at home, with the Marchese and Marchesa Origo. She is *née* Cutting, and is some relation to Ambassador Phillips, with whom they are staying. We went on to hear Edoardo de Filippo in a new play of his called *Ventiquattr'ore di un Uomo Qualunque*. During an *entr'acte* Margherita and I went behind and talked to Edoardo in his dressing-room. We took Onorato Caetani with us, for he wanted to meet the actors. And who should we find there, in de Filippo's dressing-room, but old Vittorio Emanuele Orlando ! He and I talked, inevitably, about the war. Orlando compared the feeling in Italy today to that of the days when he and Salandra succeeded one another as Prime Minister. There is no surge of popular emotion, now, as there was then, to bring Italy into the conflict, on one side or the other. What we feel is ' A plague on both your houses ! '

April 9th. A few days ago I saw Diana's maid, Rosina, packing. I asked : ' Where is the Signorina off to now ? ' Rosina answered that she thought it might be Paris. Wherever Diana starts for, she generally ends up in Paris. This morning, I received a telegram from her, dated Etalie Straphaelvar (St. Raphael, Var ?). I understand that Danielle Darrieux is of the party. . . .

In a publication called *Le Forze Armate del Fascismo* (second edition), the Italian army is described as *forte nei mezzi e inguagliabile nello spirito.* No one knows better than the general, who signs this article, that our army is not well equipped, whatever its morale may be. Our Minister of War was asked to sell some war material abroad, and refused to do so, because he dared not deprive us of the little we possessed, hardly enough to equip six or seven divisions !

This little episode shows how people in office set out to bamboozle the man in the street and the Duce himself, who likes to be told that everything is for the best in the best of worlds. It also shows the mutability of our foreign policies. Not so long ago, the Duce was encouraging the sale of our war material, so sure was he that we would not go to war. Now he's off on the opposite tack. We may be at war any day.

There is one person who is doing his best to prevent this. I mean Balbo. He was closeted with Mussolini for hours, pointing out the danger of our losing our colonies, that we had won at the cost of so much blood and treasure, and in the teeth of so much opposition.

April 18th. Final meeting, this afternoon at the Palazzo Brancaccio, of the

Commission that is to judge the work of certain university students, who have been making a special study of colonial and Far Eastern affairs.

Before we came away, Admiral Ducci told us that at a previous meeting, this morning, of the *Comitato delle Forze Armate*, the Minister of War let it be understood that we might be at war very soon.

I walked home with my former colleague, Senator Majoni. We agreed that the country is solid against war and utterly unprepared, except for the navy. . . . Things were very different in 1935. At that time, though people may have disliked the idea of even a colonial war, the Italians felt in their hearts that their cause was a just one and that Great Britain had no real justification in preaching a moral crusade against us. In the Abyssinian campaign, the country was solid behind Mussolini.

But now ?

He is going to drag us into a European war, against his own convictions, repeatedly expressed, against the advice of his Minister of Foreign Affairs, of his Ambassadors abroad and of his Chief of Staff. . . .

Why ?

Official propaganda tries to make out that we are imprisoned in the Mediterranean. If so, how is it that we managed to conquer Abyssinia, in the teeth of British opposition ?

Mussolini himself said, after the Abyssinian campaign was over, that we were a ' satisfied nation '. And indeed, my youthful dreams of Italian expansion overseas had at last come true. Since then we have consolidated our position in the Adriatic. There is precious little for us to gain in a war against England and France, though much could be obtained by an honest and skilful diplomacy. As Ciano said to Diana (and since then repeated to Bettina), Italy's rôle in this tragic business is not a heroic one, but justified under the circumstances : to sit still and do the best for ourselves, while the others are destroying one another.

April 20th. The tension of the last few days has diminished. A lull before the storm. But I have had a quiet, pleasant day in the country. Margherita drove me out along the Appian Way, to take her children to see a friend of theirs, Rosemary Baroni.

A lovely spring day, full of the scents of flowers and the fragrance of resin from the cypress trees that stand sentinel between Roman tombs. Our conveyance was a rustic *biroccino*, or buggy, having between the shafts a pre-historic animal, with legs at the four corners, who goes by the name of Pippo. He jogs along, wearing an expression of inspired pessimism, as if meditating an Ode to Melancholy. He cheered up a little when unharnessed and allowed to graze on the feathery grasses alongside the road that was built by Appius Claudius.

The children played around, happy to have shed coats and mufflers, and the dogs, with pink tongues hanging out and quivering tails, hunted lizards, poking their noses into the clefts of the brickwork, in ivy-grown ruins.

I sat on a stone and read the *Corriere della Sera*, from which I learnt that Katharina Schratt had died in Vienna, aged eighty-seven. I used to see her at Schoenbrunn, where there is a small zoological garden : a plump little woman, wearing a brown straw hat, with a quill in it. Her friendship for the Emperor Franz Josef was one of the consolations of his last years. Her suburban villa, near the Imperial residence, offered bourgeois comforts, such as Monarchs love. Our own King, Victor Emanuel, escapes from the fanfarronade of Fascism, by hiding himself in a secluded villa, out of town.

In Katharina Schratt's household, the Emperor was known as ' the Colonel '. They would play cards of an evening (the ancient game of *tarok*). To make up a four, two neighbours would be called in, one of whom was a Jew, and the other, Mr. Palmer, a banker. ' The Colonel ' smoked cheap cigars, called *trabucos*, and would make sarcastic remarks about rich bankers, who could afford Havanas, such as Mr. Palmer allowed himself.

This is ancient history. So are the tombs of the Appian Way. Such things are pleasant to dwell on, while the breeze blows off the Alban Hills, in an everlasting wash of air.

May 6th. Diana has been lost to us for some time. The last we heard of her was from St. Sebastian and she appeared to be once more with the Russian dancers, as when she fraternized with them in Paris. They were on their way to Madrid. Now she is back in Paris again, and I received the following Epistle to the Romans :

HOTEL LOTTI
PARIS, *4th May 1940*

Dearest Pà,

I have been rushing all over the world. I went to Madrid even. When I got back to Biarritz, whom do I find but Marcellino ! So we all went back to Spain. And after two days, we left again by car for Paris. A marvellous journey !

Spain is very much changed since I saw it last. Every one here, I mean there, are grands mutilés de guerre, walking with crutches and without a leg or an arm, or an eye. And all so young ! I went over the zone de guerre, and the banlieux of Madrid are simply devastated.

Marcellino is going to Rome, so I will come back with him, and he can look after his [sic] valises.

As for France, it hasn't changed a bit. People tell me that it is une guerre gagnée d'avance. The Germans bombed the airport of Le Bourget, and everyone in this hotel rushed out into the street in their pyjamas, to see what was to be seen. As to going into shelters and wearing a gas-mask, no one thought of it, except one old gentleman, who suffers from asthma. He put on his gas-mask, but it gave him a fit, and he nearly died.

I forgot to say that, when in Madrid, I looked up our old Copenhagen colleagues, the Raneros. But they were not there. They are en poste in Holland. They chose that, because they wanted a nice quiet place, after the civil war in Spain. I don't know that Holland will be as quiet as all that . . .

A bientot . . .

What Diana says about people in France talking of *une guerre gagnée d'avance*, corresponds to the general opinion that it is ' a phony war ' or ' a war of boredom '.

John Crane is here and dropped in after dinner. He says that the great advantage Hitler had over his enemies was that they thought him crazy. People just sat back in their chairs and did not take him seriously.

As a matter of fact, I believe it true that the Führer is not all there. Did he not once have an attack of hysterical aphasia ? For some time he was without speech ; now, once he gets started, he can't stop talking. When he begins haranguing them in one of his interminable monologues, people like Neurath and Goering shrug their shoulders and say : ' *Der Adolph ist noch ein mal in die Luft verschwunden !* ' (' He's up in the air again ! ').

May 24th. When England declared war, in September last, *The Times* had a heading in huge type, telling us that she did so TO SAVE THE WORLD. I abstain from the obvious comment.

Today I have received a book from London, saying—can you believe it ?— that Great Britain went to war to please me.

The book is one just published by Burns Oates and called *Neutral War Aims.* Since the British remain vague about their own war-aims, they are trying to make clear what non-belligerents are thinking. The book gives the views of nine different writers, in as many neutral countries. I contributed the article for Italy.

The Preface is written by Christopher Hollis. In it, there is an allusion to my *Laughing Diplomat.*

Italians, indeed, look at the problems of the world from an Italian point of view, and Englishmen from an English. But is there not more than either a merely English or a merely Italian point of view at stake ? Are there not things more precious even than national interests, which are today in peril ? I will give an example of one of them—one of the things for which we are fighting. We are fighting for Signor Varè.

Signor Varè's exquisite courtesy would perhaps be tempted to reply that it is very kind of us, but that he never asked us to do any such thing. But can anyone doubt that it is true ? . . . Can anyone doubt that a world that was dominated by Herr Hitler and M. Stalin would be a world that would have no place for the culture of Signor Varè ?

Diplomats do not laugh either in Moscow or Berlin.

The author kindly attributes to me a superlative culture, which I fear I do not possess. Anyway I doubt whether, after two world wars, any academical culture will be at a premium. It would be more useful if I knew how to produce foodstuffs at a profit.

I fear that I will soon find myself living in a world of ghosts. Even now, my mental processes are not tuned-in to the wavelength that is most favoured by the radio-fans. Culture is an acquired taste. In a propaganda-ridden world, men are inclined to adapt themselves to that which is commonest : flamboyance, incitement to mass-hysteria, arrogance, hatred, frustration, fear. . . .

Meanwhile, I am grateful to a kindred spirit for his appreciation.

May 25th. That the Germans should have taken Abbéville and Amiens, reached the Channel at Boulogne and encircled the Allied armies in Belgium, is certainly extraordinary. But no less extraordinary, to me, are the comments on these events, as reported in French and English papers. An ' enquiry ' in France appears to have concluded with a comprehensive insult to the French army, from the humble *poilu* (who in some places fought bravely, in others surrendered in mass, giving the communist salute) to the Commander-in-Chief. The former is accused of having lost his war mentality, while sitting in the steam-heated Maginot line. The latter is described as being without imagination, audacity, creative power. Meanwhile—so I read in the papers—the British Minister points out that it was through the French section of the line that the Germans broke through, whereas the English held firm.

I really am not surprised that the Duce has the impression that Europe is falling to pieces, and that we should not stand aside, while it is remodelled on a new plan. But does that really mean we should go to war ? Or is he afraid that the victorious Germans may turn on Italy, to punish her for having kept out ? At the bottom of most wars there is fear.

Bettina tries to find distraction in detective stories, saying that it is a relief to read about only one individual being murdered, and not many hundred thousand.

Pierre Mille has an article in *l'Europe Nouvelle* in which he looks forward to the Germans being utterly defeated, after which he proposes a sort of super-Versailles, which should impose the teaching of history in all the schools of Europe as written only by French historians, to the greater glory of France. And what about the ' enquiry ', quoted above, defaming the French *poilu* and the French commanders ?

May 30th. I have been to see Nella Grénier (*née* Caetani). She is *Dame de la Cour* of the Queen Mother of Belgium. She says there may well be a civil war in that country. It is not clear what has happened. The King is accused of having capitulated, without warning the Allies, only a few hours after a meeting in which a common plan of resistance had been agreed upon. Others say that the King was right in deciding not to sacrifice the flower of Belgian youth, while the English and the French were making for home.

Bettina is much worried about it all. She is anxious about the fate of three cousins of hers, who are now in Belgium (or in France ?) : Nicky Daniel, John Stansfeld, and Oswald Phipps (Marquess of Normanby).

I saw Ciano a moment, under the *portone* of the Palazzo Chigi. I asked him what the Duce was doing. The answer was : ' He is taking lessons in politics from the cat in the Villa Torlonia. He says that cat never makes a mistake.'

Ciano disappeared into the lift. After which (I am much gifted with what the French call *l'esprit de l'escalier*, the reply that you think of just too late), I thought we might suggest to the Duce that his cat probably does not interfere in other cats' quarrels.

People here are surprised at the fact that the British Government and General Staff have shown themselves unprepared for the German tactics. They say : ' The English have been talking for years of the threat of war from Germany. How is it that they now show themselves unprepared to meet it ? ' I don't know what the answer is, unless it be that the British military experts saw the danger as a receding horizon, never nearer than five or ten years off. . . . More likely, as in the case of Ethiopia, or of Spain, the opinion of experts was never taken seriously, since they have little or no influence on elections.

Before coming home to dinner, I looked in to see how Giovanni (Colonna) was getting on. He is very ill, but not quite bed-ridden, and this evening he had managed to get as far as a *chaise-longue* on the little open terrace, where he lay among the geraniums, looking out into the sunset behind the spire of Santa Maria delle Fratte. I gave him the news and asked him where his sympathies lay. He was very grumpy, and said that his sympathies lay nowhere. ' *Odio tutti i forestieri e mi sono antipatici gl'italiani !* ' (' I loathe all foreigners and I dislike the Italians ! ')

I wonder if we won't all be feeling that way, some day. . . .

June 5th. Andrea Celesia tells me that the French have offered us Jibuti and better conditions for the Italians in Tunisia, on the understanding that we keep out. . . . This same offer, made before the war, or at its beginning, especially if made in agreement with England, might have prevented us reaching the present pass. But I imagine that no French government could have remained in power, if it had made such a sensible gesture in time. . . . (We might have given something in exchange.) So now the offer comes, as it would seem, too late. It is made out of fear and not out of friendliness. Italy would not cut a very fine figure, if she accepted—though, perhaps, that would not matter as much as the fateful decision to go to war. Anyhow, the telegram from Guariglia, in Paris, containing the proposal, though it arrived at the end of May, has not yet been answered. And it looks as if it never will be.

The English are against any concession being made to us—or so I understand. They point out that, if they lose the war, the French offer, even if accepted, will not be enough. On the other hand, if they win the war, concessions of any kind will have been proved unnecessary.

It may be true that they put this veto, or it may not. It is very *vraisemblable*.

Whenever a French government has shown willingness to come to some agreement with us (as in 1934) the English have done their best to keep us apart. The French would never have agreed to the policy of ' sanctions ', unless they had been forced to do so by British pressure. That policy was so unpopular in France that the British Embassy in the Rue St. Honoré had to have police protection. Those sanctions have made possible the present situation.

I hear that the Americans (by which, I suppose, is meant Mr. Roosevelt) have also made some practical and desirable proposals to us. I don't know what they consist of, except the assurance that, even if we are not belligerents, we shall be admitted to take our seat at the Peace Conference. But Mussolini appears to be quite incapable of realizing what potential strength there is in the U.S.A., just as he does not understand the tenacity of the Anglo-Saxon character, which hangs on (see the old simile of the bull-dog) even when its own interest would advise it to come to terms. Mussolini thinks that if England were invaded, the war would be over. Yet it is well known that, even if an invasion of the British Isles were successful, the Empire might carry on from Canada. I am not predicting that the English will win the war. Indeed, it looks very much as if they might lose it. But even so, I feel in my bones that our old traditional Italian foreign policy, dating from my father's time, is still the right one. *Con tutto il mondo in guerra, ma non con l'Inghilterra.*

I do not write this—or say this to anyone who will listen—only out of sympathy with England. It is principally of Italy I am thinking. And I do feel a moral discomfort that is akin to shame. It is not thus that a great nation goes to war.

What I and elderly gentlemen like me think matters very little. A war against England is now possible, even in the teeth of opposition from the specialists in foreign affairs. It is the youth of the country that counts, in moments like these, with a régime like the Fascist régime. Unfortunately —as Bettina was saying the other day—the young men of Italy have no recollection of a friendly England. They have been taught, when reading recent history, of the promises made to us in the Pact of London and at St. Jean de Maurienne, promises that were broken at Versailles. And they remember sanctions. They are full of generous impulses, and they are what propaganda has made them.

June 10th. At six p.m., I listened in at the radio to Mussolini's speech. He said that at four-thirty Ciano had handed our declaration of war to the English and French Ambassadors.

Strange to say, the general feeling is one of relief. The trying period of uncertainty is over. The die is cast, for better or for worse.

The King left Rome last night by train. The station was in darkness. Somebody who was near to him told me that they were speaking of the German's advance on Paris, and calculating the distance that still remained to be covered. The King said : ' *Sarebbe come se fossero a Maccarese.*' He meant, I suppose, that they were within an hour's motor drive, going slowly . . .

As the train moved off, a few voices shouted, ' *Viva il Re !* ' from out the shadows. The tail lights showed for a few seconds and were reflected on the burnished rails. They twinkled and were gone.

Many people have a feeling that, if the King approves, it must be all right. We had snails for supper. We had never had them before. Rather tasteless, I thought. Bettina is evidently of the opinion that it is prudent to get used to this sort of food in war-time.

Letters that Never Reached Him [1]

MANY years ago, an Italian cruiser dropped anchor opposite the Bund of Hankow, on the Yangtze. Soon afterwards, a boat put off from a Japanese man-of-war and a little officer with slanting eyes approached and made his way up the gang-way. He was received on deck by a young midshipman, and the following conversation took place :

The Jap : ' I have—come—to bring—to—your Captain—the compliments—of my—Commander ! '

The Middy : ' I—have not—the knife—of my uncle—but I have —the umbrella—of—my aunt ! '

Salutes, bows, and the Japanese officer went back to his ship. When paying ceremonial visits, these Orientals would learn a few English phrases by heart, and reel them off staccato, stopping to suck the air in through their teeth. It was pretty safe to answer with a phrase out of Ollendorff's conversation book.

The Italian midshipman who figures in this story was Maurizio Bensa. He will be remembered by those (if there are any of them left) who knew Peking between 1901 and 1924. He came of a rich Genoese family, but was parsimonious to the point of avarice. (It is well known that the Genoese will pare between the rind and the cheese.) He did not stay long in the Navy. Being endowed with the gift of tongues, he learned Chinese and joined the staff of our Legation in Peking.

[1] In the heading of this chapter, the reader may recognize the title of a novel by the Baroness von Heyking. In that book, the letters that never reached their addressee were those written to him, during the siege of the Legations, in Peking, in 1900.

It was in Peking that I first met him, in the days when China was still a country of palaces and pagodas. When he retired, he went to live in Indo-China, where he bought a large property and lived a peculiar life of his own choosing, with big-game shooting as his principal recreation.

In 1940, when Italy entered the war, Bensa was put into a French concentration-camp, and died there shortly afterwards.

For many years we kept up a correspondence, though sometimes it was limited to a letter a year. In this way I kept in touch with the Far East, and he with Europe. As far back as 1937 he wrote to me that the Orientals felt war drawing nearer and nearer, a war into which the East would inevitably be dragged. One day I received a telegram from him that appeared to be a quotation from Goldsmith. It ran : " *The man recovered of the bite—The dog it was that died.*"

A fortnight later the explanation arrived by post. While on some shooting expedition in the interior, Bensa had been bitten by a mad dog. It was evident that he expected the letter, in which he told me about it, to be his last. And he asked me to do what I could to help his Chinese servants, who had been faithful to him, during a life-time. But the bite had gone through his putties, and that perhaps prevented his getting the infection.

Although it seemed a hopeless thing to do, I continued to send off letters to Bensa, even after June 1940, posting them to a mutual friend in a neutral country, to be forwarded to their destination. Following the habit acquired in twenty-five years of diplomatic service, I kept carbon copies, and these form an occasional record of current events.

I heard of Bensa's death through Monsignor Costantini of the ' Propaganda Fide ', but only when the war was over.

ROME, *2nd July 1940*

MY DEAR BENSA,

We are home again, after a fortnight in the mountains, at Fiuggi. Bettina started painting again, and was thoroughly happy : it kept her thoughts off the war. Gianmarina found a school-chum in the hotel ; also a boy-friend. So *she* was all right ! The place was full of babies and of expectant mothers, who had come away from Rome, for fear of bombardments. I counted thirty-five babies in our hotel and an equal number of dogs. We had Pucky with us and he fought all the other dogs, except, of course, the lady-dogs.

Since we got back, I have been talking with several people about the signing of the Armistice with France. That is to say, I have spoken with Rulli, who was Secretary to our delegation, and with Celesia, who is Chef de Protocol.

Chief of the French Delegation was General Huntziger, an Alsatian. You may remember him, for he was out in China. Even then, he struck me as having something teutonic about him, but at the same time possessing many of the characteristics of the French officer, at his best. While in Rome they were sumptuously housed at the Villa Madama, where Carlo Frasso once resided in more than Oriental splendour. But they met our delegation—headed by Badoglio—at the Villa Incisa, a few miles out on the Via Cassia. Celesia says that they all looked very glum and haggard, until the article was read out, saying we made no claim on their navy. Then they appeared less anxious.

The terms having been read out, they declared themselves willing to sign. But the various copies had still to be prepared, and this would take time. Military operations would therefore continue throughout the day, until the French delegation could telegraph home that the Armistice was signed, after which the order to 'cease fire' could be given.

But Badoglio said he was quite ready to accept General Huntziger's assurance that he would sign. They might telegraph home, if they liked, that the Armistice had been concluded. This would mean a gain of some five or six hours. Badoglio expressed himself in execrable French, but no one minded that. What he said was : ' Celà ne fait rien. . . . C'est firmé (sic) sur la parole. Télegraphiez immédiatement à votre governement. Comme ça il y aura moins de morts ! '

This pleased the French. Huntziger said : ' Vous êtes un vrai soldat, Badoglio, et non seulement un général. . . .'

Darlan was silent, but his tears fell on the papers as he signed them.

General Huntziger's conduct, all through the proceedings, was so impeccably correct and dignified that Rulli could not refrain from expressing his admiration. The Frenchman bowed in acknowledgement of the tribute, but said nothing.

Friday, 14th September 1940. We naturally do not correspond direct with England in these days, but Bettina had a letter from her mother, via America, telling about the cousins in the British Army. The news is confirmed that John Stansfeld is a prisoner since Dunkerque and that Oswald Normanby is missing. I went to the German Embassy here and saw Prince Bismarck about them. He advised me to write to our old friend Georges Wagnière, formerly Swiss Minister in Rome, and who is now the big noise at the International Red Cross at Geneva. Bismarck was willing to do his best for me, but he remarked : 'I understand that we took very few prisoners at Dunkerque.'

I took his advice and wrote to Wagnière, and now I have an answer, giving John's address, in Germany (Oflag. VII D.) and saying that we can send him letters and parcels.

Wagnière writes that he receives an average of 60,000 letters a day at the International Red Cross, and most of the work is done voluntarily by Swiss ladies. In spite of this pressure of work, Wagnière finds time to protest to what I say at page 189 of my *Laughing Diplomat*. He objects to the following comment : ' Most of the Geneva women are so ugly that they would calm St. Anthony at the worst moment of temptation.' It *is* a bit strong.

Bettina and Gianmarina go down to the sea most days, to bathe. Not by car, as in former years, but by tram and train. I go more rarely. The last time I went, I met Ciano in the water, and we stood out on the sandbank and talked. He introduced a General Muti to me : the type of adventurer to whom war is a godsend. In fact he ran away from home at the age of fifteen to join in the first world war ; was brought home, and ran away again. He now has rows of medals ' to valour ', but you would hardly call it ' valour ' with him : danger is the very breath of his nostrils. The day he and I and Ciano stood and talked with the water up to our necks, Muti had arrived half an hour before from Rhodes, after having bombed Haifa with a squadron of aeroplanes.

Diana has just come back, by air, from Spain. She and her mother and sister met in the bathroom, where they all were getting the sand out of their shoes. Bettina and Gianmarina had been bathing at Castel Fusano, and Diana, at the same time this morning, had bathed somewhere near Barcelona, before starting to fly home. The world is getting very small (if you will excuse a platitude). Diana has been in France, crossing the Spanish border. The Germans were very kind and nice to her. By some fluke, she was driving a car that happened to be the only one allowed to circulate. Someone had lent it to her from our Embassy in Madrid. She returned with letters for the Queen of Spain and for the concierge of the flat she used to occupy, when in Paris (I never knew anyone with so varied a visiting list as Diana). She has troubles of her own, poor girl, and tries to forget them by never keeping still for more than twenty-four hours. Diplomat's children have a restlessness in the blood, a residue of childish years, when they were planted and uprooted time after time, to follow their parents' wanderings.

Diana has now some idea of going for a cruise in the Adriatic, in a *trabaccolo*, an old fishing-boat, done up so luxuriously that it has even been written about in *Vogue*. It used to belong to Sert, the painter. I don't know who owns it now. Possibly Diana !

ROME, *12th November 1940*

Supposing it is ever delivered, this letter is to give you the sad news of the death of Giovanni Colonna di Cesarò. I remember that, when you two met in my house, you liked each other. I think this was partly because of something contrary in both your characters. You were kindred spirits.

In politics, Giovanni was born to be in opposition. Though not a Fascist, he entered Mussolini's first cabinet, and left it after the murder of Matteotti. Giovanni once gave it to me as his opinion that the cause of the rise to power of Mussolini (apart from foreign politics) was due to the pig-headedness of the Socialist party in Italy, which refused to collaborate with any other party, but wished to remain ' pure ' of contamination. In this way they played the game of the communists, who could domineer over any government that might be formed. The socialist leader, Filippo Turati, would have collaborated with Ivanoe Bonomi in forming a government, but his followers would not consent. So it was left to Mussolini to drag the country out of the slough of despond into which it had fallen. And Giovanni was willing to give him his support.

Since he broke with the Duce, Giovanni had been shadowed by a police-agent in plain clothing. This troubled the suspect not at all. He and his guardian angel were on such good terms that police supervision only served to afford him an extra and unpaid retainer.

Margherita's Alsatian has broken a toe in her front paw and wears a leather boot, that gets cleaned with the family's boots and shoes, in the morning. Our house, as usual, is rotten with dogs.

Gianmarina has reached an age when the principal amusement appears to consist in going to the cinema (preferably to a tragic one), with a school-chum (there is one called ' Mousy ', and another called ' Josette '). They weep copiously at the sad parts, and this seems to please them very much.

NAPLES, *26th June 1941*

I am writing to you from Posillipo, where we are the guests of Leo Salom at the Villa Gallotti. It is a lovely place, on the sea-shore, built up against an old powder-magazine dating from the days of the Kings of the Two Sicilies. Behind this house, the hill is hollowed out, and one can use those colossal cellars to store wine, or to take refuge in, during air-raids. A balcony runs alongside of the house and juts out over the sea itself. Our rooms open out on this balcony, and the waves beat against the wall underneath, almost as if it were the hull of a ship. A rise of green waters is followed by a dull thud and the seething roar of the wash-back.

You will not be surprised to hear that Bettina began at once to sketch the openings of the caverns on the hill-side, with festoons of cactuses falling from above and swaying in the breeze. There are also curtains of ivy-leaf geranium hanging like tapestries on the sides of the paths.

What used to be called the ' Villa Rosebery ' is next door. The Princess of Piedmont is there now with her children. The youngest, a little girl, is busy learning to walk. Farther on, the Baraccos are rebuilding the ' Villa

Emma ', where Lady Hamilton used to live. Indeed, it is called after her. Nelson would drop anchor just in front of these villas. It was very convenient. . . .

Last Sunday, at eight o'clock in the morning, Leo burst into our rooms in a great state of excitement. He had been listening to the English radio, and heard that Germany and Russia were at war, since the preceding midnight. . . .

So the invasion of the British Isles has been given up.

Here arises the old situation, as with Napoleon. He too gathered an army at the camp of Boulogne ; failed to invade England, and then launched a campaign against Russia.

Hitler himself said, not long ago, that Russia was a closed door and nobody really knew what was behind it. Well, he is breaking down the door and we'll all find out.

Russia is a country in which the mentality of the people is some 300 years behind that of the West. Into that mentality, the Soviets have injected a serum, which has produced reactions that hitherto have not been understood abroad. Who could predict the result—shall we say ?—of setting up universities in such places as Samarkand ?

Our aviation people here are anxious, for now the German aviators will have a new front to control, and the Mediterranean will be neglected.

Before this war broke out, there were a few people who declared that the best thing that could happen would be a war between Russia and Germany : a war on which the other powers could look on. I have heard this saying attributed, among others, to the American Ambassador, William Bullitt.

Now the desired situation has arisen. Unfortunately Russia and Germany are not the only belligerents. But perhaps this gives Great Britain the opportunity of emerging from the conflict, stronger than she has ever been before. All she has to do is to keep her head and not lose her nerve during aerial bombardments. She should help the Russians fight the Germans. But she should not help them too much. . . . When both are exhausted, then should come the turn of England.

And what about us Italians ? I think the best we can hope for is to survive.

ROME, *12th August 1942*

When one writes but seldom, as we do to one another, there is either too much or very little to say.

Life here is getting difficult for everybody, and the prospect of another war-winter is pretty grim. Carrots are as expensive as red orchids ; coal is as rare as black ivory ; the gas by which we are supposed to cook has become a sort of *ignis fatuus*, that will-o'-the-wisp that flickers over marshes and church-yards. Potatoes represent a buried treasure, and cheese a lost illusion. The butcher's shop is closed four days out of five.

But one gets used to everything, even to the modern uses of aircraft in war, which now include the deliberate machine-gunning from the air of bathers on the sea-shore, of children coming out of school, and of peasants working in the fields.

The mentality of the Italians is becoming used to violence and to blood-shed. This is a war that very few people wanted, and such as no one could have wished for. The mass of the civilian population, in Italy, feel a dull resentment at having been dragged at Hitler's chariot-wheels. And now even Mussolini talks of making a huge cemetery, to bury in it all the German promises to us. (This was told me by Ciano.) The people gave their sons unwillingly, but made the best of a bad job. They never had their heart in the war, but were resigned, and hoped it would not last long. Now we have seen our colonies torn from us : the colonies that had cost so much blood and treasure, and on which we had founded so many hopes. All the wealth, and the international connections, hardly won by Italian emigrants in the West and in Africa, have gone with the wind. So far, popular ill-will takes the form of passive resistance. But how will it end ?

People are bored, and have very little to distract their thoughts from their hardships. This may explain why, some time ago, I was asked to give a lecture on ' The Changing East ' at the I.S.M.I. (Instituto del Medio e Estremo Oriente). I am glad you were not there to pin down my fallacies !

I arranged for my audience to have something to look at : Bettina's paintings of old Peking, and my own collection of Chinese silks, brocades and embroideries.

I never saw such a mixed audience :—former secretaries and colleagues of my own ; a sprinkling of bishops, actors and musicians. Tucci represented Central Asiatic exploration, Giovanni Gentile philosophy, and Federico Tesio the racing world. There was even that former comrade of Lenin's, Bombacci, not to mention various Fascist *gerarchi*. There were several Roman princes, and Vittoria Sermoneta, Daisy Robilant and the Princess of Candriano who asked me how much did I think my silks might be worth, in coupons !

The Duke of Spoleto could not come, owing to the recent death at Nairobi of his brother, the Duke of Aosta. I was fond of that boy. We shared the passion for Italy's expansion overseas. And now he has died, a victim of it. And I am left to mourn for our common ideal, and for him.

No one is a prophet in his own family, or a hero to his daughters. Diana and Gianmarina did not find time to attend. But Margherita was there, with my youngest grandchild, Nicoletta (aged nine), who stared round the crowded hall and asked : ' Does grandpa know all these people ? '

ROME, *16th October 1943*

This time there should be plenty to say. . . . The difficulty is to know where to begin.

On the 2nd of October I went in to the Palazzo Chigi (there were German soldiers on the stairs), to see Augusto Rosso, who was giving up the post of Secretary General to the Foreign Office. I had nothing particular to say to him, but just wanted to hear his opinion of the situation, which is rather more than catastrophic. I found him in a small office, among the débris of official correspondence, like Marius among the ruins of Carthage. He said it will take two generations to set Italy on her feet again, and only if the Italians can put aside their factious dissensions and work together for the common good. I doubt if that could ever happen. Just now, it looks as if we might have a massacre, as in the Sicilian Vespers or the Night of St. Bartholomew.

It was strange to walk in and out of the rooms where I used to see Mussolini and Ciano, and to find them empty. I might have sat down at the big writing-table in the Sala delle Vittorie, and written out telegrams and signed them, with about as much real authority as anybody else. If I had, somebody might even have sent them off, and followed my instructions. Changes of government, in times of stress, have often occurred that way. . . .

Well, that was a fortnight ago, and things have got worse, if anything.

This morning, Margherita came home with the milk (except, of course, that there *was* no milk), having got mixed up—voluntarily, of course—in helping young men of military age to escape being rounded up by the Germans. This occurred in the purlieus of the Piazza Campitelli, in a labyrinth of little streets that, in the days of Papal Rome, used to form the Ghetto. The Germans were also rounding up the Jews that still live there. Margherita seems to have had a hectic time, climbing in and out of windows and scurrying along roofs.

She saw two Jewish children, who had been slightly wounded when a machine-gun was turned on the crowd, clinging to their mother, who lay in a pool of blood, and crying : ' Màmma, màmma . . . do not die ! What is to become of us, if you die ? ' The utter lack of altruism does not make the plea any less pitiful.

I lunched at the Club, which still is there, much as usual, in the Palazzo Borghese. And I found Vittorio (' Tojo ') Solaro del Borgo, boiling with rage, because he had seen an old Jewish woman thrown into a truck, by German soldiers, much as if she were a sack of potatoes. After lunch, I went and had a snooze on a divan, in the huge end-room, where hardly anybody ever goes, except for Club meetings. When I awoke and sat up, I found Francesco Macchi staring at me from a neighbouring sofa (he too had been asleep). He exclaimed : ' Oh, it's you ! I thought it might be some poor Jew, who had taken refuge here during the night's pogrom ! '

Diana met Pepi Salom in the street, by chance, and brought him home with her. He passed the night in our house, one of many refugees who do so in these days. He is a Jew himself, and used to direct a clinic in Trieste, and later in Milan. He says that the persecution in Lombardy is worse, if possible, than it is here, and predicts that, if the Allies break through on the

Volturno, Germans will massacre all the Jews before leaving Rome. It appears to be *une idée fixe* with them, as with Hitler. Apart from any more serious consideration, it seems to me such impertinence, to come and massacre the Jews in a country that's not yours ! On the Lago Maggiore, the Germans took the Jews out in boats, shot them, and threw the bodies into the lake. I feel I will never be able to go fishing there again, between Baveno and Ferriolo, without thinking of bodies floating ashore. Mass hatreds are terrible things, and they are not confined to any one people. I am told that the Croats are massacring the Serbs in Bosnia (or vice versa), yet they pretend to be fellow-countrymen, all Jugo-slavs !

Pepi Salom is one of the few people I have met recently who speaks of the Germans with a quiet serenity. When their Gestapo occupied his clinic in Milan, finding that he could speak German fluently, they were most kind and polite to him, and even punished a soldier for having stolen some of his cigarettes. I have noticed, myself, and so has Bettina, that it makes all the difference, speaking their language. As long as the Gestapo stayed up there, Salom had no trouble. When they left, they advised him to change his name and to go south, which he did.

I went yesterday to the ' Propaganda Fide ' and talked matters over with Monsignor Costantini. The Vatican's point of view is a little more aloof than that of us common mortals. He exclaimed : ' It has come to this : that the populace longs for the arrival in Rome of a victorious enemy.'

He points out that there can be no justification of the German excesses. It is not *the people* who have betrayed their ally. And anyway, sympathies cannot be imposed by force. But it is no longer a question of sympathies. The Germans are out to despoil the country of everything they can carry away —cattle and grain and wool, medicines and machinery, gold and silver and art-treasures ; also to round up the young men who might be enrolled to fight against them. The walls of the town are plastered over with proclamations, signed ' Rommel—Feldmarschall ' and threatening the death penalty for this, that and the other. This same Fieldmarshal was once saved from capture in Africa, by our Bersaglieri, when the British had surrounded him and his staff.

But I must tell you something more about ' our refugees '. I am always meeting unexpected guests in my house. Luckily, they do not seem to require more than a relative safety from capture. Some days ago, on entering my study in the morning, I was met by a bearded young man, whom I did not know from Adam. He had passed the night on the yellow divan, among my Chinese cut-velvets, and brocades from the Western Tombs. Somebody had let him in, after I had gone to bed. I asked him where he came from. He answered :

' From the south. I am attached to the 8th Army.'

' You are an officer ? '

226

' Yes. A naval officer. I have come to establish secret radio communications. I passed through the German lines, up in the mountains.'

' Is there anything I can do for you ? '

' Yes. If you would be so kind . . . I want some naphthaline.'

' Naphthaline ! ! ! ' I think I would have been less surprised if he had asked for the Holy Grail. But he explained :

' When I was in the mountains, they followed me with dogs. I may have to go back in a few days, and it might happen again. I am told that, if you put naphthaline in your clothes and boots, the dogs find it impossible to track you. I don't know if it's true, but I may as well try.'

I got him some naphthaline from where our furs are put away in the attic. He was very grateful.

Again, a few days later, after dinner, when I was thinking of going to bed, Diana came in and said she had brought two Germans with her. They were downstairs, in the dining-room, and wanted to pass the night there. She said they had come off a boat on the Tiber. The boat was moored under the bridge, close by, and they had left one of their party in it.

All this sounded very mysterious, and I decided not to go down and speak to them, so as to be able to say, if I were ever questioned, that I had never seen these men. But Bettina's curiosity (or kindness) induced her to go down and see them. She told me they were very nice, very distinguished, and from their accent (she spoke to them in German) they might have been Austrian or Bavarian gentlemen. They said they had come from Anzio, and that they did not want to go to the German Command so late at night. . . . . Bettina seemed to think they might be deserters from the German Army. They gave no trouble, and asked only for a towel to dry themselves with, after washing in the kitchen. Diana seemed much taken with them, and—to explain to whose house they had come—showed them the German translations of my books.

They left early in the morning, and we have not heard of them again.

ROME, *31st August 1944*

I have written to you, before, about the various ' refugees ', who seek sanctuary in our house.

I did not expect to have any after the Allies had occupied Rome, but there is one (in fact three) in the house at this moment. No, not Fascists, or Germans ; at least I don't think so. Let me explain.

Some weeks ago, an officer in the British Army, but of Austrian nationality, foisted his dog on us : a mongrel fox-terrier lady, named ' Spotty ', who was expecting to have puppies almost any day. She had married for love and not for pedigree, somewhere in the desert of Libya. Her master, after arriving in Rome, was about to proceed for the front, and it did not seem prudent that a happy event should occur in an army motor-truck. So the expectant mother took up her abode with us, and preparations were made for the *accouchement*. For two days, she stayed with us quite happily, accepting the arrangement. But one afternoon, she saw some British officers who had dropped in to pay a call on Bettina, and the sight (or the smell) of their uniforms awoke the desire to go and find her master again. A few minutes later she was nowhere to be found.

We were all in despair. A lost dog is always a pitiful thing (unless it's off on the razzle-dazzle, as Pucky so often is !). The fact of Spotty being in the family way, and not knowing her way about Rome, made it all the more harrowing. We imagined her having her puppies under a bush in some public garden and no one to feed her, or to help. . . .

Margherita commandeered a very important Allied general, who docilely took her round in his car to all the rest-centres and camps in and around Rome, but no Spotty . . . Then, sixteen hours after she had disappeared, she turned up at the house of a friend, where last she had seen her master. We brought her home in triumph.

Some days ago, the puppies arrived, two of them, one with a black patch over one eye, and one all white. An announcement of their birth was immediately sent to the service newspaper, the *Union Jack*, to be inserted in a coming number, so that the master might read about it at the front : ' Born to Spotty, two puppies, Domino and Snow White. Mother and offspring doing well.'

It requires—or it did in the first days—quite a lot of courage to go and put on Spotty's collar and chain, to take her out for an occasional constitutional. She was so very fierce in defence of her basket and the puppies. But it is all ' look-see ', as the Chinese say, and she is perfectly good-tempered, as soon as we get outside the door.

These may seem to you to be childish things to write about, in times like the present. But, if you knew how grateful we are for the homely events that make us smile. Things such as the doings of these small creatures. There is tragedy in their lives too, but not the bitterness and the hatred that makes life among human beings no longer human.

We are all much pained and impressed, in these days, by the suicide of a friend of my daughters, Count Fecia di Cossato, one of our commanders of submarines. He sunk some 100,000 tons of shipping and saved most of the lives of the people on board. A fine officer in every sense of the word.

When the Armistice came, he took his ship—as commanded—to an enemy port, acting against all the natural instincts of a brave sailor. But such was the order given in the name of the King. Now he finds that the King himself is *sub judice* and that the monarchy may not survive. The so-called government of the country is in the hands of people who have not taken oath of allegiance to the Sovereign. Mere loyalty to the Crown is a back number. . . . In these circumstances Fecia di Cossato felt that his private honour had been besmirched for a reason that could hardly be considered valid. Not even to himself could he justify, any more, the act of passing over to the enemy. And so he committed suicide. Here is a typical *caso di coscienza*, in a man who had a fastidious sense of honour. I doubt if we are qualified to judge him. Perhaps it is he who has judged us. He chose a way out that I cannot approve, but can well understand. It is not Fecia di Cossato alone, who feels that the nation's honour has been compromised by the Armistice and that which accompanied it. So many sacrifices, so much wasted heroism, and then to be told in the end that we had made a mistake and had been fighting, all the time, on the wrong side. This may be good enough for politicians, not for an officer and a gentleman.

I, myself, am not a soldier. I realize that one must consider national problems from a point of view that is more aloof than that of one's private conscience. But, if I had worn a naval uniform, I feel I might have done as he did.

Machiavelli Junior's Radio Talks

IN the immediate aftermath of the war, it was a source of puzzlement to me why I was never put in prison, nor in a concentration-camp. Not that I did—to my knowledge—anything to deserve arrest and imprisonment. That is not the point. The same might be said of two-thirds of the people who crowded Italian places of confinement between 1944 and 1948. They were arrested for their presumed political opinions and imprisoned for the offices they held. Not a few were persecuted first by the Fascists and then by the anti-Fascists. The latter could count on the protection of the Armies of Occupation, which many of them had accompanied as camp-followers. It was thus that the communists all but succeeded in getting a strangle-hold on Italy.

There were times when I felt rather hurt at the fact that I was never admitted into the not very exclusive society that congregated at the Roman prison, incongruously named ' Regina Coeli '.

I thought my time had come, at the end of September 1944, when I was questioned by two members of the American ' Security '. One was a German-American, the other an Italo-American. They wanted to know what political activities I had pursued—if any—during the war. I said that I had spoken on the radio, in English, to the enemy, under the pseudonym of ' Machiavelli Junior '. And I handed them the collection of my radio talks. They read a few of them through, with an occasional grunt, or a chuckle, as some point went home. They, themselves, cannot have held very orthodox views, for they were obviously delighted with a malicious paraphrase of Christopher Marlowe's famous verse : " Was this the face that launched a thousand ships ? "

I had substituted *jeeps* for *ships*, and the allusion was not to Helen of Troy, but to Eleanor Roosevelt.

The two enquirers stayed to tea, and we parted on the best of terms.

The only person in our family who got into trouble over the matter was Bettina. Some pip-squeak of a petty officer in the British Contingent of the Army of Occupation, drest in a little brief authority, got hold of a copy of my radio talks and would not admit any Italian could speak better English than himself. He accused Bettina of having prepared my broadcasts, a heinous crime for one who was English-born.

As a matter of fact, Bettina had nothing to do with the matter. It was Loreto, the parrot, who was responsible ! This is how it came about.

The Roman radio station of the E.I.A.R. is close to my house, and its employees pass under my windows, on their way to and from their work. Sometimes, on summer evenings, they would notice a small crowd, standing on the pavement opposite my study window, which is about fifteen feet from the ground. This crowd would be composed of errand-boys, nurses and children, not to mention the attendant swains of the nurses, all staring open-mouthed at Loreto, where he sat on the window-sill, singing *Amami Alfredo* . . . out of the *Traviata*, alternated with improvisations of his own, not to mention a vulgar comic song that my daughters had taught him, called *Evviva la Torre di Pisa !*

Loreto is a cantankerous bird. Though ready to oblige with these lyrics, to obtain the applause of people in the street, he turned nasty when the employees of the radio station tried to persuade him to talk and sing before a microphone, for the benefit of an unseen audience. When this happened, he just shut up, ruffling his feathers, scratching his head, and giving himself (and his surroundings) a shower-bath out of the water-tin in his cage.

It appears that, somewhere in America, a parrot had made a speech of seventy-five words, which had been put on the air, to the delight of an audience all over the U.S.A. It was hoped that Loreto might consent to do likewise. But he wouldn't hear of it !

Failing to engage Loreto, the pundits of the E.I.A.R. tried to get me. This was at the end of 1940, but at the time I did not consent. Then it happened that John Cavalletti got killed in Greece (his mother is English, hence the anglicized form of his Christian name). John's father worked at the E.I.A.R. Even on the day that he heard how his son had died of his wounds, on the frontiers of Albania, poor old Enrico said his piece into the microphone. It was then that, meeting his wife in the Piazza di Spagna, I offered to prepare some material for him to use in his broadcasts. I began with a radio talk, called 'The Friends of China', which procured for Cavalletti the felicitations of the American Embassy, whose members were astonished at his knowledge of the Far East.

Soon after, Enrico Cavalletti fell ill of nervous exhaustion and a cough (he had been gassed during the first world war). To relieve him, I began, myself, to go to the E.I.A.R., and spoke in his stead.

Never, at any moment, did I feel inclined to bless the enemy I had come to curse, as Balaam did. But I might be compared to Balaam's companion and adviser, who expostulated. That modest biblical character, Balaam's ass, has always been a favourite of mine. He voices the protest of the humble workers, who ask only to be allowed to accomplish their daily task, without interference. Instead of which they are dragged, by some short-sighted seer, into international complications that interest them not at all. And unfortunately, when the prophet beats the ass, not always does an angel come to its defence.

War-time Hostess

IT is a moot point whether Boccaccio really was in Florence in the year 1348. Anyway, he claims that he and a small group of friends, seven ladies and three men, met ten days running in the garden of a Florentine villa, and sought, in each other's company, to forget the horrors of the plague that raged around them. In these grim circumstances, the genius of Boccaccio (as John Addington Symonds wrote of him) " proclaimed the beauty of the world, the goodliness of youth and strength and love and life, unterrified by hell, unappalled by the shadow of impending death ".

To pass the time, the friends in that garden told stories : the stories that form the *Decameron* (in them you will find the pathetic figure of Patient Griselda, that reappears in Chaucer).

Six hundred years later, a tiny garden, up on the first floor of what was once the Palazzo Orsini, offered a pleasant oasis from the oppression of the war to a few friends of the present owner of the palace. Our hostess, to pass the time, had begun a book that much later appeared with the title taken from *Childe Harold* ('Sparkle Distant Worlds'). I was busy on a fairy-tale called *The Doge's Ring*. These tales have not the licentiousness of Boccaccio's *Novelle*, and therefore could be told, on war-time afternoons, in the house of the Duchess of Sermoneta, *née* Vittoria Colonna.

No one is less in need than she of being introduced to the public. The list of her friends would read like the *Almanach de Gotha*, combined with the telephone directories of Rome, Paris and London, and the *Social Register* of New York.

She has written memoirs both of Edwardian times, when we were young and frivolous, and of the grim years of the second world war. Also a history of her English forbears, the Lockes of Norbury.

Robert Hichens spoke of her, as 'the reigning beauty of Rome'. Alfred Austin, the poet laureate, described how he met her at Merton Hall.

" The door opened, and I saw before me the living impersonation of the Italian Renaissance, who said to me : ' I am Vittoria Colonna.' "

And he wrote in the guests' album, the following verses :

> Lady of the Race Divine
> From the land of fig and vine,
> In whose limbs the tide still flows
> Of the goddess white that rose
> From the morning-freshened foam
> And whose offspring founded Rome
> When the Trojan city fell ;
> You who blend with Southern spell
> Northern candour, and combine
> With your Latin lineage, mine ;

Along English lawn and lane,
When the woods were on the wane
With me wandered round and round
Sabine tread on Saxon ground.
Is it fancy that you share
With the sounding name you bear
Her great soul and soarings high
Who beneath Tyrrhenean sky
Wedded early, widowed long,
Soothed her twilight years with song,
And if Heaven will grant to me
All I wish that you may be
You will have but half her fate :
Without loneliness be great ;
And could time but backward flow,
I, your Michelangelo.

Her father's house (now her cousin's) is in a part of Rome that has belonged to her family for more than ten centuries. At the time of writing, she acts as hostess in her own palace, whose foundations (on the Theatre of Marcellus) were built before the birth of Christ, when Virgil was writing the *Aeneid* in the newly founded Augustan Empire, and men still spoke Latin in Rome.

In Vittoria's character, I seem to recognize the large simplicity of the earlier Gods. Like them she is capable of the most arrant nonsense. Let me quote one of her own stories of the time when she was staying with her relative, the Empress Eugénie, at Farnborough, together with a party of cousins, including the Dukes of Alba and Peneranda, Princess Clément Metternich, and others of that ilk.

Being young and light-hearted, the Spanish cousins and I used to indulge in the silliest jokes. Once, at luncheon, I served one of them—I think it was Isabelle Metternich—with a catch that had been invented that year and has now sunk into the oblivion it deserves.

' Have you seen Arthur ? ' is the question (the joke does not come off in a house that really contains an Arthur).

Instinctively everyone answers : ' Arthur who ? '

' *Our thermometer.* '

There was such a roar from the end of the table that the Empress wanted to know about it : ' *Je veux entendre la plaisanterie de Vittoria.* '

Her English has always been very limited, and of course it was impossible to translate the joke into French. I struggled to explain and all the cousins tried to help, but it was no good.

*' Je ne comprends pas ce que Arthur ait à faire avec un thermomètre. Arthur . . .
qui est Arthur ? Non. C'est vraiment trop bête ! '*

One afternoon—I think it was Bank Holiday (*Ferragosto*) in
August 1944, I was drinking iced tea and consuming home-made
cake in the little pensile garden in the Palazzo Sermoneta, with
tangerine trees, clipped laurel and seven fountains where the birds
come to drink. Vittoria was talking to her sister-in-law, Margherita
Caetani, about the family estates at Ninfa and Sermoneta, on the edge
of the Pontine Marshes (what Macaulay calls ' the never-ending
fen ').

The tide of war had left the buildings intact, but all the furniture had been wantonly destroyed, except for a few long tables.
Perhaps as a precaution, all the plates had been thrown into the
river.

Margherita Caetani was saying : ' Some day, we will clean out
the river bed and collect those plates again.'

' Why ! ' exclaimed Vittoria. ' Those must be the plates that
Gelasio had made. Once, when they were cleaning out the moat,
up at the castle, they found a lot of old plates lying in the mud at
the bottom. He liked the design, and had it copied for a dinner-
service.'

The same incident of the dinner-plates being thrown into a slow-
moving river, or a castle-moat, has occurred in the Caetani family
during two different wars, one in the fifteenth, and one in the
twentieth century. No wonder they end by acquiring a different
outlook on contemporary history from that of people who can trace
their ancestry no further back than four or five generations ! It
would not surprise me if they did not find some day, on their estates,
the household goods that Aeneas carried away from Troy.

As Quiller-Couch said, in a lecture on ' The Lineage of English
Literature ' ; " A Roman noble, even today, has some excuse for
reckoning a god in his ancestry, or at least a wolf among his wet-
nurses : but of us English, even those who came over with William
the Norman have the son of a tanner's daughter for escort."

Such ancient lineage, even if legendary, has its romantic appeal.
Prince Massimo may, or may not, be descended from the ancient
Maximi of republican Rome, but, as his great-great grandfather said

to Napoleon : " It is a rumour that has been current in my family for the last thousand years."

It was natural that Vittoria and I should look upon events from a different angle. Of us two, she was by far the less despondent. But then I (if you will forgive a hackneyed quotation) had seen the things I gave my life to broken. She regarded it all from an Olympian standpoint. Politics had little interest for her. But she never made any mystery of the fact that she was pro-English, anti-German and anti-Fascist. I was merely pro-Italian and nothing else. But she and I had a fellow-feeling about the disgrace of the way Italy had entered the war, and the equal disgrace of the way she got out of it.

' I feel ashamed,' she said to me, at the end of 1943, ' of the people who do not feel ashamed ! ' And she quoted a phrase out of Kipling's *Brushwood Boy*, something about the training that teaches there are ' things no fellow can do ! ' (Whatever these things are, we Italians seem to have done them all !)

Meanwhile, both she and I came down in the world, and became more and more proletarian in our daily lives. One noticed it, of course, more in her than in me, for she had further to fall !

Her idea of a pleasant evening was to dine out and then play a game. But because of the war, she had to give up her car and have recourse to taxis. Then the taxis failed us, and she had to go about strap-hanging in buses and trams, like any common mortal. And she took it all in her stride :

' When I get into the old F.R.,' she said to me, speaking of the electric omnibus that ends its run just opposite her door, ' and we trundle down the Corso on the last lap home, after an evening's bridge, I feel almost as if I had reached my own bedroom and could begin to undress ! '

Soon afterwards, even the buses failed us, and Vittoria had to limit her dining out to those evenings when some foreign diplomat, or the Queen of Spain, would send to fetch her in a car.

These are very minor troubles, amusing to look back on. But there was tragedy behind it. Her house, like mine, harboured its refugees. There was a man working in her garden, whom she alluded to as *l'homme au masque de fer*, and she played backgammon with him in the evenings. She herself was liable to be taken, any moment, by the Germans, as 'a hostage'. An alarm came, in due course, and Vittoria escaped by a back entrance, while her son, Onorato, talked with the Police Commissioner, who had come to effect an arrest. The Spanish Embassy to the Holy See offered her sanctuary. She and her maid, Gerty, were in hiding from January to June. She passed most of the time writing; her only distraction was her daily lunch with her hosts.

Such are my memories of Vittoria in war-time: one more link in a chain of recollections that goes back to when we took riding-lessons from old Pieretti, in the *manège* of the Palazzo Rospigliosi.

Roman palaces, English country-houses; old Lady Walsingham's drawing-room in Eaton Square; Mrs. Mansel's rooms in Clarges Street, which Vittoria and I have occupied alternately, when in London. Her sister Isa's palace in Siena, and the windows from which we watched the *palio*; the Roman campagna in February; Bond Street in May. Fresh violets and sweet lavender!

The Death of Ciano

ROME, *20th January 1944.* It is now ten days since we heard the news of Galeazzo Ciano having been condemned to death and executed, together with several others, including old de Bono. They were judged by a 'special tribunal' (the very name stinks of injustice), sitting in the beautiful old Castel-vecchio of Verona, where the green waters of the Adige flow under Roman bridges (though I believe that these have been destroyed by enemy bombers).

The prisoners believed, up till the last moment, that the sentence would not be carried out. Such grim functions generally take place at dawn, and the sun was already high in the heavens. . . . But no reprieve came.

A film was taken of the execution, but subsequently suppressed. Ciano—so I am told—recognized the cinema operator, who had often photographed him before. He remarked on the suitability of that man not being absent from the final scene of the drama. The poor boy died bravely, and encouraged de Bono, who must have been eighty years old, and had to be carried to the execution ground on a stretcher. They were made to sit on chairs, with their backs to the firing-squad, but at the last moment Ciano turned his face to the guns.

Although it offers a typical example of that 'Saturnism', by which a revolution ends in devouring its own sons, I could never have believed that so foul a judicial murder would have been carried out in Italy. And will it end here?

I doubt it. Who was responsible? Mussolini, or the Germans that forced his hand? Time may show.

If Fascism is less a matter of political convictions than of temperament, Galeazzo should never have represented it, at home or abroad. His father, that sturdy old buccaneer, might have figured as a character in *Treasure Island*, but Galeazzo would not have made a good pirate, though he might pose as one, in ladies' drawing-rooms. His principal defect was *leggerezza*, or flightiness : a lack of principle, or conviction. Once, towards the end, he said of himself that he had only been a convinced Fascist between 1936 and 1938. This may be true of others as well.

Up till the summer of 1939, Ciano had imagined that the war he had talked of so lightly would not come for many years. Had not the Germans promised not to start one till 1943 ! It was at Salzburg that he began to feel around him *le cose più grandi di lui*. Events were getting out of hand. Even Mussolini could no longer control them.

Other things happened about that time, things that confirmed Ciano's *leggerezza*. On arriving back in Rome, after the meeting at Salzburg, he said to Helfand (the Russian Chargé d'Affaires) : ' So a Russo-German agreement is really a *fait-accompli* ! ' And he expressed great pleasure about it. Yet it was not true. Indeed, negotiations were hanging fire. Ciano's light-hearted banter was based on a minor incident. During the meeting at Salzburg, Hitler and Ribbentrop had received a communication from Berlin, reporting that Schülemberg (German Ambassador in Moscow) had telegraphed to say that Stalin was willing to accept certain proposals that had been submitted to him during the preceding days. This did not mean that any final agreement had been reached. Flattered at having been shown a private communication between the German Ambassador and the Führer, Ciano subsequently revealed the fact to Helfand. His words were telegraphed at once to Molotov. And the negotiations between Berlin and Moscow were expedited, because they appeared to be so favourably considered in Rome. It was a childish piece of exaggeration that, paradoxically enough, brought the matter to a head. Yet Ciano, himself, did not believe in any lasting agreement between Moscow and Berlin. And he was flabbergasted when, on the 21st of August, he telephoned to Ribbentrop, asking for another meeting, and was told that this could not take place at once, because the German Minister was leaving for Moscow, to sign a Non-Aggression Pact. . . .

*   *   *

Ciano's character deteriorated as he neared the pinnacle of a too rapid ascent to power. Before then he gave proof of intelligence and foresight.

As far back as 1924, he wrote an article for the daily paper, *Il Tempo*, in which he maintained that a dictatorship would be the ruin of Italy. The article was never published, because old Costanzo, who was a violent-tempered man, flew into a rage and boxed his son's ears !

In 1935, Ciano was in our colony of Eritrea, as an officer in the air force. The Abyssinian crisis was then acute, but war seemed to have been averted by the Hoare–Laval Pact. To celebrate this agreement, Ciano gave a big dinner-party, and he said : ' If we go to war with Ethiopia, it will probably mean war with England at the same time. If not, the English will nurse a grudge against us (' *se lo legheranno al dito* ') and will remain on the look-out for some opportunity to take their revenge.'

Ciano possessed a keen brain, but little strength of character. Some bad fairy must have put an evil spell on him when in his cradle. It was his fate nearly always to represent a policy of which he disapproved, but which he lacked the strength of will to oppose.

When he became Minister of Foreign Affairs, he began to keep a Diary, and took a certain pride in it, so that he would often read out a page or two for the edification of a friend. He once showed me an entry mentioning ' Margherita Campello ' (my daughter). It was dated 6th March 1942, and referred to a remark made by General Gambara, who was a friend of Margherita's and who had said : " I hope to live long enough to march on Berlin, at the head of an Italian army." This had pleased Ciano, even though it was in strident contrast with the policy that the Fascist Government was following at the time.

*   *   *

BENITO MUSSOLINI, 1926

GALEAZZO CIANO

When he arrived in Peking, in 1927, to serve under me as First Secretary of our Legation, Ciano was twenty-five years old. He formed part of a group that centred round Margherita and Diana, then barely seventeen and fifteen. Life for those young people was as buoyant as their hopes, which turned, like marigolds, ever towards the light.

As a sportsman, he did not shine. He *could* ride, and did so when necessary, but took no pleasure in it. He played a pat-a-cake game of tennis, and disliked walking.

I had rented a temple in the Western Hills, and Ciano would come out and pass an occasional week-end with me. But he did not show any enthusiasm when I dragged him to the top of some neighbouring mountain, and pointed out the view of the Summer Palace shimmering in the afternoon sunlight, and the far-distant bastions and gate-towers of Peking. He sympathized with my *maître d'hôtel*, a Roman of the Romans, who made no mystery of the fact that Chinese temples were not for the likes of him.

Ciano's passion was for motor-cars, and he had not been long in Peking before be bought himself a two-seater Fiat and raced up and down the few miles of road that were available for motor traffic.

Though he took only a mild interest in the Orient, as such, Ciano was delighted with Peking. The position he graced in the Diplomatic Body was slightly above what a man of his age usually occupies, but he had no reason to feel out of place. After he left Peking, this could never be said of him again.

Even during the years when he was with me, Galeazzo began to suffer from an excess of reflected prestige. His father was too influential for the son's career to run its own course unassisted (and unencumbered) by favouritism. Galeazzo once complained to me that, at home, he never got any credit for merits of his own. And his promotions followed each other in such rapid succession that— so he said—he might have followed the diplomatic career five times over. And yet, if he had enjoyed no family influence whatever, I believe he would have done well. He might have made a good diplomat.

While he was in Peking and in the middle of a pleasant love-affair with an American lady, at home in Italy his mother and Mussolini were arranging a marriage between their children. When he first got wind of this plan, and hints were thrown out that he might apply for leave, young Ciano showed considerable reluctance, and he did his best to stay where he was. A telegram on his birthday, in which Mussolini greeted him as a father might have done (*ti saluto come padre*) did not by any means fill his heart with filial piety. In the end, his own father had to feign illness to serve as a pretext for his son's recall. When he parted from us at Shan Hai Kwan, he was in tears.

He came back to China, as Consul General at Shanghai, with his bride, Edda. I stayed with them during a week, and they seemed happy. Indeed Ciano candidly confessed to me that he was happier in his married life than he had expected to be. He also told me an amusing story about his departure for the Far East, soon after the wedding.

When the bridal couple embarked on the *Conte Rosso*, at Bari, all the family came to see them off in state. The ship came in from Venice and berthed alongside the quay, opposite the hotel. It stopped there only for an hour or two. Mussolini and his family, Costanzo Ciano and *his* family, numerous authorities and officials, backed by a crowd of admiring populace, were standing in a semicircle, when the gangway was let down. Some people came off the ship, and were hustled aside. But a few minutes later, a tall, slim figure in white ducks and wearing a sun-helmet, was seen descending the steps of the gangway. This was Mario Pansa, who was going out to Colombo, having been appointed Consul there. He wore sandals on his bare feet, and was accompanied by a dog on the leash. It was not possible to see what kind of a dog it was, for it was swathed in white bandages. Evidently it had got into serious trouble. On stepping off the gangway, Mario found himself in the centre of the semicircle. For a moment, all those important people forgot the bridal couple and focused their attention on the much-bandaged dog. It was Mussolini himself who asked the question that everyone else had in mind.

' What is the matter with that dog ? '

Mario Pansa answered : ' He had a fight with a cat at Trieste.'

Mussolini made the obvious comment : ' It would seem that the cat got the best of it ! '

*   *   *

When passing judgment on Ciano, it should be remembered that he was balked in his natural aspirations and affections, taken out of the career that he had chosen for himself, married against his will to the boss's daughter, pushed into the blinding limelight that shone on those who stood close to Mussolini, dragged at the chariot-wheels of a God-in-the-car, courted, fawned upon and flattered by a host of time-servers, who abandoned him on the day of his fall. No wonder that his character was spoilt and his mind warped ! He hoped, some day, to become Mussolini's successor. The mantle of Elijah was to have fallen on the shoulders of Elisha. And whereas Elijah had been the prophet of the wilderness, Elisha was to have been the prophet of the drawing-rooms. Whereas Elijah was the messenger of vengeance, Elisha would have been, as in the days of Ahab, the messenger of mercy and restoration. It was a fine ideal, in its way.

With surprising naïveté, Ciano counted on his numerous friend-ships to help him out, should misfortune overtake him. But not many of his former friends gathered round him, when he was in danger. And these could do little, or nothing, to help. I am glad to say that my daughters went often to keep him company, during the last days when he was in Rome, virtually a prisoner in his apartment in Via Angelo Secchi. One afternoon, when he was preparing some coffee for himself and Diana, he quoted the verses that figure in the title of this book (he possessed some knowledge of Kipling, which I think he had acquired from me !). Diana did not say so to him, but she told me afterwards that, in her opinion, Ciano faced Disaster better than he had met Triumph.

At that time, he hoped to escape, with his wife and children, to Spain or Portugal. But the next I heard of them, they were in Germany.

A letter written to Edda, when she was about to return to Italy from what he calls ' this dirty little house in Allmaushausen ', contains what might be described as Ciano's spiritual will and testament. It was meant to be shown to a few friends, among those who had not turned their backs on him in the day of his downfall. I was one of those to whom it was brought.

When he wrote, Ciano was contemplating suicide. Later, he decided to leave to others the responsibility for his death. He defends his own reputation, in the hopes that his children may not have to bow down their heads in shame.

He denies the accusation of having amassed a great fortune, saying that the greater part of what he possessed had been left to him by his father.

He confirms the general impression that he had no responsibility for Italy's entry into the war, omitting however to say that he had often approved of the idea, when war seemed only a distant possibility. Indeed, he maintains that he opposed it from the first, convinced as he was that his country should not have become ' the accomplice ' of the Nazis, and that Rome ought not to contribute to their victory. He expresses approval of the action taken by King Victor Emanuel III, in detaching himself from the German allies (" Would that *we* had done so, while there was yet time ! "). And he defends the Italian people against the German accusation of being betrayers, saying that, if he were given the opportunity of doing so, he could prove that, on the contrary, it was the Italians who had been betrayed.

He admits that it showed a foolish trustfulness on his part to have accepted the German offer to help him and his family leave Italy and reach Spain :

But when you have three children whom you love, and you see black danger growing daily more threatening, and suddenly a means of escape offers itself, it would not be in human nature to refuse. If I had been alone, it would have been different. . . .

In this same letter, he excuses himself for not having resigned from office, when Mussolini decided to enter the war on the side of Germany :

Perhaps, once our intervention had been decided, I should have slammed the door behind me, so as to clamorously manifest my dissension. I do not hide from you that I long contemplated doing so. If I abstained, it was because I did not wish, by such a gesture, to give official character to a crisis that was still latent, but already deeply radicated in the heart of the Italian people. I did not wish it to be my fault to have determined, or even merely to have revealed, the fatal split. Add to this my personal relationship to your father, which acted as a brake. Maybe I was wrong to have acted thus, but I do not repent, even if I myself have to suffer.

In the days of the Attic tragedians, Ciano's rise to power, his fall and death, might have formed the subject of one of the lost plays of Aeschylus, to reveal the gradual rousing of the slumbering Furies, the pity and the terror of the *Oresteja*, the poet's brooding thought-fulness on deep questions, the jealousy of the gods towards those who are too successful, the dark mysteries of Fate !

The Tigers and the Wild Pigs

> When the Cambrian Measures were forming, They
> promised perpetual Peace.
> They swore, if we gave them our weapons, that the
> wars of the tribes would cease.
>
> And when we disarmed, They sold us and
> delivered us bound to our foe
> And the Gods of the Copy-book-headings said
> ' Stick to the devil you know.'
>
> RUDYARD KIPLING, *The Gods of the Copy-book-headings.*

JUST after the first world war, I had a conversation with Colonel House, that might have been repeated, word for word, at the close of world war number two. He asked me how it was that the Venetian Republic had the reputation of having created a school of diplomacy, so much so that even foreign Kings went to Venice to learn how to become good diplomats. Was it only an excuse to enjoy the frivolities of carnival ?

I admitted that it might be so, and as Colonel House appeared really to be interested, I told him about a former ambassador, Marino Cavalli, who represented Venice at the Court of France, when the French King, Francis I, was at war with the Emperor, Charles V. Each of these two potentates was trying to gain supremacy in Europe, and England had allied herself with the Emperor, with the object of maintaining the balance of power. But—as Cavalli reported to the Venetian Seigniory—the enemies of France did not seek her utter ruin, but only to *travagliarla alquanto*, to diminish her power and her pride. Therefore military operations were accompanied (*fiancheggiate*) by an intense, though confidential, diplomatic activity. I compared these clandestine negotiations between enemies, to those that Colonel House had endeavoured to set in motion, with Sir Edward Grey's collaboration, in 1915. (The Allies subsequently refused to take advantage of this offer.)

At the time of my conversation with Colonel House, I had not yet written *Laughing Diplomat*, or I might have added that it was Marino Cavalli who had given me the idea of writing some memoirs and including in them extracts from a ' Handbook of the Perfect Diplomat', which *he* called *Informatione dell' Offitio dell' Ambasciatore*. This was a collection of precepts, put together by the author, in the year 1540, for the instruction of his descendants, should the latter be sent on diplomatic missions abroad. Questions such as the importance of the cook in an Ambassador's household, the duties and conduct of his secretaries, the upkeep of his horses and the care of his armour, are gone into with the experienced sagacity of a traveller in distant lands.

Questions of international import are treated with the same penetration and acumen. Old Marino had very definite ideas of how peace should be negotiated among States that were at war with one another, and he held up as an example the conduct of the enemies of France, as mentioned above.

It was a beautiful thing that these two Princes, who were such great enemies, and waged war against each other with so much hatred, never ceased, during this time, to negotiate, by various means, with the object of reaching an agreement and concluding peace. Which thing was very well done (benissimo fatta) *not only because those efforts were ultimately crowned with success, but because it showed great wisdom. One should never face so determinedly in one direction, as not to be able to keep an eye on the other.*

Cavalli goes on to relate that ' the Most Christian ' King of France once said to him how it behoved the three mightiest sovereigns in Europe (the Kings of England, of France, and the Emperor) to have three faces, like the Trinity, so that each should have ' respect of his companions and of himself '.

At the time I met Colonel House, I could not repeat verbatim to him these passages from Marino Cavalli's writings. But he, himself, put the same idea into other words. He quoted a letter written to him by E. S. Martin, who pointed out that, when you killed off all the tigers in the jungle, the wild pigs multiplied exceedingly, and the crops in the neighbouring district were in danger of being destroyed. Similarly, the equilibrium should not be destroyed among nations, for it may upset the very balance of nature itself.

If my meeting with Colonel House had taken place after the second and not the first of the world wars (shall we say, in Rome, in 1945 ?) I would have asked him to accompany me to an exhibit of ' displaced pictures ', in the Palazzo Venezia. These pictures had been entrusted to the Vatican, for safe keeping in troublous times. Among them were many masterpieces of the Venetian School. I have other, older memories of the Palazzo Venezia. They begin with dances given there by Count Széczen de Temerlin, Austrian Ambassador to the Holy See, and they end with interviews with Mussolini.

The spirit of Venice and of Venetian diplomacy—in which Colonel House sensed a political wisdom similar to his own—seems to haunt the halls of the great palace, built by a Venetian. Over the doors is the inscription, *Paulus II Venetus*, with the armorial bearings of Pietro Barbo. Pope Paul II came of a family that, like the Colonnas and the Massimos, claim descendance from the patricians (if not the gods !) of ancient Rome. Perhaps for this reason, while raising for himself a huge fortress-dwelling, at the foot of the Capitoline Hill, Pope Barbo used materials taken from the Colosseum. In the vast courtyard he reproduced, in superimposed porticoes, two stories of open arcades, such as surround the Flavian amphitheatre. Blocks of marble, quarried by the Emperor Vespasian, became ' Stones of Venice ' under a Venetian pope.

I can imagine myself strolling with Colonel House on the covered terrace and looking down at the garden that the old buildings enclose. Just below is a fountain with a large basin, full of fat, red gold-fish. The marble figure of a woman in a Doge's cap, on a little platform supported by Tritons and surrounded by dolphins, is meant to represent Venice. Tall palms, cedars and magnolia-trees rise above the level of the roofs opposite. To the left is the belfry of the church of St. Mark's, apparently leaning against the corner-tower of the palace itself. Swallows circle in the sky, and ducks preen their feathers at the edge of the fountain, while pigeons strut and coo on the gravel paths.

It is still a mystery to me how Mussolini, passing his days in such surroundings, should not have been influenced by the atmosphere of cultured sagacity and discretion, not to say the sound common sense, that was characteristic of the Venetian diplomats who once lived in that palace. But perhaps the trouble with him was the lack of any wise councillor on whose judgment he might rely. He believed in nobody but himself. His was the sin that the gods never forgive : the sin of pride. Some touch of this there may have been, towards the end, also in President Wilson. But he *did* trust his ' independent self ', as he once called Colonel House, during many years. That same sin of pride insisting on ' unconditional surrender ', can now be laid at the door of our victors in the second world war. A frivolous formula, light-heartedly adopted by the self-styled ' peace-loving nations ', cost the world millions of men and destroyed the means of livelihood of Central Europe. They destroyed all the tigers in the jungle, and let the wild pigs overrun our vineyards and our cornfields.

*   *   *

Other and more recent parallels rise inevitably in the mind of the historian, besides those evoked by the centuries-old reports of a Venetian ambassador. In the Encyclopædia Britannica's biography of Lord Castlereagh, it says of him : " His aim throughout has been to rescue Europe from military domination ; and when he found that Russia and Prussia were pursuing ends incompatible with the general interest, he did not hesitate to take a new line."

After the fall of Napoleon, the victorious allies did not hesitate for three years before taking a new line to counter the threat of military domination by the Russia of Alexander I.

Looking Back (*an impression of Benito Mussolini*)

In my Diary for the 31st March 1947, I find the following entry :

Socialist and Communist party organizations held a celebration, yesterday afternoon, of the murder of Mussolini. In the Basilica of Maxentius, facing the Forum, a degenerate-looking individual in a basque cap spoke to a crowd of people, most of whom, presumably, were the same that used to shout

LOOKING BACK (AN IMPRESSION OF BENITO MUSSOLINI)

'Duce ! Duce !' under the balcony in the Palazzo Venezia. He described his own prowess as an amateur, self-appointed executioner. This, so I gather, qualifies him for a seat in the Chamber of Deputies. (But why did he have to murder, at the same time, Claretta Petacci, the woman who remained faithful to Mussolini, to the end ?)

Crowds in the Roman Forum have listened to other orations, not to praise, but to bury, a murdered statesman. Yesterday's oratory, Moscow-inspired, had nothing classical about it. I am not saying that Mussolini did not justly pay with his life, for all the harm he did to Italy by dragging us into war. But there is something unsavoury about these post-war manifestations of the victor's justice.

The communist-inspired celebration in the Basilica of Maxentius served to rehabilitate the Duce's reputation among the inhabitants of Rome. It brought back, to elder men, memories of the communist-inspired violence that was so common, after the end of the first world war, and which contributed to the rise of Mussolini himself. Do all reactions fall into the same errors, and repeat the old mistakes ? Massimo d'Azeglio, writing about the restoration of the Pope's power in Rome, after the French had defeated Garibaldi, says : " Like the greater part of the potentates of those days, Cardinal Consalvi took the renewal of the very causes that had produced the evil, for its antidote." A contemporary American weekly says that the victorious Allies are anxious ' to baby Europe back to the political instability of pre-war days '. Certainly, it is true that they are guilty of the identical forms of injustice and short-sightedness that caused so much trouble in the past.

The Fascist revolution had certain well-defined causes : one was the disappointment of the Italians at their exclusion from colonial mandates. The other was the spread of Bolshevism. Now that Fascism has been overthrown (and it was the Italians themselves who took the initiative), an imposed peace obliged us to renounce any claim to the restoration of our colonies, and once more the way was opened to communist penetration. The Allies handed Italy over to those native Reds, that they, themselves, had fostered abroad. This is what Demaree Bess wrote about it, in the *Saturday Evening Post* of 17th January 1948 :

The moment that American and British troops invaded Italy in 1943, the Soviet Government despatched one of its top mixers, Andrei Vishinsky, to sit on the Mediterranean Advisory Commission. Mr. Vishinsky contented himself with one modest request : that a few Italian communists, including Palmiro Togliatti, be flown back from Moscow to organize the communists in Italy. The request . . . was unhesitatingly granted.

The policy of these ' top-mixers ', as Demaree Bess calls them, was quite simple : to egg the Italians on to civil war, only to find, at the end of it, that they had exchanged Fascism for Communism.

Sanctions against Fascism acted like the sickle-shaped return-boomerang of the Australian natives. They recoiled on the democratic heads of those who imagined they were destroying the devotees of a past totalitarian régime. Instead of which, it was the devotees of another totalitarian régime that benefited. *Le Fascisme est mort. Vive le Fascisme !*

Huey Long, that blustering American demagogue, once was asked : ' Governor, do you think we will ever have Fascism in this country ? '

He answered : ' Sure, son. But we'll call it Anti-Fascism ! '

Fascism and Anti-Fascism faced each other for many years across a sulphurous gulf of incomprehension and hatred, representing the proverbial extremes that meet.

★   ★   ★

In his *Storie Fiorentine*, Machiavelli wrote that too much power corrupts a man (' *quati sempre gli nomini, quanto pui autorità hanno, peggio la usano* ').

Most dictators are true to type. The supreme example is that of Napoleon. He is unique in his qualities of military genius and civil administrator. His defects reappear in dictators of lesser calibre. The considerations in Lord Rosebery's book, *Napoleon : The Last Phase*, are often applicable to Mussolini. But a far more striking resemblance is that with ' Rienzi ', or Cola di Rienzo, whose ' Life ' in English has been written by Bulwer-Lytton and by the Marchesa Iris Origo.

In Rienzi, as in Mussolini, we have the same sudden acquisition of power within the state, the same mirage of restoring the greatness of Rome, the same high ideals, the same crimes, the same mistakes, and finally the same ignoble end at the hands of an infuriated mob, mad with the lust of cruelty. The revolting scene in Piazza Loreto in Milan (April 1946) had been enacted in Rome, in October 1354, near the Church of San Marcello. Even the particulars are the same, such as the hanging of the victim's body up by the feet, to expose it to the insults of the mob.

*   *   *

I first knew Mussolini at Lausanne. At that time, Lord Curzon alluded to him as ' that absurd little man '. But not long afterwards, foreign statesmen began to show him more deference than they had ever vouchsafed to the liberals, who had governed Italy before him.

I knew that he had been a school-teacher, a mason (his hands were those of a man who had known manual labour), a corporal, wounded in the first world war. I knew also that he had been instrumental in bringing Italy into that war, on the side of the Allies. I was told that he had known hunger and slept under the bridges. It was not surprising that Lord Curzon should resent having to treat as an equal a man who, not so long before, had been a poor Italian emigrant. On the other hand it was not long before I was asking myself if such a man might not be the champion of those aspirations for Italy that had long been the object of my own dreams. Indeed, he was destined both to realize those dreams and to shatter them.

Maffeo Pantaleoni, who had been my teacher in political economy, became a devoted admirer of Mussolini, considering him as an exponent of economic liberalism, as opposed to state interference. And so indeed he was, in the first years after he came into power. Thanks to Mussolini, the state monopoly on insurance (imposed by Nitti, some years before) was abolished. The telephone system was restored to private ownership.

In 1927, Winston Churchill, after an interview with Mussolini, held a press conference at the British Embassy, and declared to the assembled journalists that, had he been Italian, he would have been wholeheartedly a Fascist. There was nothing surprising in this. Any fair-minded person, knowing something of recent history, had to admit that, with us as in France, a multiplicity of parties had reduced our parliamentary system to hysterical nonsense. Nor was Italy rich enough (as France was) to be able to support an inefficient system.

Just after the murder of Matteotti, I discussed with Antonio Salandra (this was at the Hotel des Bergues at Geneva) the possible duration of the Fascist régime. Salandra had been Prime Minister in Italy in 1915, when we declared war on Germany. He said to me that Fascism would naturally follow a parabola, but he did not think, at the time of speaking, that it had run its course. And he believed that only Mussolini could govern Italy at that moment. He hoped, when the régime fell, that it might end like Cromwell's rule in England, leaving behind it the good it had done. This meant that the descending curve of the parabola would have to be a gentle one.

Why did people like Pantaleoni, like Scialoja, like Salandra, like myself, consent to collaborate with Mussolini ? Why did so many impartial foreigners sing his praises ? Does the explanation lie in the resemblance to Rienzi ? Of the latter, Iris Origo writes :

Not necessarily men of great intellectual power, or even of outstanding character, these leaders owe their pre-eminence to the fact that their genius is a focal point, a concentration of the spirit of their time. Such a man, in the transition between the Middle Ages and the Renaissance, was Cola di Rienzo.

Such a man, in the transition period between the world as I and my generation have known it, and the ' brave new world ' that awaits us, was Benito Mussolini.

The faults of his régime were not all his own. The responsibility for many errors and exaggerations falls on the Italians whom he ruled. Framed on the walls of many public offices, one often saw the slogan *Mussolini ha sempre ragione !* It might be translated ' Mussolini right or wrong '. At least this hero-worship was not foreign-inspired. As an Italian ideal, it was better than ' Stalin right or wrong ', the slogan that communist agents subsequently taught to Italian and French youth. *Allons enfants de la Russie !*

*   *   *

In recalling my personal reactions to past events, I must plead guilty to a certain *esprit de contradiction*. I often resented Fascism, when I saw it blatantly triumphant ; and its fanfarronade set my teeth on edge. But when I heard it misjudged, and saw its honest votaries persecuted for their opinions, I could not but feel disgust with the hypocrisy, the political versatility, and the even worse excesses of its opponents. There is no excuse possible for the cowardly policy that, under the protection of a foreign army of occupation, set out to hunt down and despoil those Italians who, in various fields of human endeavour, loyally served their country's interests under a régime that, in common with so many people abroad, they considered as well suited to Italy.

If a future historian wishes for a balanced and concise judgment on Italian Fascism, he will find it in a report written by Mr. Turner, Commercial Attaché of the British Embassy in Rome, and published in the London *Times* of 2nd November 1933. Mr. Turner called is 'a great experiment', admitting that it suited Italy, 'which is, of course, no reason why it should suit other countries, which differ from Italy in geographical conditions, in the stage of their economic development and in the characteristics of their individual citizens'.

To the credit of Italian Fascism should be placed also the fact that —unlike Russian Communism—it was never afraid of the friendship of democratic states. There was no Iron Curtain on the Italian Alps.

Elderly statesmen might maintain an attitude of mildly critical detachment. But it is an undoubted fact that most of the youth of Italy was filled with an ardent spirit of renewal, which welled up with the advent of Fascism, lighting a veritable passion to reaffirm the intellectual and moral influence of Italy in the world. There were times when I too shared this passion. Were I to deny it today that Fascism is fallen and so many turn-coats have abjured their faith, I would feel as Saint Peter must have felt when, in his declining years, he heard a cock crow !

*   *   *

Failing health is often the ruin and the excuse of statesmen wielding great power. So it was with Roosevelt when, at Yalta and Teheran, he surrendered to Stalin many of the advantages gained by the defeat of Hitler, and secretly consigned thousands of innocent people into slavery.

The tragedy of Mussolini (and our tragedy !) was the physical and mental degeneration that belied the promises of his earlier days. During the initial period of his rule, he was eager to learn, being

251

conscious of his own ignorance even in such small matters as table manners and clothes. He was modest and approachable. When learning to ride, he willingly took hints in horsemanship from my daughter Margherita, then aged fifteen. And they exchanged photographs of each other, on their favourite horses.

On the occasion of his one and only visit to London, he got out of the train at Charing Cross, carrying a heavy stick (*un randello*), not unlike an Irish shillelah. His Chef de Cabinet, Paulicci, realising that such a cudgel was not in keeping with the amenities of a friendly visit, snatched the sapling out of his Chief's hand, while he was still on the station platform. Mussolini gave him an indignant stare, but made no verbal protest. Nor did he ask for his stick again.

During that visit, Mussolini told Lady Curzon that he was learning English, and promised to write her a letter in that language, in two months time from then. Two months later, he remembered his promise, but his English was not yet up to the mark. So he asked me to write the letter for him. He added that he wanted this epistle to be characteristic of his personality, so I concocted a piece of prose with a certain swing in it. He read it over and objected : ' You forget that I'm Prime Minister.'

' Isn't that what you want ? To forget your official rank and to make the lady forget it too ? '

But he seemed to think that I'd overdone it. So I indited a painfully banal letter, with the usual hackneyed expressions. And he took it away to copy out.

When I first met Mussolini, he had ' the lean and hungry look of the dangerous man, who thinks too much '. When I last saw him, he was thin again, after a period of corpulence, and he had a large, disfiguring wart on the side of his shaven head. There was a notable failure in the sequence of his ideas. Indeed, the Chief of Police suggested to Ciano that the Duce should do a cure of some sort, for he had become ' perfectly intractable '.

At what precise date he lost the balance of his faculties, it is impossible to say. For many years, his cool, calculating shrewdness was at least in proportion to his ambition. In the last years, one might observe an irritability, a want of decency and control, a recklessness of cause and effect. This was in part the reaction from the intoxicating moments when, as from an exceeding high mountain, he had seen the kingdoms of the earth spread out before him. In his early days, he encouraged a certain *camaraderie* among his subordinates. Later, he began to expect fulsome adulation as his due.

Only a physical and mental decadence can explain how Mussolini fell under Hitler's influence. He disliked and mistrusted the Germans. From the very beginning, the ' Axis ' had never functioned save to our loss. A golden opportunity came in 1939 for its decent burial, when the Germans reached an agreement with Russia. After that, an Anti-Comintern Pact had no *raison d'être*. Mussolini could have backed out gracefully and made it up with the Western Powers, as Hitler had done with the Eastern. But to do so would have required courage and foresight, such as the Duce no longer possessed.

In those days, Ribbentrop's star was in the ascendant. At his request, Grandi was recalled from our Embassy in London (as later Attolico from our Embassy in Berlin). When war broke out, Grandi declared himself in favour of Italy's remaining neutral. This—in his own words—is what happened :

In the Cabinet meeting of September the first 1939, Mussolini communicated to us the declaration of Italy's ' non-belligerence '. This was the first time that I took part, as Minister of Justice, in a meeting of the Cabinet after my brusque recall from London, on demand of the German Government. After we had been informed of Italy's abstention from entering war against England, France and Poland, on the side of our ally, Germany, I proposed that the above-mentioned declaration of ' non-belligerence ' be replaced by an explicit announcement of NEUTRALITY, accompanied by a formal denounciation of our alliance with Germany, as signed on March 22 of that year. Simultaneously, a ' Green Book ' should be published making clear to public opinion, the world-over, the reasons of Italy's policy, and our unquestionable right to resume full liberty of action.

When asking the Head of the Government to accept this proposal, I based my request on two considerations : (*a*) Mussolini himself, when setting forth to us the situation arising out of the recent Ribbentrop-Molotov ' Pact of Non-Aggression ', which had been prepared and concluded without the knowledge of Italy, had not hesitated to describe the conduct of the Nazi Government as an act of premeditated ' betrayal ' of the agreements (both open and secret) previously entered into by Germany in regard to Italy, in the Treaty of Alliance ; (*b*) the events of August-September 1939 were the exact repetition of the treatment experienced by Italy 25 years before, in 1914, when the Kaiser's Germany (then, as now, our ally) had conducted herself, in regard to the Italy of Salandra and Sonnino, in exactly the same way as Hitler's Germany now conducted herself towards the Italy of Mussolini.

While listening to what I said, Mussolini showed growing signs of irritation. He did not reply, but closed the meeting.[1]

To another Italian Ambassador, Dino Alfieri, who replaced Attolico in Berlin (April 1940), I am indebted for particulars as to how Mussolini finally came to the fatal decision to enter the war on the side of Germany.[2]

This decision was taken by him some time after Ribbentrop's visit to Rome in March 1940 (see my Diary for March 13th, ' the Ides of March '). The German Minister's official visit to the Pope served as a pretext for his being accompanied by a huge retinue of officials, all well primed for propaganda purposes in Rome. Ribbentrop saw Mussolini twice, but made no request for the abandonment of our non-belligerence. It was to Ciano that he spoke, ' not as one Minister of Foreign Affairs to another, but as a comrade speaks to a comrade '. He pointed out that it was to Italy's own interest not to be absent at the moment of victory, for though ' a German victory would be an Italian victory ', the fruits thereof would naturally be in proportion to the effort made and to the sacrifices. . . .

While Ribbentrop was trying to influence Ciano, the German Minister's staff was busy encouraging the Fascist extremists to bring pressure to bear on the Duce.

Apart from such pressure, Mussolini feared to remain in the background while Europe was reconstructed by Hitler, with the acquiescence and support of Stalin. He had lost all faith in the Western, democratic, Powers. Their enmity appeared less dangerous than that of their Eastern rivals. And their friendship (vide the aftermath both of Dolfuss's murder, and of Stresa) was not worth having. Italy's neutrality, the neutrality of a Mediterranean power, must necessarily (so the Duce reasoned) be favourable to Great Britain. To punish such favouritism, Hitler might well, one day, send his Panzer divisions over the Brenner into Lombardy. Add to these political considerations, Mussolini's personal jealousy of the Führer.

During his visit to Germany, in 1937, the Duce had been shown

[1] Extract from a letter, dated San Paulo, 23rd November 1948, from former Ambassador, Dino Grandi, to the author.

[2] See Due Dittatori di Fronte, by Dino Alfieri (Rizzoli, Milan, 1948).

the wonderful war machine that had been put together at Essen and elsewhere. When that machine carried everything before it, Mussolini visualized Hitler remodelling the world, and he himself standing by, inactive and impotent. Also, he may have had some project, as an active ally in arms, of using his own influence to moderate the Führer's post-war claims.

In the early morning of the 30th of May, after a restless night, Mussolini, acting against the wishes of King Victor Emanuel III, and without consulting any of the members of the government, wrote a personal letter to Hitler, announcing that he would declare war on the 5th of June, unless the choice of a later date were shown to be advisable.

You may call it a crime. Talleyrand would have said : ' It was worse than a crime. It was a mistake ! '

*   *   *

A Chinese proverb says : ' Everybody gives a push to a tottering wall.' At the time of his fall, every hack-journalist, every minor politician and cheap demagogue, seized the opportunity to prove his superiority to Benito Mussolini. On the other hand, many Italian soldiers died for him, nor grudged the sacrifice of their lives. And I who served him for many years, to the best of my ability, prefer to be generous to his memory, rather than just.

A Diary of Defeat (1946)

Le roman est fini. Nous rentrons dans l'histoire.

PRINCE METTERNICH (after the fall of Napoleon).

Rome, 3rd January 1946. I have sold Bettina's diamond necklace and my mother's diamond rings, also my Chinese *objets d'art* : the lacquer panelling of a room (in black and blue and gold), the Tang horses and some *blanc de Chine* porcelain.

This is one way of making money in these difficult times. Another is described in the following story, brought back by Margherita from Naples :

A lady of our acquaintance, looking out of the window of her apartment, saw a handsome young woman, begging at the street corner, with a coal-black baby in her arms. She seemed to be getting a lot of money from passers-by. This went on for several days, till the lady stopped in her walk to the nearest tram-station and questioned the young woman, asking if she had not got a husband.

Yes. She had got a husband.

Was he black?

Indignant denial from the young woman!

' But what about this baby? '

' Bless your heart! If you see this baby in the evening, after he has had his bath, you will find him as white as I am! '

She spoke of the painted baby as a *nennillo pittato*.

January 5th. Doctor Manlio Cace came in to see me this afternoon. He is a native of Zara. He tells me that, in the Italian towns on the Adriatic, the Jugo-slavs have set up ' Tribunals of honour', where they judge the richer Italians, accused of *collaborazionismo*. They have got this word from the French. The Italians are accused of ' collaborating' with other Italians, during the twenty years or more, since the Treaty of Saint-Germain gave us those territories, and the Treaty of Rapallo confirmed the agreement. The crime of the local Italians is to have respected these two Treaties, and thus contributed to maintaining the Italian rule.

Among those accused of *collaborazionismo* are the two Luxardo brothers, though it is well known that one of them has died in a Jugo-slav concentration-camp. The motive of the whole proceeding is merely to justify the whole-sale confiscation of valuable property, such as the Luxardo distilleries, at Zara.

You would think that some of the owners of the shiny motor-cars that one sees waiting outside the Italian ' Constituent Assembly', would have the courage to denounce these things. But no! The Communists and Socialists successfully obstruct any move in defence of the Italians of the Eastern Adriatic. The attitude of the Allies is that of Pontius Pilate.

January 10th. It is natural, indeed inevitable, that there should be some queer fish in the armies of the United Nations. One of them came to tea with us today : Diana's friend, the Baron Antoine Allard. His mother is a Princesse de Ligne. Although he is Belgian, he has been wearing British uniform during the war. And he got into trouble with his commanding officers, because he insisted, despite regulations to the contrary, on giving medical aid to Italian children, whenever he thought they needed it. And he distributed British medical stores among them. For this he was court-martialled, but he got the better of his judges by assuring them, in indifferent English, that he had read the International Conventions on the subject and found that his conduct was justified by them. He also affirmed that he would continue to give medical aid to any child he thought might require it. If this was a crime, they might shoot him for it.

One of his judges asked him sarcastically if he thought he was a soldier. He answered mildly : ' I am dressed like one.'

What can you do with such a man? His judges were not of the type of Englishman that burned Joan of Arc, so they condemned him to a few days imprisonment, but considered that he had already served his sentence, and they let him go. He is now spending large sums to set up an international institution, to stop war!

January 20th. The Signora Agresti tells me she is giving English lessons to a young man, by name Barbolani, the son of a former Italian Consul General in Ethiopia.

The elder Barbolani came to Italy in 1935, entrusted with a confidential mission from the Negus, offering to consent to an Italian protectorate, on the lines of the former one that existed between the years 1890 and 1896. But he was arrested and put in prison. He was freed in 1941, but died soon afterwards. Now Barbolani's son wants to return to Ethiopia. The Negus is his god-father, and would welcome him back.

But the British authorities, true to their policy of keeping Italians out of Africa, have put a veto to the return there, even of single individuals ; engineers and other professionals. They have discovered that we are not so unpopular with the Ethiopians as they would like to make out.

January 30th. Here, in the Viale Mazzini, not far from us, there lives a government official, with a wife and six children. He has been put *sotto inchiesta* (under enquiry) by the authorities that are directing Sanctions against Fascism. The charge against him is that he obtained his post ' by favour of Fascism '. Otherwise there is nothing against him. You might say the same of every official who has not been hibernating, like a dormouse, during 25 years. Fascism came into power when he was a young man. How could he be expected to rebel against a government that was accepted by a democratically elected Parliament and recognized by the foreign powers ? The judges who conduct the enquiry may be as guilty as he was, but more prompt in turning their coats.

Anyway, his pay has been suspended since 1943. He owns a small house in Naples, but the present rents take no notice of inflation and they are controlled, so that they cannot be raised. The house brings in just enough to pay the taxes. He has let some rooms in his own apartment in Rome, but that again was before the devaluation of the *lira*, and he cannot now alter the terms of the lease. He possesses no other source of income. His family has one meal a day—a bowl of soup from the Vatican Soup Kitchen, at the Circolo di San Pietro. One of his little boys is the friend of some children I know. They give him food, but he is so little used to food that is cooked and with sauces, that he hardly knows how to eat it. He never sees such food at home. His smaller brothers and sisters cry themselves to sleep at night, and wake up hungry before morning, when there is no breakfast for them. If some extra food can be procured from kind neighbours, the elder children generally manage to gulp it down, before the tiny tots get a chance. The eldest boy, aged fifteen, has twice run away from home, and once he took some clothes of his mother's to sell. *Mala suade fames.*

If this was only one case . . . But, although they are not apparent to the casual observer, they are so numerous that I have the feeling of utter helplessness that I used to have, when I travelled through a famine-stricken province in China. This sort of thing makes for Communism, even though the people who vote the communist ticket are not those who go hungry, but those who are anxious to obtain some political pull.

Such cases are not contemplated by war charities. Children starve because their parents are subjected to persecution. They will probably die, if not of 'malnutrition', of tuberculosis—as do 140 per thousand of the Roman children today.

Political persecution is conducted under the protection of foreign bayonets, to the greater glory of ' democracy '.

There is nothing new in all this. It is a recurrent evil. In his *Promessi Sposi*, Manzoni tells of the *untori*, suspected, in the year 1628, of intentionally spreading the plague, by smearing the outer walls of the houses in Milan, and the pillars in the cathedral, with an ointment that carried the contagion. The authorities tortured and hung these innocent victims of popular clamour. Similar victims were hung on Gallows Hill, during the witchcraft delusion at Salem. The spirit of the Inquisition is ever with us, hunting out the heretics. The burning of witches is a burning question even today.

February 12th. Diana is much impressed by a letter to the Editor, that appeared in the Roman daily, *Il Tempo.* I think this piece of prose may have been edited by Virginio Lilli, of the newspaper's staff, but it certainly interprets the feelings of many Italian veterans of the two world-wars.

Diana has translated this letter for the benefit of some English and American friends.

Un reduce decorato (a returned soldier, with medals) asks :

" What shall I do with my medals ? For I have some medals for military valour.

" Of all those wars, that mud, that cold, that sweat, that fear, of all the dead I have seen, the cries I have heard ; of all the dust that powdered my face, the thousands of kilometres that I have tramped ; of all the hospitals reeking of disinfectants ; of all the lice, the curses, the secret implorations before a battle ; the ' Dear Father ', ' Dear wife ', ' Dear Son ', that I wrote by the light of a candle-end ; of all the fasts, the vigils, the advances, the retreats . . . nothing is left to me but three little pieces of metal, three medals ! What shall I do with them ?

" I did not want the wars in which I was given those medals ; the wars claimed me. I was against them from the first moment when I was called out to kill and to be killed. In one war after another, my youth has faded away and my country has collapsed. Most of my brothers-in-arms are dead, lying now at the four corners of Europe and of Africa, each under a wooden cross and a steel helmet. We who survived presented arms at their graves and went on fighting. We behaved like all the soldiers in the world, who are worthy of the name. We didn't tremble, we didn't weep. We stood by our flag. But our enemies proved stronger than us. God had determined that our country should not prevail over those countries, but should itself be overpowered and defeated. The war was lost. And then our fellow-citizens said : ' Curse the soldiers that fought this war ! Blessed be those that fled, those that deserted ! ' So now even the dead we buried are accursed. Those who have earned a medal are even more despised. What shall I do with my medals ?

" I can't put them in a frame and hang them on the wall, to recall the days of my youth to my declining years, as if to say to me : ' You were young once, and a soldier, and strong . . .' My family, looking at those medals, would have pity on me who earned them. They would think : ' He is a vainglorious and foolish old man ! ' Neither will I leave them to my children, for my sons are growing up in an atmosphere that curses all my generation. Standing before my medals, when I am dead, my children would shake their heads in commiseration, remembering that their father fought shoulder to shoulder with a barbarous people, at the orders of a tyrant, so as to be able to tyrannize over other countries. The fathers that belonged to my generation are already judged by their children, they are already condemned. . . .

" My medals are in a drawer in the writing-table, together with three sheets of paper, three documents, to certify that officer so-and-so ' kept up an unequal fight, until exhaustion, etc. etc.' and that ' he defended with great daring, etc. etc.'

" How my heart leaped with pride, when I first received them !

" Now it seems to me that a voice whispers in my ear : ' Your life has been wasted ; your country is laid waste ; it were better if such memories did not live on. . . . Those sheets of paper are turning yellow. They bear the signatures of commanders who have been disavowed and degraded. . . . Give all this up ! Give up your medals ! '

" And yet I know that those three little pieces of metal will never be tossed into the waste-paper basket. . . . I will never tear up those certificates. Though Destiny has reserved for my generation the supreme bitterness, though she would have us blush for having been soldiers of our country, for having endeavoured, even on the battlefield, to live up to that sense of dignity in man that should govern his life. But it is not I that will blush !

" I will not give up my medals ! "

April 7th. I went to see Alberto and Maria Blanc, who are now living in two tiny rooms in Via Lima, their own palaces and villas all being requisitioned. They don't complain. They consider themselves lucky to be alive at all, and with a roof over their heads. They had to fly from their country-house, by the sea, at Viareggio, and take to the hills. . . . While they were encamped somewhere near Camaiore, a village near-by was razed to the ground by the Germans, who set it on fire and mowed down the inhabitants with machine-guns, including a young mother, seventeen years old, and her baby. These were 'reprisals', because a boy, driven crazy by ill-treatment, had thrown a bomb at his tormentors. A woman who had absented herself the night before, on returning home, found no more village, no more home, no more parents . . .

My conversation with the Blancs, in spite of their experiences, was about a common friend of ours, a German, and a victim of his nationals, no less than the villagers who saw their homes set on fire. They told me about the von Hassels. Ulrich von Hassel was German Ambassador here, before von Mackensen. His wife was a daughter of Admiral Tirpitz. Nice people. A daughter of theirs married an Italian, Pirzio Biroli. Von Hassell was a diplomat of the old school, very reserved and rather distant in manner, especially since the Nazis came into power. He was no Nazi himself, and this got him into trouble with Ciano, who used to conduct our diplomatic relations with Berlin over von Hassel's head, and finally asked for and obtained his recall. I don't know that I can blame Ciano, under the circumstances, for von Hassel hardly concealed the fact that he did not take Ribbentrop seriously and that he considered Hitler as a dangerous *exalté*. It would appear that he was not exclusively a diplomat. He could also be a conspirator. And he was mixed up in the Beck-Goerdeler plot to assassinate Hitler. The plot failed, and von Hassel was executed in the prison of Ploetzensee, on the 8th of September 1944.

His daughter and her two children were first put in a concentration-camp together, but then the children were taken away from their mother, and placed in a kind of asylum, where the Nazi authorities collected the children of the people they were persecuting. These children were deprived of their names and cut off from their families. After the collapse of Germany, the grandmother, Ulrich von Hassel's widow, went in search of her daughter's children, among the 15,000 that the Nazis had collected, destroying all traces of their identity. The grandmother could not be sure of recognizing them, and it was unlikely they would recognize her—they had been so tiny, when they had been taken away. . . . The only hope was that they might remember a few words of Italian, and the name of their Italian chauffeur, and the name of their dog. . . .

It was by these means, so Maria Blanc told me, that, in the end, they were found.[1]

---

[1] Ulrich von Hassel left a Diary, which has been translated and published (it was hidden—so I understand—in his garden).

He speaks of that other Germany, *Das andere Deutschland*, that endeavoured to rid Germany of Hitler, before it was too late. Perhaps, if it had succeeded,

A DIARY OF DEFEAT (1946)

April 10th. For the second time in a few days, Diana and I have been to a reception at the Grand Hotel, given by the Press Bureau of the *Presidenza del Consiglio*. The first was in honour of Walter Lippmann. The second in honour of a group of French journalists. All these people—so I understand—are visiting Rome, as guests of the Italian Government.

Diana was much pleased to hear French spoken again by people of wit and culture. But I find the conversation of these present-day Frenchmen rather startling.

I have known French journalists ever since old Henri de Blowitz, in a *rédingote* and side-whiskers, used to come and call on my mother, at the Hotel Saint-Romain, whenever we happened to be passing through Paris. He got into trouble with the German Ambassador, Count Muenster, at the time of Prince Bismarck's dismissal. But he ran no risk of being shot or put in prison.

I asked the principal French journalist, Monsieur Henri Lévin, for news of my former friends in his profession, for example, Jules Sauerwein. The answer was : ' *Vingt-quatre ans de travaux forcés.*'

Then I asked about André Lejeune, who used to run the newspapers of the Paternotre group. This time the answer was : ' *Fusillé !* '

I remarked to Monsieur Lévin that they seemed to have overdone it in France, but he did not agree. He said that they had not shot enough people there, and he added ' or in Italy '.

The French are often utterly ruthless toward their own nationals, and at present many of them appear to have lost their bearings, being more surprised than anybody to find themselves on the winning side. They refuse to admit that this is the merit of the British, the Americans and the Russians. Therefore they try to prove to themselves that they deserved and attained victory. And they persecute those who nourished openly the same doubts that they did. French ferocity towards ' collaborationists ' and *attentistes* is in part the reaction of a bad conscience, and in part resentment at having to acknowledge that, between 1940 and 1944, France ceased to be a great power, and the main current of events passed them by. For this they have to find a scapegoat.

May 10th. Victor Emanuel III has abdicated and will leave for Egypt. Most people think that he ought to have done so long ago, so as to give his son a better chance, and the Monarchy a chance of surviving.

You would think that the Communist and Socialist papers would be jubilant.

---

the ' United Nations ' might not have demanded ' unconditional surrender ', with the result of creating a vacuum in the heart of Europe, into which the Slavs could pour their destructive hordes.

Von Hassel's wife, in publishing his Diary, added the last letter he wrote to her, a few hours before his execution. It is a beautiful letter, telling her to remain strong and brave, for their children's sake, and *not to be embittered.*

At no time did I ever think of Ulrich von Hassel as an enemy, or I might quote Ovid : *Fas est ab hoste doceri.*

261

On the contrary, they are full of abuse, for they fear that, by clearing out, even as late as this, in favour of Prince Humbert, the old King's gesture may still be effective.

May 19th. I hear it is a popular joke in Germany that Hitler was right in saying that the Nazi régime would last 1,000 years. Twelve years under him, and nine hundred and eighty-eight years under ' denazification '!

Conditions in post-war Europe are the same today as in the time of Tacitus. He was an eye-witness of the reign of terror in the last years of the Emperor Domitian. A revolt in Upper Germany was followed by a contemporary ' denazification ', in which the Emperor got rid of all whom he disliked. No man of eminence was safe against him. Tacitus has his parallel today in General Patton, who describes the situation much as the Roman historian did in his *Life of Agricola*, less than a hundred years after the birth of Christ (" You always find the ' outs ' making charges against the ' ins '. The ' outs ' are saying that the ' ins ' are Nazis.')

General Patton got into trouble by so much frankness. *Toute verité n'est pas bonne a dire !* Yet my experience of what goes on now in Germany and in Rome, shows me that both Tacitus and Patton judged the situation correctly.

June 7th. The reign of a month is over. King Humbert will be leaving soon. I went this morning to the Quirinal to say good-bye.

It was with mixed feelings that I mounted the shallow steps of the spiral staircase that I have known since I was a little boy, and crossed the *sala vetrata* to enter the well-remembered rooms. The King had come out of his study and was in the room where the Marchesa di Villamarina used to sit. He was pale and a little dazed. I just shook hands and said nothing. What was there to say ?

On my way out, I was accosted in the Piazza by a little woman, who, from her accent, I guessed to be from the Trastevere. She had tears in her eyes and said : ' *Non lo faccia partire !* ' (' Don't let him leave !') I shook my head in silence and pressed her hand. Again, what was there to say ? [1]

June 10th. The papers announce the proclamation of the Republic at the Capitol, this afternoon at six o'clock. The public remains indifferent to this event. There is no trace of the heroic republican faith that once animated men like Mazzini and Garibaldi.

People are hungry, and therefore apathetic. And I fear that love of country blossoms more easily when the state is victorious and laurel-crowned. Yet patriotism is greater—or should be—when our country, defeated and down-trodden, has need of everything and can give nothing.

I have heard it said that the Americans wanted us to become a Republic, because they thought this might be to Italy's advantage. The English also

---

[1] The fall of the monarchy in Italy is treated more amply in the author's *Twilight of the Kings* (John Murray, 1948).

AXEL MUNTHE
From a drawing by Sir William Rothenstein, 1936

wished it, knowing that it would weaken us. It is doubtful if a Republic can hold the loyalty and the imagination of the Italian people as the Monarchy did.

September 19th. The Allied Army of Occupation has an irritating, dog-in-the-manger habit of requisitioning quarters that they don't really seem to want, and don't use. (This reminds me of their ' colonial ' policy towards Italy.)

The huts on the sea-shore at Castel Fusano, where we used to meet all the rank and fashion of Rome, are now requisitioned by the British, but not one hut in fifty is occupied, even though summer lingers and the sea is quite warm enough for bathing. The less attractive bathing-establishments at Ostia are crowded to suffocation with Roman women and children, who face the uncomfortable journey from town, and return home in the evening, in the electric train.

Diana has discovered a beach which she now considers her own, and she has taken me down to it several days running. It is what they call *la spiaggia libera*, a far-flung stretch of coast in the direction of Castel Porziano, and what used to be the royal domain, where the King held shooting parties. On the edge of the dunes, where the high-road ends between the sands and the pine-forest, there is a ramshackle hut, such as you might see on a cabbage-patch. It has been put together, with considerable ingenuity, by an Italian ex-officer (a major) and his wife, with bits of matting, rubble, some wooden poles, and the usual odds and ends that one may pick up along an unfrequented beach. No hope to come upon the storied hulls and precious cargoes that may be washed up on the Gulf coast of Texas (where fortune-hunters still dream of finding the lost galleon of Cortez), but there is plenty of such humble wreckage as may turn up (especially after a war) in the crescent arc of a coastal bend. And this is enough to reward such modest beach-combers, as so many of us are nowadays.

When the breeze freshens, windy sprays of fine dust are thrown up on the sides of the sandhills, where the thick-stemmed grasses grow bravely.

The St. Martin's Summer habitués of this humble *plage* include Diana and myself, a ' lady ' belonging to the oldest profession open to women (she lives at Ostia), a Russian propagandist and a few other stray dogs. The major and his wife keep beer and aerated waters, besides some sour new wine. They will cook us an omlette, or a plate of spaghetti.

Diana says our little beach-combing group reminds her of the various people that met on the bridge of San Louis Rey, before it collapsed. A similar heterogeneous lot of people, human flotsam and jetsam, have been thrown up there by the tide of war, just as the flotsam and jetsam of which the hut is built, was thrown up by the sea.

There must be innumerable little groups in Europe today, living in impro-vised huts, people who have been salvaged somehow out of the general wreck. And these are the fortunate ones !

In Italy alone, there are now some 250,000 people who figure in lists made out by the victors as 'surrendered enemy personnel'. They attain a freedom of sorts, as their guards become inadequate to keep them herded in camps, and then they scatter among a population unwilling to absorb them. Among them is some good human material, badly needed wherever 'reconstruction' is really under way. It is painful to see so many young men going to seed in enforced idleness, or engaged in unfamiliar work, most of which had better be left undone. Here we find recruits for the black market, traffickers in food, tobacco, foreign *valuta*, precious stones, stolen army-stores, and prostitution.

Diana and I meet with and talk to people of this type, half a mile from where we used to sit and gossip with ' the smart set'. I'm not sure that our present-day acquaintances are not the more amusing of the two.

September 27th. The day is approaching when the verdicts will be pronounced that close the Nuremberg trials. An officer tells me that they had great difficulty, in England, to find magistrates who would accept to sit on the bench. But now the *Illustrated London News* publishes a full-page portrait of an eminent judge, of whom it says : " He has, perhaps more than any judge in history, established before the world, in an international court, the true principles of British justice. . . ." Likewise, a judge of the U.S. High Court impersonates ' American justice ', and so on with the Russian and the French. None of them claims—or so it would appear—to impersonate mere justice, without any national qualification. Not to have had a neutral (or even a German) judge, sitting with the others, was a mistake such as only nations intoxicated with victory could have committed.

There is something here that leaves a bad taste in the mouth. That a great many war criminals (guilty of crimes against humanity) deserve to be hung, *cela va sans dire*. They have violated rules of war that are older than Grotius. But everyone knows that the same crimes for which Germans will be condemned were committed also by Russians and Jugo-Slavs. Yet a Russian judge sits on the bench ! These magistrates, appointed by the victorious powers, apply laws from which they exempt themselves and anyone who fought on their side. Their scales of justice admittedly require two weights and two measures.

If it were vouchsafed to us, the vanquished, to bring war-criminals to justice, we would ask to see in the dock whoever was responsible for letting the Moroccan troops loose on our countryside. A few days ago, the Signora Agresti quoted to me some remarks of Professor Silvestri, who said that, three years after the Allied advance in Italy, there is still a ward in the hospital of Naples, where are some of the unfortunate women who were victimized by our Moroccan ' liberators '. The day is distant indeed when Lord Chatham denounced the government for employing Red Indians in the American War of Independence. (This time the Holy See protested.)

Final query : Supposing the ' United Nations ' had not won the war, how could they have justified Nagasaki and Hiroshima ?

November 5th. Despite hard times, some of us still look forward to radiant morrows, *les lendesmains qui chantent.*

Ill-advised statesmen may ' cry havoc and let loose the dogs of war ' but they can't prevent young people in the opposing camps falling in love.

When this happens, we feel again the taste and perfume of an old familiar vintage, to sweeten the cup that we had imagined would be bitter to the dregs.

In a few days, Gianmarina is going to be married to an Englishman : David Grose, flag-lieutenant to Admiral Warren.

The wedding is to take place at Ravello, on Sunday, the 17th. Everyone asks me : ' Why Ravello ? Aren't there any churches in Rome ? '

As a matter of fact, it's for economy's sake. If the wedding were to be in Rome, we would have to ask (between Gianmarina's friends, our own friends, David Grose's friends and brother-officers) something like two thousand people. A reception, at the present prices for refreshment, would cost a king's ransom. Let it be Ravello by all means.

November 7th (at Ravello, above Amalfi, on the Gulf of Salerno). Motored down here with Gianmarina and her fiancé, to make the necessary arrangements. After something like a two-years' drought, it has begun to rain. ' And the windows of Heaven were opened,' as in Noah's time. The newly repaired asphalt roads, when wet, are as slippery as toboggan tracks. Just before Terracina, we came upon a group of armoured cars and trucks, piled up in a pyramid in the middle of the road. The drivers appeared to be Poles. They could talk no language known to me.

We lunched on fish-soup at Terracina, and stopped again to re-fill in Naples, at a gasolene station, opposite the cemetery of Poggio Reale. I was thirsty and asked where I could obtain a glass of wine. A Jew from Palestine (wearing British uniform) advised me to try a flower-shop, where they sold wreaths and crosses, to put on the tombs. I accepted the suggestion and obtained some excellent wine and a ham sandwich. The shop catered for the quick and for the dead.

Arrived at Ravello by moonlight, and put up at the Albergo Villa Rufolo. Very nice and clean. An excellent supper, at a little table set near the wood-fire, beside the fireplace in a corner of the room.

November 8th. Called on the *parroco*, a jovial priest called ' Don Ciccio ', and visited the cathedral. Gianmarina has chosen the altar at which she is to be married : not the high altar, or even a side-chapel. It is a tiny Byzantine altar under the Ambon (this is a piece of church furniture, dating from the early Romanesque period, A.D. 1030, part pulpit, part lectern, for the reading of the Epistle). The Ambon in the cathedral of Ravello is described in the *Encyclopædia Britannica.* It is made of sculptured marble with mosaic inlay.

Gianmarina has taken a liking to Don Ciccio, and wants him to celebrate the marriage. But the Bishop in Rome wishes to officiate himself. They must fight it out between them.

We strolled about Cimbrone, the Villa that belongs to Lord Grimthorpe. I had known it when Ernest Beckett was still alive and remember ' Moony ' acting as hostess, and making us all dress up in an improvised masquerade. It is a lovely place, poised above the sea. Wagner was here, when he was writing *Parsifal*, and the villas of Ravello inspired scenes in the Garden of Klingsor.

November 10th (back in Rome). On our way home from Ravello, we stopped at Amalfi and made the acquaintance of an extraordinary lady, known along this coast as ' Connie of Peckham '. She is married, I believe, to an Italian, who is an invalid. Her cockney accent reminded me of the flowergirl in Bernard Shaw's *Pygmalion*. To hear her talk, you would think that the Allied landing in the Gulf of Salerno was intended to reach her !

Among other activities, she now sends parcels of lemons, oranges, nuts, raisins, etc. etc. to people in England. I gave her some addresses of friends and relations in the British Isles, and a very moderate sum, to cover expenses. During the war, I used to send off parcels to Bettina's cousins, who were in Officers' Prison Camps in Germany (Oflag VII, etc.). Now that the war is over, and the English are among the victors, I still send them edibles from Italy !

We motored to Rome, by the inland route, and passed what used to be Monte Cassino : once a temple of peace, and throughout the centuries a refuge for those who were tired of hating. The hillside is there, with bits of foundations sticking up, but even the rubble has been taken away. From a little distance off, you would hardly guess that the place had ever been built over at all. There are only a few modest huts, recently put together, at the side of the road, for motor-cars to stop at. Many of the surrounding hill-towns have been destroyed, but the walls are still standing, though they are nothing more than façades. It seemed to me, as I looked at them, that they were symbols of the old Europe. Even the big powers, England, France, Italy, are but the façades of what they were before this war. Still, even a façade is something. It keeps up appearances, till you get going again.

November 18th (in Rome again, after the wedding at Ravello). This time, we got back late at night. A very pretty wedding. The tiny, candle-lit altar, in its niche under the Ambon, made a quaint, old-world setting. Village children, peering through the encircling foliage of palms and other potted plants, appeared as rosy faces without bodies, like Correggio's cherubs.

The Bishop arrived from Rome at the last moment, and Don Ciccio had to play second fiddle at the nuptial ceremony. The rain kept off till we came out of the church ; then we had to run through the crowd in the piazza, not to wet our wedding-finery.

I think everybody who was there will remember the soufflées at the wedding lunch ; lemon soufflées and chocolate soufflées. They were brought in in a continuous stream till we all (to use a child's expression) felt our buttons. After lunch, the rain having stopped for the moment, we walked about on the terrace, overlooking the Gulf of Salerno. The honeymoon couple remained on at Ravello. The guests came away. We were about a dozen Italians, including Pier Maria Pasolini, the Joris, the Bishop (who, during lunch, ate the salted almonds with his knife !) and Don Ciccio. The others were English and American officers and their families. They are the only people who can travel about in motor-cars, in these days. Gianmarina bossed those Admirals and Air-Marshals, as if they were so many recruits.

Every dog his day.

It was no joke, getting to Ravello, or away from it. The floods were out on the countryside. Every now and then, the road dipped to cross an impro-vised bridge, alongside of an old one that had been blown up. Then, the yellowish water surged up over our mud-guards, and the exhaust bubbled, as in a motor-boat. Many cars were damaged, going and coming. But it was all very festive, very cordial. It was nice of all those people, to come. . . .

December 6th. Nothing is quite so characteristically Fascist as extreme Anti-Fascism.

Ignazio Thaon de Revel has lent me a French book called *Décombres* (rubble), by Lucien Rebadet, published in 1942 in the Edition Denoel. The author has now been shot, and so has his former colleague on the staff of *Je suis partout*, Pierre Gaxotte. This reminds me of my conversation, last April, with Monsier Henri Lévin, at the official reception for the French journalists.

Apparently it is considered a crime, today in France, to possess a copy of Rebadet's *Décombres*. He was shot—so I understand—for having written it.

He paints a realistic picture of France and the French Army at the beginning of the war. Merely to mention one item : he describes the C.O.R.A. (*Centre d'organization automobiles de l'Armée*), with its superb park of armoured cars, the interminable lines of trucks, both large and small, fresh from the great *usines* of France, and from the most modern motor works in the U.S.A. (White, Dodge, Studebaker). No other army possessed finer material. Yet the French *état major* and the *train d'équipages* proved themselves—according to Lucien Rebadet—as utterly incapable of dealing with all this war material, as a band of Red Indians might have been, to use a *linotype*. The *parc d'auto-mobiles* moved only once, and in retreat.

Rebadet's prose reveals a man of whose love of country there can be no shadow of doubt. It is love of France that inspires his most furious diatribes, his most bitter invective (and there are pages that seem to emit sparks of rage !). For this love of country, he is condemned as a criminal and shot. He must not love France in his own way.

There was an article about him in the *Figaro*, signed, if I remember rightly, André Maurois. He called Rebadet a *polémiste*, and seemed to conclude that, if he had been shot, it was because he was an excellent journalist. If he had been a bad one, he would have been left in peace.

My own conclusion is : *Il n'y a que la verité qui blesse !*

It must be because Rebadet's criticisms were well founded that the French authorities were so anxious to hush them up and to condemn the critic as a criminal.

And the French Army, described as so corrupt and inefficient, now attitudinizes as a conqueror. It parades its coloured troops up and down the Corso in Rome (a thing the English and the Americans have never done), to make us realize who are our victors. Yet the Italian Army, ill equipped and unprepared as it was, held out for three long years. Our soldiers, our officers, our commanders, performed miracles, with the scanty material at their disposal.

Christmas 1946. A very quiet Xmas. Only myself, Bettina and Diana at home.

Things are going badly in Palestine. Terrorism, armed attacks against railway-trains, bomb-throwing, curfews and reprisals. It was safer in the time of Herod.

If Jesus Christ had been born today, the Wise Men of the East, instead of bringing gifts of gold and myrrh and frankincense, would be trafficking in the Black Market !

I am not trying to be irreverent : only following the general tendency to bring the facts of the Nativity down to ' present day ', and adorn them with the image of familiar things. So did our ancestors, when they had their portraits painted, hobnobbing with the Holy Family. So do Picasso and his contemporaries, when they paint St. Joseph smoking a pipe, or sitting under an electric-light bulb.

When I was last in Peking, I commissioned a Chinese painter (a Christian) to paint me a picture of the Three Kings, coming to Bethlehem. He dressed them in the robes of Chinese Emperors of the Ming Dynasty.

Our peasants in the Appenines repeat to their children the story of the birth of Christ, describing conditions that have nothing to do with the Holy Land. A tiny hut stands alone in a broad valley, where a silvery light makes everything as bright as day, even though there is no moon. The mountains are snow-covered, but the snow has the colour and the perfume of roses. The Christ-child lies in his manger, kept warm by the breath of the kine . . .

Sentimental Journey

AVENIDA PALACE,
LISBON, 19th October 1948

LAST Monday, at six p.m., I was walking down the Viale Mazzini, when I noticed a hand-cart proceeding along the street in front of me. On it was a coffin. This struck me as a bad omen, for in a few hours' time, I was to start, with young Prince Alliata (the son of a former colleague in diplomacy), for a nocturnal flight to Lisbon. We were going to see our former King, Umberto II. There was no particular motive for our visit. It was a sentimental journey. To be preceded down the street by a coffin, on my last outing before we started was not encouraging.

At half-past eight, Alliata's motor came to fetch me. I was to pick him up at the Grand Hotel, on our way to the airport. As we drove through the lighted streets, the car suddenly swerved, and only just missed running over a black cat (another bad omen).

When we reached the Grand Hotel, Alliata came out and joined me in the car. He was looking rather glum. Apparently the last person he had spoken to, before starting, was known to have the evil eye. This was the third of the bad omens. I said so to Alliata, and told him about the other two.

A few minutes later, we were proceeding down the Via Merulana, when again the car swerved. The chauffeur had perceived (too late to stop) a jeep coming at us full tilt out of a side-street. He managed to avoid being struck broadside on, but could not escape the inevitable collision. The jeep struck our car on the side I was on, glanced off, and ended up inside a café at the side of the street. I found myself sitting on a much lower level than before, and was aware of a sharp pain in my left hand, that made me think the little finger must be broken. Our car had subsided over a crumpled wheel.

Alliata took the matter calmly. Indeed, he seemed pleased. He remarked in a tone of some satisfaction : ' *Abbiamo superato la cassa da morto, il gatto nero, e Don* ——*!* ' (I avoid mentioning the name of the *jettatore*. Merely to do so brings ill-luck !) I too felt much

269

relieved. The three portents had been justified, and the danger was over. We could now face the journey by air with confidence and pleasurable anticipation.

An hour later, having reached Ciampino in a taxi, we were sitting in a ' Constellation ', while they tried out the engines. At a signal from the control-tower, the huge plane addressed the runway, roared fiercely till it disengaged itself from the concrete strip, and soared, all silvery, into the moonlight.

At five next morning (after an hour's stop at Madrid) we swooped down, with ears popping, on the airport outside Lisbon. The flight had been steady and smooth as that of a homing dove. But the shock of the car-smash must have done me some injury, for I have felt sick for the last few days and am still shaky. Before I went in to be received by the King, at Cascaes, his gentleman-in-waiting had to give me some brandy. The climate of Lisbon, which is very lowering, may have something to do with it. I have been advised to drink lots of the *vin-du-pays*, otherwise port-wine. This should bring up my blood-pressure, which is abnormally low. I have begun this cure and can only regret that we are starting back to Rome tomorrow, and the treatment cannot be prolonged.

★   ★   ★

It was sheer joy to see the King again, even though it pains me that a man so well-fitted to be Chief of the Italian State should be relegated to the weary role of a *roi-en-exil*. For me, Italy without the House of Savoy is like a face that has lost its smile. What other princely house can show a rule of nearly one thousand years, and never once a tyrant ?

To the Americans, monarchies appear no less out of date than *The Prisoner of Zenda*. Was it not to escape monarchies that their first forebears left Europe ? But their allies in victory are not sorry to see the Italian nation deprived of an element of stability, such as the British cherish for themselves. Like them, we need something more colourful than a President of Republic to inspire our loyalty and our imagination. Indeed, de Nicola and Einaudi, our first two Presidents, never denied their monarchist sympathies. Among our higher government officials, the best men are monarchists at heart and serve the Republic because they accept it, more or less regretfully, as a *fait accompli*.

End of ' The Story of San Michele ' (1949)

IT required quite an effort of will to make once more the journey between Rome and London, after the second world war. Reason has nothing to do with this *phobia*. It is a question of nerves. Now I am back in London, after ten years' absence, and I feel that a spell has been broken.

The means of transport available today are different from those that I used to take in the past. So I missed the renewal of an old traveller's sensations in following the accustomed route. Diana and I left the Ciampino airport at eleven-twenty a.m., stopped at Marseilles for half an hour, and reached Northolt at twenty minutes to five in the afternoon. I imagine, in a few years, this will appear to be a long and weary flight.

Our departure and arrival coincided with the obituary notices of Axel Munthe, who had just died at Stockholm, at the age of ninety-one.

During these last years, he lived in the Royal Palace at Stockholm : a guest of King Gustav. A Swedish friend tells me that almost every day Munthe would enquire about his Royal host. And then he would shake his head despondently and say : ' Ah, the poor King ! He is getting very old. He can't last much longer.' (King Gustav being the same age as himself.) On his part, the King would enquire about Munthe. And *he* would shake his head and say : ' Ah, poor Munthe ! He is getting very old. He must be nearing his end.'

After Munthe's death, and just before my departure for England, I was asked to write an article about him in the daily *Tempo*, and I noticed a lady passenger reading it in the air-liner, on our way to England. That same evening I listened in, while Jock Murray spoke on the radio about our old friend. He quoted a remark of Munthe's about his own book :

' It was never intended to be an autobiography, but, if that is what it is, then I believe that the simplest way to write a book about oneself is to think of somebody else.'

' Somebody else ', for Munthe, did not always mean people. It more often meant birds, or dogs, or monkeys. These represented for him a major interest in life, as they do for my own daughter, Margherita (a trait that she has inherited, through me, from my mother). In fact, it was because of this common interest that a friendship arose between Munthe and Margherita, despite the disparity in age, as it had arisen, some fifty years before, between Munthe and me. They met at Capri, and used to talk on their favourite subject by the hour. They agreed that Heaven can have scant attractions, if animals are excluded. Surely, St. Anthony took in his pig, and St. Roch his dog?

For people who love animals so intensely, they cease to be animals at all, in the sense that the word is generally used. They are even more than persons : they are personages and personalities. To inflict unnecessary suffering on them is more than a sin against humanity ; it is a sin against the Holy Ghost.

Munthe and Margherita would tell each other stories about their pets and their livestock, and the narrative would be more vivid and arresting than any similar story about human beings. To go to the rescue of an animal in distress was more than a duty ; it was an obsession. One of the last times that I saw him, Munthe told me an anecdote about Margherita. He told it with so much gusto (and so many embellishments) that I refrained from interrupting to say that I had heard it before, from Margherita herself.

She was travelling alone, driving her car between Rome and Naples. There had been heavy rains and the water-courses were swollen. As she drove over a bridge, she saw a crowd of peasants leaning on the balustrade and gazing excitedly down into the water. Curiosity as to what might be causing so much interest made Margherita stop and get out of her car, to look too. A big dog was drowning in the canal, not being able to climb up the precipitous sides. No one was attempting to help it.

Margherita flung off her coat and her frock and plunged into the water. When she came out, having saved the dog, she gave the peasants a piece of her mind. I don't think they were impressed. She had provided an added and an attractive item to the spectacle.

★   ★   ★

From Jock Murray's obituary radio-talk, I learnt that it had been Munthe's last wish to return to Capri in the spring of 1949, and to die there. But this consolation was denied him.

No one more than he loved both Italy and England, but he could look upon both these countries with detachment. I am sorry he did not attain his desire to see Capri once more. I would have sought him out there, and talked things over. He might have quieted my nerves, in that hypnotic way of his, helping me to remove some of the bitterness that the war years and their aftermath had left in my mind.

In the days immediately preceding the war, I sometimes met Munthe in Ella Stephens's house, South Kensington. Edward had gone blind and deaf. It was almost impossible to communicate with him. Munthe managed to do so, somehow, but I could not. Mrs. Stephens was more of an invalid than ever. She lay all the time on a divan. Even to talk tired her, so she would listen, while Munthe and I conversed on various subjects.

At that time, the Stephens *ménage* was directed by an Italian butler recommended by Munthe. He had been previously in the service of the Marchese Imperiali, when the latter was Italian Ambassador in London. I once knew his surname, but have forgotten it. Everyone called him 'Charles'. In many ways, he was (and probably is still) a remarkable personality, with a knowledge of the world that few of us could equal. When he accompanied the Ambassador on his visits, Charles stayed in most of the stately homes of England and Scotland, including Balmoral. In the Stephens household, he ruled as an autocrat, and from all I heard, he was a godsend to that aged, infirm couple. Munthe, as friend and doctor, may have given some moral support to Charles. Between them, they attended both husband and wife, to the day of their death.

Edward died first, and by that time Ella was nearing her end. When I went to see her, if Munthe were not there too, it was with Charles that I conversed part of the time, lest I should exhaust her by making her talk.

One day, at tea-time, we were together in the drawing-room, Charles and a footman had brought in tea. Ella said:

'I have bought a wonderful new electric super-gramophone. Ask Charles to put on a record for you.'

Charles showed me the recent acquisition and, on his own initiative, he put on a record from one of Beethoven's symphonies. I listened for some minutes and then exclaimed : ' How beautiful.'

' Yes,' answered Charles. ' It reminds me of a phrase of Oscar Wilde's. " It is so beautiful that it makes me want to repent of sins I have never committed." '

(Wodehouse's Jeeves was a vulgarian in comparison with Charles, the Italian butler in an English family.)

One evening, I received a message to say that Mrs. Stephens wanted me to come and dine. I took this as a sign that she must be better. But when I arrived up at Harrington Gardens and met the other guests in the drawing-room, we were regretfully informed that our hostess felt so unwell that she could not come down to entertain us. Would we sit down to table without her ? There was nothing we could do but comply, so we were ushered into the dining-room and partook of an excellent dinner, beautifully cooked, beautifully served and with wonderful wines.

One of the guests was Sir Almoth Wright. The other two, whom I met there for the first time, were a brother of Sir Roger Keyes and his wife.

Half an hour after dinner was over, we sent up some kind message to our hostess, and I walked with Sir Almoth Wright as far as the Underground Station in the Gloucester Road.

Next morning, I went to enquire how Mrs. Stephens had passed the night. Charles met me in the hall. He looked very grave.

' I hope you will forgive me, sir,' he said, ' but last night I took it upon myself not to tell you that Mrs. Stephens had died a few minutes before you came.'

What a servant ! What a man !

Charles told me he meant to go back to the diplomatic service. And when next I saw Munthe, he said that he might find him a place as *maître d'hôtel* at the Swedish Legation in Paris.

Mrs. Stephens lived to a good age, and in spite of being a confirmed invalid, she led a life that was not without happiness. And this she owed to Axel Munthe and to Charles.

I never saw Munthe again. But I occasionally heard of his doings and sayings. Lady O'Malley (better known by her pseudonym of

Ann Bridge) told me she had sat next to him at a luncheon party at Sir William McClure's, on the Trinità dei Monti. She had recently published a new novel, called *Illyrian Spring*. Munthe was not aware that she wrote. He only knew her as a British diplomat's wife. When the conversation came round to Dalmatia, which was just beginning to open up to the tourist traffic, he remarked :

'I have always wanted to go there. But now the place has been spoilt—or so I hear. Some pestilential lady novelist has written a book about it, and the place is overrun with sightseers.'

No one told him that the 'pestilential lady novelist' was sitting at his side.

The caustic phrase was characteristic of the man, no less than the tenderness that is apparent in his books. And so is the clause in his will, by which he begged the King of Sweden to distribute 100·000 Kronen (about £5,500, representing his earnings as an author in Sweden) to help "the blind, the Lapps, and the birds ".

Some day a *Life* of Munthe may complete his own rambling auto-biography. But will it have the magic of his prose ? I doubt it. For he was, indeed, something of a magician. Or shall we call him an *apprenti-sorcier* ?

Mankind, today, is not content with that true balance of the sensibilities that we call common sense. It longs for magic, to relieve the drabness of our workaday existence. This may explain why so many people fall under the spell of rulers, who only offer Black Magic.

So, in medicine, the present-day mania for psycho-analysis is a form of craving for the occult. Some time ago, *The New Yorker* published a satyrical drawing, representing a drug-store, offering—as drug-stores do in America—all sorts of heterogeneous services. A queue of patients are lined up, awaiting their turn to be psycho-analysed by a shop-colleague of the cutie at the cosmetic counter.

In the East and the Far East, the old-established medical faculty is full of such psycho-analysts, who have nothing in common with Cerletti in Italy, Répond in Switzerland, and Crichton-Miller in England. Their Oriental clients regard them simply as magicians and witch-doctors. But even they might represent a reaction against over specialization in pathology, by attempting to reach physical ills also through the medium of the mind. Many of Munthe's patients regarded him as a witch-doctor, whereas he was a by-product of his time.

A *Life* of such a man should attempt to discover the source of his charm, as Vivien did, when she wrested the secret spell from Merlin, in the wild woods of Broceliande.

Once more England

WHEN she was in England, last year, Bettina was much struck by the change in the children. Except in a few families, to whom money is no object, they are no longer in the charge of nurses and governesses, nor are they expected to be seen and not heard. I too have observed this interesting social phenomenon. London babies are shoved out in the street in their prams, with a harness to prevent them falling out. Nobody in the house has time to be with them, and there is no ' baby-sitter '. But the babies don't complain. They have a busy time, throwing their belongings out on the pavement : a doll, a woollen cap, their socks, a toy dog. Simple-minded strangers pick these things up and put them back, saying a few kind words. When they've gone, the baby throws everything out again as a lure for other passers-by who don't realize that the joke is on them !

The no-servant problem has become an obsession, both in town and country-houses. Today, the little servant-girl in Dickens, whom he calls ' the Marchioness ', might receive as her due the homage that the title justifies, and this without any irony whatsoever. At Anley, in Yorkshire, where Diana and I have been staying, the few remaining retainers keep their own families with them ; their children, ignoring social distinctions (as children do), form an integral part of the household, to everyone's advantage. I admire this new Order, in which the classes are not kept asunder by barriers of convention. But one cannot help wondering if the British country-house can survive as a family residence.

From Trevelyan's *Social History of England* (i.e. history with the politics left out), I learned how the highly-capitalized British agriculture was ruined, in the eighteen-seventies, by the cheaper mass-agriculture of the United States. American farmers skimmed the cream off a virgin-soil and used the newly-built railroads and the modern Atlantic steamships to pour their products into the British Isles. If, at that time, no great change became apparent, this was because business men, enriched by the industrial revolution, were willing to bring their money to the countryside. But now there does not seem to be any class left to keep up a refined rusticity alongside the winding roads on which Mr. Pickwick travelled, and that we associate with Constable landscapes, flowering hedgerows, and indoor comfort and cosiness at the journey's end.

In London, conditions are more puzzling and complicated. As when I was last in New York, I can hardly see the wood for the trees. The big hotels are cosmopolitan and not British at all. So they always were. But if you telephone to make contacts with an English family, you will find that the servant—where there is one—is almost always a foreigner. A knowledge of languages : French, Italian, Polish, Finnish and Lithuanian, is often useful, when you ring up dwellers in Hampstead, Kensington and Chelsea.

I feel less at home here than before, which is only natural. The same cordiality, the same affectionate hospitality, awaits me among the people I knew best. But I am no longer welcome in some of my old haunts, and I have no longer a club here. There is a time-lag in ill-feeling. Wounds may heal, but they leave a scar, and the scar serves as a reminder.

There are scars a-plenty in London. If they do not make much impression on me, it is because I have seen other devastated towns on the continent. Close to Gianmarina's little house in Chelsea, a German bomb has destroyed the Old Church at the corner of Cheyne Row. Daffodils and primroses grow among the ruins, for it is April.

Perhaps because of its associations, which are not political, but literary and artistic, Chelsea appears more friendly to me than other districts of London. I found my own books in its public library, and I meet many pleasant ghosts there. After sunset, my body, like theirs, casts no shadow. The streets on either side of King's Road are haunted by phantoms of Rossetti, Turner, Swinburne, George Eliot and Carlyle. And there is one that I met in the flesh more than half a century ago. I mean James McNeill Whistler.

THE DREAM SHATTERED

He died at 96 Cheyne Walk, in 1903. And in May, last year, they held an exhibition of Whistleriana in his house. One of the pictures shown on that occasion now belongs to me : a self-portrait, painted in 1864. It has the mocking, arrogant, whimsical expression that I remember so well. But when I knew him, his hair was longer and he wore a monocle. Like many others of his pictures, it is signed with the butterfly (for example the *Nocturne, Cremorne Lights*, in the National Gallery).

The first owners of my picture were the Greaves brothers, who as night was falling used to row the artist out into the middle of the darkening river, where he memorized the crepuscular effects that he afterwards rendered in his Nocturnes. I read about this in the Fore-word, written by James Laver, for the catalogue of the Whistleriana exhibit. And he quotes a paragraph from Whistler's *Ten O'Clock* :

When the evening mist clothes the riverside with poetry as with a veil, and the poor buildings lose themselves in the dim sky, and the warehouses are palaces in the night, and the whole city hangs in the heavens, and fairyland is before us, then the wayfarer hastens home ; the working man and the cultured one : the wise man and the one of pleasure cease to understand, and Nature, who for once has sung in tune, sings her exquisite song to the artist alone, her son and her master—her son in that he loves her, her master in that he knows her.

Whistler's Chelsea was different from Gianmarina's. When he first came to live there, with his mother, in 1866, there was no Embankment. Big shady trees grew along Cheyne Walk, at the edge of the mud-flats, left uncovered by the tide. No chimney-stacks towered up above an electric-power plant. No brightly-lit motor-coaches, returning from the country at dusk, streamed past the Old Ferry and Pamela Wharf. But the grey-blue dusk itself lent then, as it does today, a tonality to the landscape, such as we find in Whistler's paintings. Nature, in Chelsea, does not overload the colours, any more than he did. And withal, Chelsea is as English as Alice in Wonderland.

★   ★   ★

I could now add some further comments to what I have already written in my scrap-book, about changes in the character of the English. In their docile acceptance of austerity, people here have

JAMES McNEILL WHISTLER
Self-portrait, 1864

become queue-minded. They seem to take a lugubrious pride in standing in line for every imaginable reason. With us, on the continent, it would often end in a free fight.

I forget who it was that said, after the Napoleonic wars (if indeed that is the right date), that England had saved herself by her exertions and the world by her example. Last October, among the *azulejos* of Lisbon, King Umberto spoke to me about the English. He said : ' They have given an example to all the world, with their discipline.' This is perfectly true. But of the Italians it might be said, with equal truth, that it was by their lack of discipline that Italy was saved.

The average Italian is not law-abiding, but he *is* hard-working. The old legend of *il dolce far niente* was born when there was not enough work to go round, in a country that was not rich in those natural resources which are necessary to modern living-conditions. This was not true in the versatile days of Lorenzo the Magnificent. Nor is it true today, though the economic consequences of defeat may bring back once more the old enforced idleness and hunger, in the shape of unemployment, or under-employment, of the masses, whose former outlets have been closed to them.

Everybody here with whom I have spoken on the subject is willing to admit that, in spite of communist sabotage, and in spite of the undeniable fact that ' white-collar ' labourers in Italy do not earn a living wage, the national effort towards recovery is marvellous. Recent Italian films, such as *Paisà* and *L'Onorevole Angelina*, made— as the Hollywood people say—with a shoe-string, reproduce, with photographic accuracy, the hard life of the people. But the picture is incomplete.

Some foreigners, touring the continent on a limited *valuta* allowance, have been a little shocked because, *chez nous*, they have seen beautiful women, in lovely clothes, eating wonderful food, drinking vintage wines, and obviously enjoying themselves. Can this be the same world, where the victors practise austerity, and where so many people struggle to sustain an unhappy physical life, while seeking spiritual means to escape it ?

Italy is a country that exports luxuries. So it is natural that people should drink wine, eat peaches and grapes, wear silk, and breed horses such as Tesio's Nearco (now in England). Italian labourers may, or may not, work harder than their opposite numbers in Great Britain. Certainly, they have more incentive to exert themselves. The British Labour Government's economic ideal may be founded on wisdom, but it is not encouraging. As a French cook said of a dish, prepared by him under war conditions : ' *Ce n'est pas affollant !* ' A planned mediocrity may have its advantages, but it is incompatible with liberty, and one cannot raise much enthusiasm over the prospect of ensuring for everybody a mathematically equal slice of a not very edible cake. Italian workmen do not enjoy the same sense of a moderate domestic and economic security as workmen in England. But, if they work hard enough to earn them, the amenities are not denied them. The rewards are worth striving for.

Except by ruthless taxation, successive Italian governments have not done much to ensure a material austerity in our lives, but they have shown themselves very anxious to purify the body-politic, by an *epurazione* that passes us all through a sieve, intended to allow only true democrats to attain salvation.

Such conscientious efforts of the powers that be, to reduce humanity to one pattern of perfection, reminds me of a story once told me by Barry Pain. It was a fairy-story, on the following lines (I tell it again in my own words) :

Once upon a time, there was a king, a widower, with only one child, a daughter. Like so many other fairy-tale princesses, she was the most beautiful in all the world. Young Princes came from far and near, to ask for her hand in marriage.

But the King, her father, was determined that she should only wed the most worthy and respectable young man possible. The Princess, herself, was not so sure that this was what *she* wanted, but being a dutiful daughter, she let the King make such arrangements as he thought fit.

The Royal Palace, in that fairyland, was situated at the top of a high mountain with very precipitous sides. Only one road led up to it from the plain below. This gave the King an idea, which he promptly carried into effect. He built a pleasure-resort, a kind of Luna Park, at the foot of the hill, with all sorts of places of entertainment : smart hotels, bars, theatres, cinemas, music-halls, and other hostels that offered entertainment of a character which I may not specify. The suitors had to pass through this Venusberg on their way up to the Palace. They could stop there to rest after their travels, and refresh themselves, and change their raiment, before taking the steep road up the hill. If they were really worthy and respectable young men—or so the King argued—they would not tarry among those attractions. They would resist temptation and hurry on. . . .

The King told his daughter of this idea, and she did not show much enthusiasm. But she raised no objections, and the old man went on with his plan. . . .

The result was not satisfactory. Lots of suitors came, and they stopped at the foot of the hill. But they never got any farther. And meanwhile, time passed and the Princess remained single.

At last the King began to realize that there must be something wrong somewhere. He admitted as much to his daughter.

' I am afraid,' he said, ' that I may have overdone it. These young men will never come up to so high a standard as mine. Meanwhile, your youth has been wasted ! '

' Not entirely wasted, Papa.'

' What do you mean ? '

' Well, you see, when you set up those establishments at the foot of the hill, I thought it only prudent to make my own arrangements.'

' And what were they ? '

' Merely that I was one of the attractions.'

★   ★   ★

I see much in England that is admirable and new (though sometimes it savours strangely of Fascism !), but I do not possess the opportunities for observation that I enjoyed before. My time is now occupied in little family affairs and in dealing with the Controller of Enemy Property, whose day is long in the land, as D.O.R.A.'s was after the first world war.

In Gianmarina's house, I am surrounded by an aura of youthful domesticity, the delights and trials of a *jeune ménage*. I am practising *l'art d'être grandpère*. The baby, Benedetta, cannot talk yet, but has a lot to say. She expects me to sing to her, and I have furbished up memories of lullabies, such as Eleanor Farjeon's *Presents from Heaven*, and the French berceuse :

> *Le long des quais, les grands vaisseaux,*
> *Que la houle berce en silence,*
> *Ne prennent pas garde aux berceaux,*
> *Que les bras des femmes balancent.*
>
> *Mais viendra le jour des adieux,*
> *Car il faut que les femmes pleurent*
> *Et que les hommes, curieux,*
> *Tentent les horizons qui leurrent.*
>
> *Et ce jour là, les grand vaisseaux,*
> *Fuyant le port qui diminue,*
> *Sentent leur masse retenue*
> *Par l'âme des lointains berceaux.*

Here is the old antithesis between love of home and the spirit of adventure : cradles by the hearth and ships that sail the high seas. But in these permit-ridden, servantless days, the *Wanderlust* is subordinated to the concession of a visa, and no one has time to rock the cradle !

And once more : Butterflies under the Arch of Titus

> And Pharaoh awoke, and behold, it was a dream.
>
> GENESIS xli. 7.

At the end of the last century, excavations in the Forum had brought to light the buildings of Imperial Rome. Since then, Giacomo Boni and his successors had delved to lower levels, through layers of brick, marble and tufa, and corresponding stratifications of history, down to *vestigia* that were already ancient in the legendary times of Romulus. But the atmosphere of the *Foro Romano* is still much the same as when I spent a morning there, with Giosuè Carducci, in 1895, and the mild air was full of Red Admirals, Painted Ladies, Chalk Blues and Cloudy Yellows.

No better background could be found for a great writer than the ruins of a past civilization. Even as the clouds gather and sweep over broken colonnades and deserted amphitheatres, so do the centuries circle, phantom-like, round the brow of a poet. We look to him for inspiration, as the generations succeed one another. This is still the Italy for which Dante suffered and Petrarch rhymed and Machiavelli thought.

I often walk over the Palatine and through the Arch of Titus. With every return of spring, the Forum is fragrant with the scent of flowers. Birds give the mating-call and young couples wander along the shady paths under the ilexes on the slope of the hill. From beneath a jewelled mantle of wistaria and climbing roses, the crumbling ruins seem to whisper a warning : ' Time flies, *tempus fugit*. Love each other while you may ! '

Once, near the Temple of Castor and Pollux, where the Great Twin Brethren washed their bloodstained horses, after the battle of Lake Regillus, I picked up a poor dead bird, a mere handful of feathers that were still warm. Some cruel boy may have killed it with a catapult. The fancy took me to bury it at the foot of the Rostra, where Mark Anthony spoke a funeral oration, and the people made a ring about the corpse of Caesar. Throughout the centuries, we who live in Rome may well have mourned, in the Forum, for the ideals, illusions and affections that lie buried there. Such things must pass. The Emperor, riding in his chariot of ivory and gold, as he figures in the bas-reliefs under the triumphal arch, remains to us only as a vague memory, connected with the fall of Jerusalem. Today, the greatest temple that stands in the Eternal City is dedicated to a poor fisherman from Galilee.

The famous verse *chi le farfalle cerca sotto l'Arco di Tito ?* seems now to hold for me a different meaning, for every year the butterflies come back.

Empires rise and fall in an epic cycle ; civilizations pass and recur, as do the melodies in a *Liederkreis*. But ideals do not die. Like butterflies, they are born and born again.

Can it be that only our dreams are immortal, in the abiding childhood of the world ?

INDEX